Woman of Means

Woman of Means

of

A

c.1

THOM LEMMONS

Multnomah•Publishers *Sisters, Oregon*

WOMAN OF MEANS
published by Multnomah Publishers, Inc.
© 2000 by Thom Lemmons

International Standard Book Number: 1-57673-612-1

Cover illustration by Dean Williams
Design by Stephen Gardner

Multnomah is a trademark of Multnomah Publishers, Inc.,
and is registered in the U.S. Patent and Trademark Office.

The colophon is a trademark of Multnomah Publishers, Inc.

Printed in the United States of America

For information:
MULTNOMAH PUBLISHERS, INC.
POST OFFICE BOX 1720
SISTERS, OREGON 97759

00 01 02 03 04 05 — 10 9 8 7 6 5 4 3 2 1 0

Acknowledgments

I gratefully acknowledge my debt to the following resources:

The Perseus Project (http://www.perseus.tufts.edu), an online resource for the study of ancient Greece; Gregory Crane, editor-in-chief; Tufts University, Medford, Massachusetts.

Everett Ferguson, *Backgrounds of Early Christianity*, second ed. (Wm. B. Eerdmans Publishing Company, 1993) and *Early Christians Speak: Faith and Life in the First Three Centuries*, revised ed. (ACU Press, 1981).

Richard Oster, *The Living Word Commentary on Acts*, vol. 2 (ACU Press, 1984).

Argos (http://argos.evansville.edu), a limited-area search engine for ancient and medieval online documents and resources; Anthony F. Beavers, managing editor; University of Evansville, Evansville, Indiana.

I also thank the following people for their support and encouragement:

Cheryl, who still believes in me after all these years;

Heather, Jessica, and Austin, who put up with my vacant stares and aimless wandering;

Charme Robarts, my colleague and friend, who has been known to run with the boys;

Stephen Weathers, award-winning fiction writer, professor, and sympathetic listener;

Sherry Rankin, whom I appreciate for her writing, but even more for her camaraderie;

Al Haley, a novelist's novelist who finds time to nurture the craft in others;

Rod Morris, my editor and safety net.

PART ONE

The Runner

The old woman was dying; she knew it as well as anyone in the room. That wasn't what bothered her.

"Don't you think she looks a little better?" asked the one with the blotchy skin. "I think she looks better today."

"Oh, yes. Why, I expect she'll be up and about any day now," said the other one. Her voice was high-pitched and irritating; it reminded Lydia of a mewling cat. She fussed with the linen blanket covering the old woman, as if she were coddling a child or primping a pet.

"I'm dying, but I'm not deaf," said the old woman, without moving or opening her eyes. "If you must talk foolishness, at least keep your voices down." Wherever did Euodia dig up these dim-witted girls?

"Now, now, Mother Lydia. You mustn't talk that way."

"I've lived long enough to talk any way I please. I'll soon be gone and you won't have to listen to me any more. Take off this blanket. I'm hot."

Lydia wished they'd think to open the shutters. During the

short moments when she had the strength to hold her eyes open, she could see the rich yellow light of day streaming through the cracks between the shutters. She felt the moist spring air moving over her face; smelled the freshly turned earth in the fields below the town. It would be good to die in spring.

Her room was at the northwest corner of the house, across the atrium from the kitchen, where the two girls spent most of their time. Lydia wished she had had the walls repainted last summer, when she had had the chance. She had a single window, high on the north wall, and two smaller ones on the west wall. She didn't especially like having the window on the north wall; it opened onto Short Street, and sometimes the noise was aggravating. But they were the only two outside walls, and the cross-draft made summer evenings more bearable. The room was sparsely furnished: just the couch on which she lay, a small lacquered table, a chair, and a stool or two. Even the woven hemp mats that used to cover the stone floor were gone, rolled up and sold, and the money given by Crescens or one of the other elders to someone in the community who needed it.

In her busy younger days, Lydia had fashioned this room into a refuge: a small triclinium for the times when she wanted to have one or two guests for an intimate meal, several large water ewers in one corner to save her the trouble of going to the well, a small chest for her perfumes and cosmetics, even a few decorative plants in clay pots. The climbing jasmine was her favorite. On summer nights, it wafted a gentle perfume into the air around her bed.

But she didn't need much these days. Just a place to lie and a small table to hold a water cup or a bowl of broth. A place for one or two visitors to sit. Over the last months, as her illness had worsened, Lydia had gradually sold or given away most of her furnishings. It surprised her to realize how much clutter she had accumulated.

Lydia wondered if the runners had reached Thessalonica. It probably didn't matter. Hermeia knew the way to Philippi. Why should she return now, after all this time?

"Here, Mother Lydia. Try to drink this." One of the girls had her hand under Lydia's neck, lifting her up. She felt the cold water against her parched lips and managed a weak swallow or two. They tried to get her to drink more, but she pressed her lips together and turned her face.

Lydia remembered the first time she had drunk from the springs at Philippi. It was in the late summer, during the nineteenth year of Tiberius Caesar's reign. With her two little children, she had arrived here from Thyatira—alone, her resources dwindling rapidly. Traffic on the Via Egnatia was heavy that day, she remembered. They had crossed the wide, marshy plain from the port at Neapolis, surrounded by creaking, overloaded drays. More than once she had snatched little Parmenes from beneath the wheels of one of the carts. By the time they reached the forum at Philippi, she was worn thin with fatigue. Everything she owned was in two bundles slung across her shoulders, the purse hidden beneath her robe, and the small pack on Hermeia's back. She stood in the bustling forum, gripping the hands of her children and wondering how she would gather the strength to make inquiries for her uncle's house, when she heard the sound of water splashing on stones. At the center of the forum, opposite the temple of Dionysus, was a fountain. Lydia suddenly realized she had had nothing to drink since debarking early that morning. She pulled Hermeia and Parmenes through the crowds and knelt beside the low stone wall rimming the fountain. She ordered Hermeia to hold her little brother's hand and cupped a handful of water to her mouth. She splashed cool water on her face and rubbed it on the back of her neck. She turned to ask Hermeia if she wanted a drink and realized her children were gone.

Lydia leaped to her feet. She darted a glance all around the fountain, thinking maybe they had wandered along while she drank, dangling their fingers in the water. Not there. She stared around the forum. "Hermeia! Where are you?" A few passersby glanced briefly at her as they went on their way. To her frantic eyes, the whole forum was a blur of moving, unfamiliar shapes. She wheeled around and stared back the way they had come, started back toward the highway, then stopped and looked. Which way to go? How could she guess? "Hermeia! Parmenes!" Her voice sounded high-pitched, brittle.

She began dodging through the crowd in a rapid, back-and-forth course. Her path took her across the forum toward the bema. Knots of wealthy-looking men stood about on its steps and on the dais itself. A group of them parted to reveal Hermeia and Parmenes, sitting with folded hands and rapt faces in front of a bald, fat man. He wore a robe pieced together from haphazard scraps of garish, ill-matched colors, and he grinned at the children as he spoke, touching them now and then with odd, twitching gestures. The children's mouths hung open as they watched him.

"Hermeia! I told you to watch your brother." Lydia rushed up, giving the strange man a suspicious look as she gathered the children away from him.

"You told me to hold his hand," the girl replied. "He walked away and I stayed with him, holding onto his hand."

"No harm, dear lady, no harm," said the fat man, turning his grin on Lydia. "Just old Xerxes, telling them a story. Just a little story."

"Thank you. But she knows better than to let her brother wander off. He's likely to jump down a well, or worse."

"No harm, no harm." The man gave a cackling chuckle. "Just a little story." The children's eyes had already turned back to him. He grinned and waved at them. He made silly faces.

"Come on," said Lydia, gripping her children's hands firmly as she turned toward the steps of the bema. "We have to find the house of Menippus."

"Menippus the wool merchant?" asked the bald man.

Lydia looked back at him. "Yes, but—"

"Ah! Xerxes knows him! He can show you the way."

"Thank you, but I'm sure we can manage, if you'll just point—"

"Ah, no harm, no harm," chuckled Xerxes, springing to his feet and dusting off his clothing. "This way." He started off down the steps and through the forum, crooking a finger in the air behind him. "This way. Xerxes will show you."

Lydia pulled her children with her, shaking her head as she followed the figure in the weird robe.

"Shouldn't we try to get her to eat?" asked Cat Voice. Euterpe—that was her name, Lydia suddenly remembered, feeling a vague twinge of guilt.

"I don't know. She looks like she's asleep," said the other one.

Clystra, Lydia reminded herself. "I'm awake, but I'm not hungry," she said. "Has anyone heard from my daughter?"

In the pause that followed, Lydia knew without opening her eyes that the two were looking at each other, neither willing to touch the answer.

"Never mind. Give me a little more water. Would you,

please, Euterpe? And then I might try to swallow a little broth."

They had just propped her up and brought a bowl of broth when Euodia breezed in, trailing two of her domestics. "Wait! Let me see that broth. Lydia's condition is delicate, and I won't have her touching anything that might harm her. Uncover the west windows; the air in this room is too dank. And couldn't you find anything better to cover her than this threadbare old blanket?" Clystra and Euterpe, along with the two domestics, scurried back and forth like cornered mice, all of them trying to follow each of Euodia's directions at once.

"Dear Euodia, how good of you to think of me," murmured Lydia. "Won't you please come in?"

Though barely six years younger than Lydia, Euodia's back was still straight, her movements brisk and decided. She had to use the henna more often these days, Lydia suspected. Euodia wore her hair in an elaborate, backswept style, and Lydia could see the narrow line of gray along the roots above her forehead. Poor dear. As Euodia tucked in the thicker blanket brought by one of the serving girls, Lydia could see the liver-colored spots on the backs of her long, thin hands. Her friend carried her years well, Lydia thought, but aging was such a nuisance for those who denied its approach.

"Are these girls taking good care of you, dear?" Euodia leaned close to Lydia's face, placing a palm gently against her withered cheek. "Are they making you comfortable?"

"Only God can make me comfortable, and he seems to be taking his own time about it."

Euodia clicked her tongue. "You're hopeless. You'll frighten them, talking that way."

Lydia winced as a spasm lanced her bowels. She felt Euodia's hand slide into hers.

"Are the pains getting worse?"

Lydia let out a slow breath and made a small nod. "Honeyed wine used to help, but now it just comes back up."

"Can I have my physician come to you?"

"No. Tell him to spend his time on those who can get well."

Euodia smiled at her friend. "You aren't about to make this easy for anyone, are you? Yourself, least of all."

Lydia managed a slight shrug and the wisp of a smile. "You've known me too many years."

Euodia dismissed the servants, telling them to come back at lamplighting. By the speed with which they left the house, Lydia guessed they weren't too sorry to be sent away. Euodia sat down beside Lydia's couch. "Do you need anything?" she asked.

Lydia shook her head. "Thank you for sending them away. Euterpe and Clystra do try so hard, but I sometimes wonder how they manage, with such little sense between them."

"They displease you? I can send someone else."

"No, no. At least I'm accustomed to their silliness. No use starting over with others." Lydia cut her eyes guiltily toward her friend. "And I suppose it wouldn't be overly kind to expose any more of your girls to a dying old woman's harshness."

Euodia patted her hand. "Now, now. No need for false humility, dear. It's unbecoming."

Lydia managed a ghostly chuckle. She sucked in a quick breath and gripped Euodia's hand until the sudden pain passed. "I might drink a little broth," she said when her breath was easy again. "Sometimes it helps."

Euodia brought the bowl from the small, black lacquered table beneath one of the west windows, testing the heat of the broth with a fingertip. She dipped a wide, wooden spoon in the thin broth and brought it to Lydia's lips, cupping a palm beneath the sick woman's chin. Carefully she tilted the broth into Lydia's mouth, a few drops at a time, until the whole spoonful was swallowed. "It tastes good?"

"As good as anything. And I think it will ease my stomach. I'll try some more."

After the fifth spoonful, Lydia turned aside her face. "No more, just now. Let's see how that does. Your trade is well?"

"Well enough. Domitian's new settlers are anxious to prove their pedigrees; purple goods are in brisk demand. I keep my people busy."

"Does it ever bother you that we made our living, all these years, from the vanity of other people?"

Euodia laughed. "I never thought of it that way."

"I think of many things differently these days."

Euodia patted her friend's arm. There was a silence.

"Syntyche was here yesterday," Lydia said. She felt the slight movement of Euodia's fingers where they rested on her arm. Without opening her eyes to see, she could imagine the straightening of Euodia's back, the sudden tautness around her eyes. "Even after all this time, Euodia?"

"I show her no disrespect."

"True enough. But you also show her no love. Isn't it time to put all that behind you?"

"And what of her? Is she blameless?"

"She isn't here."

Lydia felt Euodia withdraw her hand; heard her robes rustle as she stood up quickly from the chair. There were several footsteps across the stone floor—away, then back. "I didn't wish to upset you, dear," said Lydia. "But one day, you, like me, will be almost out of time. And there will be things you, too, will wish to have said. Or left unsaid."

In the distance, the noise of a procession grew. It came down the street and skirled past the front of Lydia's house: the raucous blare of the *aulos*, the clanging of finger cymbals, the tangled chorus of women's voices singing a hymn to Demeter as they paraded toward the temple in the forum. Lydia could hear the swishing of the bundled sheaves the women waved above their heads as they went.

It was odd: Growing up, Lydia had never noticed how many religious processions and celebrations there were. Since coming to know the God of Abraham, Isaac, and Jacob many years ago, she supposed she had learned to look at Greek customs with an outsider's eye. And one of the strangest things to her was the amount of time spent in observing this special day or that festival. It seemed that something was happening nearly every other day at one of the shrines or temples. Some days, of course, were more notable than others. Maybe it had always been so.

She felt the nervous tensing of her stomach muscles as she approached the starting mark. The race began here, at the granite plinth that marked the boundary of Thyatira's *pōmērium*. They would run along the main road and through the center of town, toward the finish line in the forum in front of the temple of Apollo Tyrimnaios. Lydia looked up and down the line of runners. She had never raced against boys before. It was a mark of her father's standing among the guilds that she was here at all. "She has already beaten all the girls her age," he had told the priest. What harm would it do to let her run against boys? The priest still looked doubtful, but his eyes stayed on the purse her father held loosely in his hand. In the end, the purse eased the priest's misgivings. Her father had patted her head as they walked home. "My little Amazon," he had called her. "I've bought you a place in the contest. Run well."

But she knew it wasn't enough to do well; she had to win. This was the beginning of the Sun Festival, the biggest civic celebration of the year. The priest of Apollo would give to the winner a laurel crown and a prize of three *tetradrachma,* along with the right to sit among the elders of the city's boule at the banquet in the forum. Lydia wanted all Thyatira to know that she was a runner to be reckoned with. She wasn't in the race as a courtesy; she was a competitor who had as much right to be there as any of the boys.

Lydia cut her eyes to the left without moving her head. Menander was there, bending and stretching as he waited for the signal to toe the line. He was two or three years older than Lydia, still in the primary school run by old Macrinus in the little building on the side street just off the forum. The oil on his skin glistened in the bright sunlight as he bent to the right, reaching over his head with his left arm, then the other way, reaching with the other arm. Menander's family lived on her street. She saw him every day, walking with other young boys and their pedagogues to his reading classes. He was maybe two fingerswidths taller than she, and he had curly, dark hair. Some afternoons, she climbed the stairs to the roof of her uncle's house, at the edge of the meadow that lay along the riverbank. In the meadow, Menander and his friends did their wrestling, running, and other daily exercises. He was the fastest of the boys, she judged, but Lydia thought she could beat him. She always thought she could win.

The starter, an assistant priest at the Temple of Apollo, called them to the line. Lydia pulled the ends of her short, linen shift up between her thighs and tucked them tightly beneath her sash. The midsummer day was hot; Lydia felt the sweat trickling down her back beneath her shift. Heat shimmered above the road into town, blurring the edges of the nearest buildings, maybe three stadia distant. The dust of the roadway was warm under her bare feet. She let her arms hang loose at her sides and leaned forward onto her left foot. Her toes were just behind the line the starter had drawn in the dust with his staff. All of them angled their heads to the right to watch as the starter raised his hand over his head. "Go!"

The line of young runners spilled over the mark. Lydia tried to find her stride. Some of the younger boys pounded quickly ahead. Let them go, she thought. They wouldn't be able to maintain that pace all the way into town.

Menander was running easily to her left, just ahead of her. Lydia decided to hang back a while to take his measure. The road wound up the side of a small, rocky rise, then down into a dish-shaped swale. She concentrated on steadying the rhythm of her breathing on the upslope, then held herself in check on the downslope. By now, the runners were strung out in a ragged line along the road, and some of those who had bounded off so quickly at the beginning were coming back to the field. Lydia shifted to the left to pass one of them, running with his head down. His breath blew loud from him, almost two to the stride. Just as Lydia overtook him, he stubbed a toe on a stone in the path. The boy yelped and fell beside the road. Should have kept his head up.

They crested the other side of the swale. Now there were only four boys in front of her and Menander. They had gone maybe a third of the way between their starting line and the town walls. Lydia felt the familiar burn beginning in her calves and thighs; felt the hot drag of her breath along her breastbone.

She pulled air in and let it go out; forced herself to keep a rhythm in her wind that would help her maintain the even pumping of her legs. It wasn't time to suck greedily at the air; that would come later, near the end, when she spent her remaining strength in an all-out rush for the finish.

That was where she often won—in that final, utter push. She had beaten many older girls who thought she was used up. Lydia had always been able to save something for the very last. It was her secret luck, her own, hidden advantage. It had always been enough.

She could see the spectators, gathered on both sides of the road on the outskirts of Thyatira. Lydia could hear the faint sounds of their cheering. It pulled at her, that sound; made her hold her head a little higher. She longed to hear them chanting her name in the forum.

Now Menander glanced over his shoulder at her. The flash of his expression was too brief to read; it could have been surprise, or annoyance, or something in between. It didn't matter, but she kept a closer eye on him. Still, Menander kept on, running straight and true down the road. Lydia thought his face was cocked more toward her, though, since he knew she was still with him.

They were maybe fifty paces from the town now, and there was only one boy in front of them. He was flagging, his paces uneven and labored. By this time they had reached the spectators. They ran down a corridor of voices and clapping hands. Lydia wanted to look around at the crowd to try to find the face of her father or one of her brothers, but she dared not take her eyes off the course or Menander. They passed the city gates and the remaining boy at almost the same instant. Now it was down to Lydia and Menander.

Her shift was coming untucked. Without breaking stride or looking down, Lydia rammed the ends of the garment back beneath the sash. Boys had such an advantage.

Lydia could see the pillars on either side of the forum entrance. It was time. She pressed herself forward, surging past Menander's right shoulder. She could feel his eyes on her. Her breath was now coming in quick, hot gasps. From the corner of her eye, she could see him pushing, straining as he tried to get in front of her. She forced her mind into her legs, her feet. She flung herself forward, ignoring the burning in her muscles, her chest.

The crowd's roar faded, drowned by the pounding of her heart, the racing of her blood. Again she could see Menander edging up; again she pressed ahead. The pillars and shining doors of Apollo's temple rushed toward her. She saw the finish line, scratched in the dust a few paces in front of the steps. Her vision blurred to black; she began to stumble. She threw herself toward the mark, arms out, reaching. The ground came up to meet her. There was a dull, muffled roar in her ears, then nothing.

Two

The noise of the crowd was the first thing she heard. Gradually, she became aware that someone was holding her. Her eyes slowly opened and she saw Menander, using a *strigil* to scrape the oily dust from his skin. He had won. She had stumbled at the very last, and he had crossed the line ahead of her. Lydia wished she could go back into the blackness to avoid the taste of her failure.

And then hands were raising her up, standing her on her shaky legs. A hand rested on her head and a resonant voice was speaking words into the air above her.

"Lydia, daughter of Threnides, I award you the winner's crown and first prize." She looked down at her hand; she held three tetradrachma. Confused, she stared at the crowd gathered in a semicircle in front of the steps of the Temple of Apollo. They were shouting *"Io! Io!"* and waving their hands in the air. Lydia's father stood in the front ranks, an odd, disturbed expression on his face. Her brothers stood beside him, applauding politely, but no more than that. Lydia looked at Menander. He scowled at her for a moment, then turned away. She brushed her hand across the front of her shift and realized it was covered with dirt. Her knees and shins were scraped and beginning to ooze blood.

The priest of Apollo towered over her. His face, looking down at her, was stern, an odd contrast to the shouting, cheering onlookers. He held out a hand to her and led her up the steps of the temple. A small wooden table stood in the center of the front portico, and resting on the table was a laurel wreath. The priest guided Lydia to the left side of the table and turned her to face the crowd. She felt the wreath settle onto her head. "*Io! Io!*" shouted the crowd again, waving their hands in the air. But Menander still wouldn't look at her.

When Lydia and her father arrived back at their house, Lydia's mother and her sisters stood in the courtyard, dressed in the leather cuirasses of hoplites. They each held a lath painted to resemble a sword, and Lydia's mother wore a tragedy mask. Her arm was lifted in a dramatic attitude as she declaimed, "'And with stout heart to raise her, as if she were a young goat, high above the altar; and with a gag upon her lovely mouth to hold back the shouted curse against her house—'"

Lydia's father had a pained expression. "Chloe, of all days for such foolishness."

She battled the air at him and continued her speech. "'Then, as she shed to earth her saffron robe, she struck each of her sacrificers with a glance from her eyes beseeching pity—'" The cuirass was too large for her and kept slipping over one shoulder or the other. She had to keep pulling it back in place with her free hand.

"Mother, these leather clothes are hot," whined Thetis, dropping her sword on the ground and tugging the heavy, ill-fitting cuirass over her head. "I don't want to play anymore."

"Me either," said Zobia, the oldest girl.

"Now see what you've done?" said Lydia's mother, shaking her head at her husband. "How can I master the divine syllables of Aeschylus without the necessary practice? And now you've caused the chorus members to quit the play." She pulled the mask from her face and dropped it to the ground with a sigh.

"Mother, I won! I won the race! I beat the boys!"

She looked at her youngest child as if seeing her for the first time. "Why, Lydia! You're filthy! What happened?"

Lydia glanced guiltily at the front of her shift. She brushed at it with one hand, gesturing with the other as she told her mother the story of her dramatic finish. "And see! The priest of Apollo gave me three tetradrachma!" She held out the coins toward her mother.

"Let me look," said Thetis, older than Lydia by two years. She grabbed Lydia's hand and reached for the coins.

"No, they're mine!" Lydia snatched them away from her sister. "I won them. They're mine!"

"Don't be such a crybaby, Lydia." Zobia held out her leather costume and her lath sword. "Where do you want me to put these, Mother?"

Lydia's mother flung a dismissing hand toward the women's quarters across the atrium. "The wooden chest in my chamber. I suppose I'll never learn Aeschylus now. And I had so hoped to present a dramatic tableau at next year's Thesmophoria."

Lydia's father made an impatient noise. "Chloe, enough of this. Look at this child. Tend to her, at least." He strode off toward the men's chambers.

"Oh, of course." Chloe knelt down and held out her arms to Lydia. "And you beat the boys. Who ever heard of such a thing?"

"I get to sit with the elders tonight at the feast."

Lydia's mother looked up at her in surprise. "Oh, Lydia! The feast will be so late! You're a little child!"

"I'm almost ten. And besides, if Menander had won, he'd be there, and he's not much older than me."

Chloe shook her head. "Girls racing with boys. Sitting with all those old men. I wonder. I wonder."

A few days after the festival, Lydia looked out on the street from the window of her room and saw Menander and his friends on their way to classes. She thought about the scowl on his face as he had turned away from the sight of her standing on the temple steps beside the priest. She went down the stairs to the courtyard and across to the gate. Her mother sat on the stone bench beside the cistern in the portico off the courtyard, a large bell krater between her knees. She leaned over it, the tip of her tongue working back and forth across her upper lip as she daubed a paintbrush across the unglazed surface. She looked up as Lydia passed. "Where are you going, dear?"

"Nowhere. Just talking to someone." Lydia tugged open the gate and looked up the street at the group of boys. They walked in a loose rank that stretched across the street and their pedagogues trailed along behind them, visiting among themselves. Menander was in the center, grinning and laughing as he talked to the boys on either side of him. He had an easy, open stride that Lydia liked. She stood very still in the recessed entry as the boys came closer. When they were abreast of her gate, she took a step into the street. "Hello, Menander."

He turned and looked at her, still smiling from the last exchange with one of his friends. The smile slowly faded. "Lydia. What are you doing out here?" She saw the scowl beginning to form around the corners of his eyes.

"I only wanted to say...I mean, I wanted to tell you

that…that you ran well in the race. I thought you had won."

"Is this the girl who beat you, Menander?" One of the other boys was looking from Lydia to Menander, a slow smirk creeping across his features. Menander gave him a sharp look, then stalked on. "Shut up, Alexander. You didn't even make it to the end, the way I remember it."

"Menander—" she began.

"Go back inside and tend to your weaving, girl." He didn't even look at her as he said it. The others grinned slyly at her as they passed. The pedagogues kept their faces turned away, but Lydia could hear their low chuckling.

Lydia felt her face stinging as she closed the gate behind her. She wandered slowly across the pilastered atrium into the women's suite. She heard Zobia and Thetis talking in the small courtyard behind the latticed screen, so she went the other way, into the main room.

The walls of the main room were painted a pale green, her mother's favorite color. Across the back wall was a fresco depicting Bacchus's revenge on the king of Thebes. Lydia's father said he never should have permitted the fresco, but her mother said she liked it. There were large, linen cushions, stuffed with wool and piled about in the corners of the room. She flung herself into a pile of cushions and wriggled to the bottom, imagining she was a naiad, diving to the bottom of a pond in a forest glade. She tossed the cushions off, flinging them this way and that. She lay on the floor and stared at the ceiling, trying to connect the cracks in the plaster into an unbroken path from one wall to another.

Lydia got up with a sigh and wandered toward the table in the center of the room. She found the vellum roll of Homer she had been studying the day before. She picked it up and went to her mother, still bent studiously over the bell krater. She sat on the bench. "Mother, can we work on reading now?"

Chloe looked up at her daughter. "Oh, dear, not now. I'm trying to get the figures right on this vase, and I can't quite seem to manage. Get Zobia to help, do you mind?" She gave Lydia a quick smile and a pat on the back of the hand, then went back to her painting.

Lydia sighed and slid from the bench. She padded back across the courtyard toward the women's rooms. Glancing down at the back of her hand, she noticed a daub of ochre from her mother's brush. She wiped it on the back of her chiton.

Lydia paused, standing next to the altar. For a moment, she looked at the painted stone figures of the household gods behind the altar: Vesta, kneeling, her head draped by a fold of her flowing robes, and double-faced Janus, standing in front of the small, painted doorway at the back of the altar niche.

Why did Menander hate her? If she had lost instead of him, she would have been angry with herself, not at him. If she burned some grain on their altar, would Janus and Vesta give her the answer? Would one of the lares or penates whisper in her ear while she was sleeping to tell her what she might do to remove the sour look from Menander's face?

Is this the girl who beat you, Menander? Alexander's voice smeared the air with the question. He made "girl" sound like a curse—the worst thing a person could be. She tried to imagine Menander's reaction if one of the other boys had won. She didn't think losing to one of his friends would bring such shame as she had seen in his face moments ago. *Tend to your weaving, girl.* As if she had violated some border, gone into some forbidden room. As if "girl" was the only thing anyone needed to know about her. Even the boys' slaves had turned their faces as they passed—as if she were a bad smell.

Thetis had left Zobia alone in the small courtyard in the women's suite. She leaned against the wall of the colonnade that ran along the northern side, working at a handloom. She never looked up as Lydia approached. Lydia stood looking over her shoulder for a while, waiting for Zobia to say something. Finally, she tapped her on the shoulder with the scroll.

"What do you want?" Zobia's fingers never paused as she passed the shuttle back and forth across the warp.

"Mother says you have to help me with reading. She's busy." Lydia thrust the roll of Homer toward her sister.

"Well, I'm busy, too. Go get Thetis."

"No! She yells at me every time I miss a word."

"Then go get Iole, or one of the other slaves."

"They can't read."

Zobia flung down the loom and glared at Lydia. "I'm not helping you. Go somewhere else."

Lydia blew an exasperated breath through her lips. She whirled around.

"What's that on the back of your clothes?" Zobia asked.

Lydia stopped and looked. It was the ochre stain from Mother's paintbrush. "None of your business," she said, stomping back toward the main atrium. Why did everyone suddenly despise her? She stood in the doorway of the women's suite and flung the scroll as hard as she could toward the far wall. Then she crossed the atrium and went out the gate.

She ran down the street toward the eastern gate, then out. She pounded along the road, fast enough to make the wind sing in her ears, to make the blood pound in her temples and drown out the angry voices in her head. Her chiton twined about her shins and she yanked it up, gathered it above her knees, and ran.

A path diverged from the main road, meandered down the rocky slope, and twined through scrub tamarisks and oaks toward a copse of plane trees that grew near the riverbank. Lydia took the path and let the incline pull her feet along. She dodged back and forth along the twisting trail until it leveled out toward the grove of large, squat-boled trees, hunkered like a group of old, heavy women in the small floodplain beside the river.

Lydia found her tree, the one she always climbed. It had easy hand- and footholds close to the ground, and soon she was up among the broad, whispering leaves. She found her favorite limb, broad enough that she could recline on it and not fear falling and high enough that she could not be seen by anyone.

She lay on her back and looked up into the shifting green canopy. She watched the tiny, white needle points of day as they twinkled through the foliage. It was cool here, up among the skirts of the tree. The harsh summer heat had less power. She felt the limb stirring gently beneath her, nudged back and forth by the easy wind. It was like lying in her nurse's lap when she was a baby, feeling the peaceful to-and-fro of her breathing as Lydia drifted off to sleep.

Lydia thought of her mother, curled over the bell krater with her paintbrush. She imagined her father coming home from the dyeworks and seeing his wife painting a pot instead of sewing or weaving or overseeing the household. He would shake his head as he had the day after the race. "Chloe, what rabbit are you chasing now?" he would say. She would answer nothing; pretend he hadn't spoken. Or she would make a mouth at him and go on with her work. She might even reply. "This krater needs my attention just now, more than the ovens or the looms," she might say. Her father would shake his head once more and shout across the atrium for one of the kitchen girls to find him something to eat.

Lydia tried to imagine herself as a grown woman. Would there be strangeness between her and her husband, as there was between her parents? Would she even have a husband? Zobia was fifteen, and Lydia had heard her parents talking about whom she might marry. Father's choice was Theonides. Lydia had seen him in the forum; he was as tall as Father, but not quite as old. His hair and beard had fewer traces of gray than Father's. Theonides had a metalworking shop and was very influential in the silversmiths' guild—she had heard Father say so.

Lydia was only nine—almost ten, she reminded herself. Fifteen seemed far away, like the thought of cool weather in the middle of summer. She tried to form a picture in her mind of what her husband would look like. Would he be serious and always busy, like Father, or would he laugh sometimes and carry his children on his shoulders? Would he be a friend?

She turned over, rolling onto her stomach with her arms and legs hanging askew on either side of the tree limb. She would probably muss the pleats in her chiton, but she didn't care. She began idly peeling strips of the loose, papery bark and dropping it onto the grass below the tree. Then, without warning, a face appeared beneath her, staring up into the tree—staring at her.

"Do you plan to peel the whole tree or just the limb you're on?" the man said. He was tall and gaunt; his head was uncovered, and his beard and hair grew wild, like a tangle of weeds on ground no one cared about. He wore some sort of animal skin for a cover and carried a staff that was taller than he. It looked like a length of tree limb with the bark peeled off. Lydia watched him, waiting to see what he would do. He wasn't from Thyatira;

she had never seen him before. She sat up slowly, unsure whether to call for help or climb to a higher limb.

"You needn't be afraid," he said, still craning his neck back to peer up at her. "I don't make a habit of eating little girls." Despite his uncouth appearance, his speech was clear and precise; his voice reminded Lydia of the priest of Apollo on the day of the Sun Festival.

"I didn't hear you coming."

"No, I suppose not. I was asleep on the other side of the tree, and you woke me up with all your scrambling and thrashing about."

"I...I'm sorry."

Then he laughed—a clear, shining sound. His teeth were strong and even. "No, child. I didn't mean to scold you. I might have slept away the morning if you hadn't come along." He looked away from her then, toward the river. He moved his arm in a wide half-circle that took in the whole scene. "With the river to sing to me, I might have slept all day; who knows?" He looked back up at her. "Where am I, anyway?"

"What?"

"Where am I? What's the town behind those walls over there?"

"That's Thyatira." He had an accent, but it didn't sound western, like the settlers from Rome. It was different than anything she had heard.

"Really? I'd never have guessed." He looked toward the town, scratching the back of his neck. "Well, suppose you come down here and tell me what I need to know about this place." He held a hand toward her.

Lydia looked at him, unmoving.

"It's all right. You can come down." He beckoned her with

his hand. Then his faced changed; became very still. "Child, as the One God is my witness, you will come to no harm."

Lydia felt her arms and legs moving her toward the trunk of the tree. A part of her mind was watching as she climbed down, wondering what would happen next. Oddly, though, she felt no alarm. Somehow, she knew that what the strange man said was true: He would not hurt her. She reached the ground and sat with her back against the plane tree's bole. She pulled her knees up to her chest and clasped her arms around her legs. She looked at the man. "What do you want to know?"

He sat down abruptly where he was, maybe three cubits away. He sat cross-legged and laid his staff across his thighs. He had used rawhide strips to stitch together the sides of his hide garment. Lydia couldn't decide if his face was old or young; his beard obscured most of it. He seemed too nimble to be old and too sure and direct to be young.

"First, I need to know why a young girl is in this place with no one else around at a time of day when she ought to be doing her lessons or working on her loom. I also need to know why she is lounging in a tree and daydreaming of things she'll find out in due course anyway."

A little thrill of fear tickled her spine. "I thought you wanted to know about the town."

"I do. I just asked my first question."

"But it was about me."

"You live here, do you not?"

She nodded.

"And why should the apparent unhappiness of one of this city's young girls not be of as much interest to me as the doings of its leading citizens?"

Lydia looked at the ground and shrugged. A long silence followed. She risked a quick glance at him from beneath her eyebrows. He was watching her with an attentive, waiting expression, like a schoolmaster who had just posed a question to a student.

"There was a race," she said, finally.

"Who won?"

"I did."

"Ah. And because of this victory you are out here by yourself, pulling the bark off a tree that has done you no harm?"

"I raced against boys."

He raised his eyebrows.

"No girl has ever done that before. Not here."

"Ah." He had a pleased expression. "Never?"

She shook her head.

"And you won?"

Lydia nodded. The stranger chuckled, rubbing his knees.

"Interesting. The most interesting information I've had in a while." He kept smiling, looking at a place just above her head. Presently, he gave a little shudder and his eyes flickered back to her face. "Well, time for you to be going along home, don't you think?"

Lydia looked down, digging her thumb into the ground beside her.

"Your place is with your family," he said in a different, softer voice. "At least for now. Perhaps, later...."

She looked up at him, her forehead wrinkled in bafflement. "How do you know so much about me?"

He gave her a sad little smile. "I will not answer that question. Still, I suppose it's only fair to let you try again, after all you've told me. Go ahead. Ask another."

Lydia thought for a long time. "Where are you from?"

Again the sad smile. "Nowhere," he said. In a single motion he rose to his feet. "And everywhere. Now, you must go."

With a start, Lydia opened her eyes and looked about her. She stood on the main road, where the path to the river joined it. She had no memory of getting up from the ground beneath the plane tree or walking the winding path up the rise from the river. But she had not been asleep! He was real, as real as the ground beneath her feet! She looked at her clothing. There was a green stain from a leaf she had crushed as she climbed the tree. There was the place her skirts had wrinkled as she lay on her stomach atop the broad limb. She had not imagined it. It was not a dream.

She walked slowly along the road toward the city gates. The sun had risen halfway up the sky, and traffic was thinning as everyone sought out shade to wait out the heat of the day. She reached the gates and turned into the street where her house was. And there, coming toward her, was Menander.

Three

His head was down and he walked with a slow, foot-dragging gait. His pedagogue walked the usual three paces behind him, but Lydia could see the slave's lips moving and the taut line of his mouth. Whatever he was saying to Menander wasn't pleasant.

She wasn't sure what to do. Should she duck down an alley, hoping she wouldn't be seen? Should she walk past him, her head high, as if he didn't exist?

"There!" The pedagogue was staring at her, pointing at her. "There is where all the trouble started! This girl who wants to run with the boys!"

Lydia felt her face burning. She stared wildly about until she saw a narrow, dark crevice between the walls of two houses. She ran toward it.

"Lydia, wait!"

Menander's voice. She paused and looked at him uncertainly.

"Young master, you must not speak to this…this—"

"Krates, this is the daughter of a citizen of this city," said

Menander in a stern voice. "Your duty is to see to my education, and I have to tolerate your scoldings as far as they concern that. But my father will not be pleased when I tell him you've insulted the child of a free family."

The pedagogue fell into a silent scowl, tucking his hands beneath his armpits and half-turning away from his charge. Lydia stared at him, then at Menander. Finally, the boy broke the silence.

"Lydia…I'm sorry. I spoke poorly to you this morning. You won the race fairly, and I shouldn't have—"

"It's all right. I understand why you did it. I shouldn't have said anything to you in front of your friends." She looked down at her feet. "I'm still not sure why I did." She heard the pedagogue's indignant sniff.

"Why are you going home, Menander?" she asked. "It's barely midday."

"Philoteles said something smart during numbers drill and I hit him. Macrinus made me leave school for the rest of the day." He dug his toe into the dust of the street. "I'm sure I'll get a beating when Krates tells my father."

"Oh, Menander. I'm sorry."

He glanced up at her and shrugged. "It's my fault. You won fairly. I had no reason to be angry."

Lydia nodded. "Well. I need to go home. It's getting hot."

Menander walked on. Just as Lydia passed him in the street, he said in a voice barely loud enough for her to hear, "Next time we race, I'll be ready."

When she looked at him, he was smiling.

Lydia's thoughts were interrupted by the sound of a table being dragged across the stone floor. She opened her eyes. Euodia had pulled the small, black table under one of the western windows. From a bag on the floor she withdrew some sort of garment, along with a needle and some brightly hued embroidery thread. She placed the extra thread and needles on the table, then seated herself in the best of the light and began to work on one of the garment's sleeves.

"That's a nice tunic. Whom is it for?" Lydia asked.

"My grandson's oldest. He's to be baptized at the next assembly, you know."

"No, I hadn't heard. You must be very proud."

"He's a good boy." She took a few stitches, then held her work up to the light with a critical eye. "His parents have taught him well." She turned the sleeve this way and that, then pulled it back into her lap and went on with her embroidery.

"Does your grandson ever ask about his father?"

Euodia's hands faltered, then resumed. She shook her head. "Not for many years now."

"I'm sorry, Euodia. It must have been very hard for him— and for your daughter—all those years, not knowing."

She shrugged and gave a little nod.

"I've lived a long time, Euodia—too long, really—and still there are so many things I don't understand."

Euodia stitched in silence for a long time. "I told her there was no use waiting. There were any number of suitable and willing young men through the years, and pining for him wouldn't bring him back."

Lydia turned her face toward the ceiling. The cobwebs had proliferated among the rafters. Someone ought to take a broom to them, but Lydia realized she didn't care enough to spend words on it. She pulled in a long breath. "She loved him very much, didn't she?"

"I suppose." Lydia heard the soft punches of the needle piercing the woolen sleeve. "But that's no reason to stay in mourning the rest of her life."

"Maybe not mourning, Euodia. Sometimes a heart can hold only one love. Or sometimes, risking such a loss again seems too dangerous." Lydia turned her head to look at Euodia, but the other woman kept her eyes down, watching the track of her needle across her great-grandson's baptismal robe.

"To the god. Threnides, son of Anaxemenes—President of the Guild of Fullers and Dyers; aedile of the trade guilds along with Philostratus; twice member of the City Council, during the praetorship of Marcus Livius Nervum and again during the praetorship of Tullius Rufus Sempronius; initiate of the Great Mysteries at Eleusis; beloved of Apollo—paid with his own funds for the building of this house for the use of the Guild of Fullers and Dyers, in the eleventh year of the glorious reign of the Divine Emperor Tiberius Julius Caesar Augustus."

At least, that's what Menander told her the words said; Lydia couldn't read Latin. The inscription was carved on the limestone blocks above the entrance to the new guild-hall.

"Your father must be very proud," Menander said.

Lydia nodded. "The high priests of Apollo and Artemis are personally offering victims at the dedication." She tilted her head back to peer at the building's imposing front, at the four tall, fluted columns and their Doric capitals. This structure had consumed her father's life for the past three years. Nearly every night he closeted himself in the men's suite with architects, masons, engineers, stonecutters, or artisans of some other kind. Zobia scolded Mother nearly constantly over the way Father was neglecting both his sons-in-law in his obsession with this monument. But then, ever since her second child had been born, Zobia had grown more and more insufferable. Thetis was still too new to marriage, still too absorbed in the novelty of having a husband, to give much trouble. But, Zobia.... Had it been allowed, Lydia would have gladly hidden herself in the *andrōn* with the men and their building talk rather than sit with Mother and endure Zobia's tirades, interspersed with the shrill scolding of her children. Lydia wondered why, if Zobia found matters so intolerable, she called on Mother and Father so often. Maybe her husband wearied so of her nagging that he sent her to her parents' home to give his ears some rest.

The limestone blocks of the guild house gleamed in the bright sun of autumn. Since its completion four days earlier, a steady stream of sightseers had circled this newest addition to the forum square.

Menander leaned close and whispered, "Have you spoken to him yet?"

She gave him a quick look. "No. He's hardly been anywhere except here or in his chambers since the building started. After the dedication there'll be more time."

"Yes, that's what worries me."

Lydia saw her brothers across the forum. "I have to go. Andronicus and Philip are looking for me."

She felt his hand touch hers, then take hold.

"Menander. If they see us—"

"I know. Go on." He released her hand.

She started to walk away.

"Lydia."

She stopped.

"Soon."

She nodded without turning around.

Lydia worked her way across the crowded square. She and Menander, from their meeting place behind the statue of Fortuna, in a small alcove on the side of the Temple of Apollo, had watched the crowd steadily thicken throughout the morning. The beggars had been first on the scene as usual, fighting each other for the prime locations. But by this time, practically all Thyatira had gathered for the dedication of the guildhall. Lydia had the thought that it would be a good day to be a thief. Surely, by now, every house in the city was vacant.

The two of them had left their houses early, both on the pretext of meeting friends before the dedication. And it had not been a lie, Lydia reminded herself. Menander was a friend in the truest sense. That what they felt for each other had deepened far beyond friendship didn't change that basic fact. Not that Mother would have noticed, anyway. When Lydia had let herself through the gate, Mother was sitting on the bench beside the cistern, plucking a lyre and composing an ode, keeping a wary eye on the door to the andrōn in case her husband should enter the courtyard. Father seemed less and less tolerant of Mother's artistic endeavors these days, and his impatience had grown more noticeable with the approach of this dedication. Mother did her best to keep such activities out of his notice. In fact, to Lydia it seemed that Mother often contrived to be almost anywhere but in her husband's presence. She couldn't remember the last time she had seen them together in any companionable setting. It saddened her to think that both of them had no one to hear their secrets.

Lydia smiled. It still surprised her sometimes: the gradual, quiet way in which that sour-faced boy who had turned away from her in the street had become her most treasured companion.

It had surprised them both, like traveling to a faraway place and seeing someone from home. Or like hearing someone say aloud what you had just been thinking. Lydia had lost count of the number of times, during their conversations, their eyes had widened as they looked at each other. "You, too?" Lydia would never have imagined the depth of her pleasure in finding another who shared so many thoughts she had assumed were hers alone.

"What are you grinning at?"

Lydia's brothers stood in front of her. Phillip was studying her with narrowed eyes. "I thought you were meeting some of your friends here."

"I did. But I saw the two of you, and I guessed it was almost time."

"Yes, it is. Father sent us to bring you inside."

She gave Phillip a bold stare. "Then why are we still standing here?"

He studied her a moment longer and turned. "Come on, Andronicus. You too, Lydia." Phillip strode away toward the guild house. Andronicus gave Lydia a quick, guilty look, then hurried to catch up with his older brother.

They passed through the milling throng and climbed the three broad steps that spanned the entire front of the building. The four pillars supported the overhang of the hip roof, which covered a large portico. They crossed the portico and passed through the entry, guarded by two ornate, bronze doors—each nearly six cubits tall and half as many wide—and into the spacious main chamber. Inside were shrines to Pietas and the Genius of Rome, as well as to the guild's patron deities. There were Roman-style frescoes along both long walls. Two courses of painted stone pillars supported the roof. At the back of the hall, behind the main altar, was a door leading to small rooms for meetings or social gatherings. The floor was paved with squares of polished marble set in alternating courses of white and black.

Father and Mother stood with the other officials of the guild, waiting for the signal to proceed outside to meet the priests and begin the dedication ceremony. Lydia looked at her father. He seemed larger, expanded. The other officials deferred to him with their gestures, their expressions. This was his day. With the dedication of this building, her father's status as a public benefactor was secured.

Mother stood a little apart from the group, gazing upward into the darkness below the roof beams, probably trying out different tunes for her ode. Then she noticed her husband staring at her from the group of men and quickly pulled her attention back to the occasion at hand. Lydia sighed. At least they wouldn't have to put up with Zobia and her unruly children today. She and Thetis would be with their husbands.

Father turned toward them. "Ah, here they are! My sons. And you found Lydia. Very good."

"I wasn't lost," Lydia said, but he had already turned back toward the other men. He talked with them a few more moments before an acolyte came and told them the procession from the Temple of Apollo was about to begin. Quickly, Father formed them into a line with himself at the head, followed by the officials of the guild, then Phillip and Andronicus, then Mother, and, finally, Lydia. They proceeded out the doorway onto the portico. As Lydia passed through the entrance, she heard the heavy doors swing shut behind her.

There was a crash of cymbals and tabors, then the sound of lyres and singing as a procession of priests and acolytes paced slowly down the steps of the Temple of Apollo and into the forum. A lane opened through the crowd as the parade moved sedately toward the front of the guildhall.

Phoebus Apollo, of thee the swan sings clearly with his wings,
alighting on the bank beside the whirling stream Peneus;
and the singer with his clear-toned lyre
sweet sounding, first and last doth always sing of thee.
So hail, O Lord, We seek thy favor with our song.

The chorus of men and young boys was robed in dazzling white linen, and each of them wore on his head a wreath of laurel. Lydia could see, at the back of the column, the high priest of Apollo, with his gold-trimmed, white, woolen cape, its shroud draped to obscure his face to anyone not standing directly in front of him. He held his hands palms up; on one palm rested the haft of the knife and on the other the blade. Beside him strode the priest of Artemis, wearing his coat of rich green, the color of the woodlands and meadows sacred to the goddess. He, too, carried before him a knife consecrated to the ceremonial uses of the cult. Behind each of the priests was an acolyte, leading on a leash a victim for the dedicatory sacrifices. The priest of Apollo would offer a pig, it appeared, and the priest of Artemis a goat. To ensure the animals' docility, their tenders had earlier mixed mandrake root with their food, Lydia guessed.

Lydia watched the yearling pig trotting along behind its keeper. It was white, a color sacred to the god, and its hooves had been painted with gold pigment for the occasion. Since its weaning, this animal had probably lived in comfort in an enclosure attached to the Temple of Apollo, fed on the best grains, with pure milk or cream to drink, petted and fussed over by the long-faced acolyte who now held its leash.

The procession reached the steps of the guildhall and divided to the right and the left. The celebrants ranged themselves along the front of the building. They continued their hymn until the priests reached the altar, a rounded block of black granite, a stark contrast to the pure white of the limestone on which it rested. Carved all around with images of sacrifice and cultic piety, the altar sat in the center of the portico, at the edge of the top step. The priests stood in front of the altar, and the priest of Apollo raised the knife, still resting across both palms, above his head. The hymn ceased; the crowd quieted.

"To our Lord Apollo Tyrimnaios, master of the life-giving sun, whose unblinking eye sees and judges all men according to their deeds; before whose face none can stand except the great Zeus, thy father, and holy Leto, thy mother; whose burning purity cleanses us of our guilt; who punishes the guilty with thy terrible bow, but sends from thy lyre songs to pleasure the hearts of the pious. Receive now, O Lord, the blood of this victim as an offering, and bless this house on which the blood rests and all the pious who enter here."

He stepped back and the priest of Artemis moved forward, likewise raising his blade above his head.

"To the great goddess Artemis and her divine brother, Apollo Tyrimnaios, we consecrate this building. O our lady, benefactress and protectress, guardian of the forests and meadows, keeper of the childbed, jealous ward of our wives' and daughters' virtue, accept these gifts as they arise from our hearts, and take pleasure in the piety of our almsgiving."

The priest of Artemis stood over the altar, and his acolyte moved the kid into position. The drugged animal never resisted as the boy picked it up and laid it on its side. Another acolyte gathered up its legs as the first pulled its head back, baring its neck. The priest placed the tip of the blade just under the animal's jawline, then, with a quick thrust, pierced its throat and sliced keenly outward. The goat kicked and struggled, splashing the acolytes' white garments with crimson, but they held it firm. Another assistant held a silver bowl below the notch in the edge of the altar and caught the bright red, foaming blood. To Lydia, the goat's blood seemed to flow forever, but at last the bowl-bearer straightened and stepped back. A temple slave picked up the goat to carry it back to the temple.

Now the priest of Apollo approached the altar.

The pig, even in its stupefied state, scented the hot blood on the altar and began protesting and trying to wriggle away. The priest's lips pressed together disapprovingly as he watched his acolytes struggling with the resisting beast. The pig's squeals grew louder and more insistent as three of the assistants picked it up and carried it toward the altar. The priest motioned impatiently to another acolyte, who stepped around to the pig's head and tried to steady it for the deathblow. The pig snapped and bit, causing the acolyte to jerk back his hands. Finally, he was able to clamp a fist around the pig's snout and clamp its head in the bend of his elbow. The priest bent quickly and stabbed the pig's throat, slashing outward. The loud squeals ended abruptly. The only remaining sounds were the thrashing of the dying animal and the gurgling of its blood as it flowed into the gold bowl held below the notch in the altar.

The salty, metallic smell of the animals' mingled blood was thick in Lydia's nostrils. She could at least avoid looking at the sanguine mess on and around the altar, she decided. Lydia allowed her eyes to rove the crowd gathered to witness the dedication. There, in the front ranks, his gaze never leaving her face, was Menander. Lydia permitted a tiny smile to tease the corners of her lips. His dark eyes answered, though he moved not a muscle.

As the pig's carcass was lifted from the altar, the two priests elevated the bowls of blood. Each turned and handed his bowl to an assistant, then dipped sprigs of laurel and juniper into the blood. Lydia and her family bowed their heads to receive the anointing. Lydia felt the warm, thick droplets spattering from the branches onto the back of her neck.

Just as the priests were about to move forward, sprinkling the blood across the portico and doors of the guildhall, a murmur began from the back of the crowd. Lydia turned to look. The bystanders nearest the place where the main road entered the forum were shifting back and forth, making way for someone to walk toward the steps of the guildhall. As the front ranks of the gathering parted, into the open space before the steps emerged the strange, bent, grizzled form of the oracle of the Sybil Sambethe.

The crone hobbled forward on her bowed legs, gripping her crooked staff with a gnarled fist. Of all the shrines and temples in and around Thyatira, the shrine of the Sybil was strangest and least known, at least to Lydia. No one knew the age of the old woman who supposedly sat night and day beside the altar of her patroness, wafting incense ceaselessly into her face and waiting for the next dream or vision. She ate nothing but the flesh of sparrows and larks, it was said, and drank only the juice squeezed from wild gourds.

Her hair was tangled and starkly white. She wore a robe of unbleached wool, gathered at her waist with a piece of coarsely woven rope. She limped forward toward the group gathered at the altar, her eyes on the ground in front of her feet. She moved slowly, thoughtfully, with no evidence that she was aware of the silent throng staring at her from all sides.

The priest of Apollo watched her approach with an irritated expression, his lips pulled to one side. The twigs now hung forgotten at his side, dripping tiny pools of thickening blood onto the white limestone pavement of the portico.

The old woman grunted her way up the first step, then the second. She detoured around the altar without a glance. Only when she stood atop the third step did she raise her face. Her eyes shifted among them, sliding quickly across the priest of Artemis and the high priest of Apollo, sorting among the guild officials, slowing as they reached Lydia's family, then halting finally on her. The hooded, dark gaze bored into Lydia. She felt the eyes of everyone in the forum on her. The old woman moved toward her, still staring into her face. She trod unheeding in a puddle of blood beside the altar. She stood in front of Lydia, took her chin in a hand that was surprisingly gentle and soft. And she began to speak.

ydia felt a hand brush her cheek. Her eyes fluttered and opened. It was Euodia, leaning near in the flickering light of her bedside lamp.

"I must leave now, my friend," Euodia said. "The girls are back. Rest well tonight, and I will come again tomorrow."

"If I rest as I wish, you won't need to come tomorrow."

Euodia gave her a sidelong glance. "It may be the Lord isn't anxious to summon such a crotchety old woman. I think he delays, hoping you'll smooth your rough edges."

"The Lord knows me better than that."

Euodia chuckled softly. "All right, then."

Lydia found her friend's hand, gave it a squeeze. "Thank you for coming."

It was unlike Father to host a banquet without telling anyone, but it appeared that was exactly what he had done. One group of slaves carried out the food vessels with their despoiled remains: the picked-over, crumbled leavings of the roasted pig—barely enough meat and sinew left to hold the bones together—the small, broken fragments of what had once been mounds of bread, the mostly empty baskets with the few, bruised figs that none of the guests had wanted, the bowls of honey, scraped almost clean enough not to require washing. And another group of servants carried in the amphorae of wine for the symposium. Already some of the men were showing signs of excess enjoyment; Lydia suspected some of them had opted not to water the wine they drank with their meal.

There were hetairae here, and that, too, was unlike Father. Some of the painted, jeweled courtesans sat on the couches with the guests, laughing and whispering and plying them with more wine. Others sat in a group in the center of the triclinium, singing an old Mysian love song and plucking lyres and kitharas. Lydia could never remember Father entertaining his guests with paid women.

The priest of Apollo was reclining near her father at the head table, a girl on either side of him. One of them was refilling his cup from a long-necked ewer, and the other was taking coins from a purse tied to his belt. When the bag ran out of coins, Lydia's father leaned over and dropped in another handful of silver.

Lydia wasn't quite sure why she was here in the first place. A part of her whispered uneasily that she should be with Mother in the women's suite instead of snooping here in the andron, seeing things she probably didn't want to know about anyway. If Father saw her, he would be embarrassed in front of his guests. Not to mention that she would be severely punished.

And then she saw Menander, leaning back on a corner of the couch, grinning like a fool at one of the hetairae who sat on his lap and made up bawdy couplets in parody of Plato. So! For this he spent all their money on scrolls and papyri—so he could appreciate the jokes of a party woman? Lydia felt the anger rising up in her, stinging the corners of her eyes. She realized the courtesan had Syntyche's face. Then Menander's form shifted and shrunk. Now it was Paul who sat there, the lamplight glinting on his bald head, his eyes burning dark in their deep sockets. He wasn't listening to the doggerel verses of the courtesan, but staring intently at Lydia—or so she thought until she looked closer. His face held that rigid, gaping look; his mouth hung open slightly. Lydia could see the gleam of spittle draining from the corner of his lips into his beard. He needed her help. She wanted to go to him, to move the Syntyche courtesan out of the way, to hold his face in her hands and speak low and carefully to him until the bluish, pinched lips moved again and the throat swallowed and he came back from whatever strange, inner landscape he traveled during these unpredictable episodes. But she couldn't move—Father would see her. She could only watch as Paul sat there, the revel swirling and breaking around him like the water of a stream.

Lydia stirred and woke. She felt the familiar contours of her bed. In the corner by the hearth, Euterpe snored softly. At the foot of the bed, Clystra sat in the chair, her head lolling on her chest. Lydia realized it wouldn't do to die in her sleep; Clystra would never forgive herself.

What a strange dream! What did it mean—if anything? Maybe more to the point: What use did she have for such a dream now, when all her dreams were about to be absorbed in the endless rest of death? If God wanted to give her a message, why didn't he just wait until she was there and deliver it himself?

Lydia wondered what watch of the night it was. Odd that she should care. Except that she had a sudden urge to see Syntyche. Maybe the dream had reminded her. When the sun was up, she would send one of the girls to fetch her.

Lydia remembered a game she used to play with herself as a child. She was always a light sleeper, even in her youth; frequently she would wake in the darkness of her chamber, likely the only one awake in the house. Lying on her couch, she could turn her head to one side and see through the latticed window to the star-encrusted night sky. Lydia fancied that the whole world was held in a huge sack and that the stars were tiny holes in the sack, through which peeped pinpoints of light from the true day. If she could only get close enough to one of those tiny holes, Lydia used to think, she could see outside the sack, to the way things really were. She used to try to find one really bright, steady star. She imagined it was the bit of light that leaked through the neck of the sack, the place where it was cinched shut, held in the grip of—what? A god? One of the Titans from before the birth of time? Or, her girl-self wondered, was it Nothing that held the sack closed? If she could fly up like Daedalus to the place where the light was, if she could find the neck of the sack and crawl through, win her way past whatever blind force or infinite will held it shut, what might she see? What might she tell the others, when she came back, of the real light beyond the sack in which the world was wrapped?

Too bad. The way her bed was situated now, she couldn't see any windows. She couldn't see the holes in the sack. When she died, would her spirit fly like Daedalus in the old story? Would she soar toward God; would she burst with a shout of joy through a hole in the sack into whatever Beyond waited on the other side? She wouldn't be coming back to bring news from there, she guessed. That was too bad, also.

Or, maybe—just as well.

Poor Syntyche, she was a mess, as usual. Lydia had given Clystra very careful instructions about how to find Syntyche's house on High Street and about precisely what to say. She didn't want her friend alarmed by having it seem to be a last-gasp summons. But here was Syntyche, flustered and disheveled, weeping over her and clinging to her hand as if this were, indeed, the final good–bye.

"There's no need to be upset, my dear. I'm dying, but not yet. At least, I don't think so. Please, sit down and calm yourself."

"I came as soon as I could, Lydia—"

"Of course you did."

"Your servant said you were asking for me, so naturally I was afraid—"

Lydia darted a glance at Clystra, who ducked her head and studied the tops of her sandals. "I did ask Clystra to bring you to me, yes. And I'm so glad you've come. Can the girls get anything for you? Some wine, maybe? A bit of bread?"

Syntyche pressed her hands to her face and took in a deep breath through her nose, drawing herself up straight. She dropped her arms to her sides and gave Lydia her best imitation of a bright, cheerful look. "No, thank you. I'm fine now. Really." She dragged up a stool and sat down beside the bed. "Now you must tell me how you've been since I saw you last." She grimaced as soon as the words were out of her mouth. Lydia gave a dry little chuckle.

"Syntyche, I've been just as you see me now. It seems I've had little time for much else."

"Oh, Lydia, I'm sorry—"

"Never mind. Ask one of the girls to bring me some water, would you?"

Syntyche motioned Euterpe over. She took the jug from the servant's arms and poured a little water into a small, shallow dish, spilling onto the tabletop nearly as much as she put in the vessel. Slowly she brought the dish to Lydia's lips. The tip of Syntyche's tongue played along her upper lip. She reminded Lydia of a young girl trying to learn to thread a needle. Lydia took a sip or two of water and motioned it away.

"I spoke of you to Euodia yesterday."

Syntyche gave her a startled glance, then quickly rose from the stool and paced toward the window, hugging herself. "Why would you spoil her visit so? Or cut it short. No doubt when you said my name, she left immediately."

"Syntyche, come here."

She turned slowly and walked back with hesitant steps. She wouldn't look at Lydia.

"It's been over thirty years, Syntyche. What will it take?"

"I tried, Lydia! I did everything except crawl on the ground at her feet, and still she—" Syntyche gestured helplessly and spun away again, narrowly avoiding a collision with the table beside Lydia's bed. "Nothing I can say will make any difference. It's her problem, not mine."

"She says much the same."

"I never meant to hurt either of them! It was a stupid blunder! How many times have I tried to tell her that?"

"But the hurt is still there, Syntyche. An arrow let slip by mistake can kill just as surely as a carefully aimed shot. You can surely have no doubt about my knowledge of this." Lydia let the words soak in a moment. "Go to her, Syntyche. Try again."

Syntyche paced back and forth, shaking her head. "But it has been so long. So many years."

"And the years haven't eased it, have they? The more time you let pass, the harder the healing."

Syntyche stopped pacing and looked at her. "Why, Lydia? Why now?"

"Because you are both my friends, and it grieves me to part from this life with the breach unmended. Because Paul asked you to do this years ago, and I still wish enough to honor his memory to prevail upon your friendship." Lydia smiled. "And because people will do things for a dying old woman that they wouldn't do for anyone else."

Syntyche stared at her.

"Oh, it's true, dear. Dying gives you a kind of power you never had while you were well. The closer you approach death, the more you are wrapped in its aura. By the time you finally go, you're nearly invincible."

By now, not only Syntyche, but Clystra and Euterpe as well, were looking at Lydia as if a gourdvine had just sprouted from her forehead. By the edgy glances the three gave each other, Lydia could tell they were trying to decide if her mind had preceded her body into the next world. She couldn't hold her face still any longer. The laugh shook her and set her to coughing.

Syntyche grabbed the water dish, spilling most of its contents in her haste. She slid an arm beneath Lydia's shoulders to help her drink.

"Ah, thank you, friend," Lydia said. "The water was good, but I think the laugh was better."

"Such things you say."

"Part of my charm and you know it."

"Yes, I think so. You can say almost anything, Lydia. As long as I've known you, you've been able to do that." She sat down on the stool at the foot of the bed and leaned forward, propping her elbow on one knee and cupping her chin in a palm. "I'll miss that. It'll be too bad, not having someone who can say whatever she likes, whenever she likes."

Lydia turned her face away from Syntyche toward the window in the far wall. Not such a great talent, really, she thought. Sometimes it's better to keep from saying what's on your mind.

"And what is my charm, do you suppose?" Syntyche asked. Now she was toying with the water dish, moving it slowly across the top of the table, dragging it through the puddles of spilled water, drawing them out into rings and arcs of smeared droplets. "What will people miss about me when I'm gone?"

Lydia turned back to look at her friend.

"When I was a girl," Syntyche said, "my younger brother was forever collecting stray dogs. My father roared and my mother fretted, but still he kept on adopting every poor, flea-bitten brute he could coax into following him home. Do you know what finally made him stop?"

Lydia shook her head.

"Longinus, one of my father's slaves." Syntyche smiled at the memory. "He was an old man, stooped and slow, but very tall and gaunt. He told my brother that when he died, he would be buried in a shallow grave on the hillside above the town, since he was not a freedman. He said one of my brother's dogs would likely dig him up and steal one of his leg bones. He would have to go into the afterlife hopping on one leg. At his height, he said, it was a long way for him to fall, even as a shade. He asked my brother if he wouldn't have pity on poor old Longinus and stop bringing home so many dogs." She stopped sliding the dish and looked up at Lydia. "Of course, that was many years ago, before I knew about God and his son, Jesus Christ. I don't believe in such foolishness, now."

"Certainly not."

"Isn't it strange, the things we remember?"

Not as strange as the things we forget, Lydia thought.

"My brother loved those awful dogs," Syntyche said. "He named them all—and he remembered their names. When he left for school in the mornings, they would play around his feet. 'Now, Scapias, move over. Get out of the way, Darkfoot, can't you see I have to go to school?'" She shook her head. "Yet, he cared more about Longinus's poor shade, hopping about on one leg."

"Everyone ought to consider the dead, don't you think, Syntyche? It eases the consciences of the living." Lydia looked down, plucking an imaginary crumb off the top blanket. "Do you ever think of Paul?"

Syntyche cupped her elbows in her palms and stared into the air above Lydia's head. "Of course I do. How could I not?"

"What do you remember most about him?"

"His voice. Sometimes so weak and raspy you could barely hear him. Then, other times, without really being any louder, it cut like a knife."

Lydia nodded, closing her eyes. Yes. The voice.

"And then, the way he talked: so earnestly and with such passion. As though he had never thought of anything else in his life except the thing he was telling you right then. I remember thinking sometimes, 'I must listen closely, if only because it seems so important to this man.' I was afraid of him, a little, I think. Weren't you?"

Lydia didn't open her eyes. She knew Syntyche was watching her face, waiting for her response. "No, I wasn't afraid of him. I think it would have been better if I had been." There. Let her make what she could of that.

A silence passed. Lydia waited. Finally, Syntyche spoke, her voice wilted a little by disappointment. "He seemed so absorbed. Completely taken up with what he was about."

"Yes, he was that. At least, most of the time." This really was too cruel. She would have to quit dropping hints about matters she had no intention of disclosing. Still, even such tidbits would entertain the gossip circles for years to come.

It had been unseasonably cool that day, Lydia remembered. The middle of summer, and yet she recalled being chilled by the wind as she sat on the grassy bank of the Krenides. She was wishing she had brought a heavier robe as she listened to Euodia's slave read from the Torah scroll.

"Abraham looked up and saw three men standing nearby," the old man read. "When he saw them, he hurried from the entrance of his tent—"

Syntyche was first to notice them. At her look, the rest of them gradually turned around to see four strangers standing at the edge of the path that ran between the city's western wall and the stream. One of them was tall, with an erect, decorous bearing. One of them was young; his eyes switched back and forth among his companions, waiting for a cue as to what he should do next, it seemed. One was short and stout, and the fourth stood slightly in front of the rest. He was short also, but the opposite of stout— rather bony, in fact. He had forward-angled shoulders and a balding head that seemed too large for his frame.

The rest of the women were watching her to see what she would do. Lydia rose to address the strangers, her eyes meeting those of the tallest one.

"Grace to you, friends. How may we be of assistance?"

The answer came not from the tall, refined one, but from his slight, stoop-shouldered companion. "As we were walking down the path, we heard the words of the Torah," he said, gesturing toward the scroll still held by Euodia's man. The speaker's voice was thin and nasal. Lydia remembered her surprise at his recognition of the Scriptures. "Since we came here four days ago, we've been looking for fellow believers in the one true God. May we join you?"

Lydia hesitated a moment. The Jewish religion was officially unpopular these last few months since Claudius's edict. They knew nothing about these men.

But the eyes of the small man burned into her; urged her with silent pleadings. She nodded, returning to her seat, and the four men moved in among them. Lydia looked at the skinny, bald man. "You seem to know the Torah. Would you like to read?"

The man nodded and all but snatched the scroll from the slave's hands. The old man tried to point to the place where he had left off, but the stranger shook his head as he shuffled the scroll back and forth, searching for some other passage. Lydia stifled her annoyance at such a breach of manners and watched as the small man's fingers slid back and forth with practiced motions along the lines of Hebrew characters. Finally, he found the place he wanted. With a grunt and a nod, he began to read.

"The LORD had said to Abram, 'Leave your country, your people and your father's household and go to the land I will show you. I will make you into a great nation and I will bless

you; I will make your name great, and you will be a blessing. I
will bless those who bless you, and whoever curses you I will
curse; and all peoples on earth will be blessed through you.'"
Carefully he rolled the Torah scroll and slipped it into its leather
sheath. He kissed it and handed it to the slave. Here was a man
skilled in the Hebrew Scriptures. Lydia suddenly realized…
maybe even a rabbi! There had been no rabbi in Philippi ever,
as far as anyone knew.

"Today I will show you how this promise to our father
Abraham has been fulfilled," he said. And he began telling them
things—things Lydia had always known, but would never have
guessed….

"Why do you think he was like that?" Syntyche wanted to know.

"How do you mean?"

"So absorbed—so constantly intent."

Lydia opened her eyes and looked at her friend. "Because he
was chosen."

As the oracle spoke, Lydia felt the droplets of blood on her neck
trickling down past her shoulder blades. She had to stifle the
urge to scratch. The oracle's appearance was a great omen, and
she knew she mustn't do anything to spoil it.

"Beyond earth and sea, beyond sun and moon, beyond light
and dark, beyond time itself dwells the Unmade," the old
woman chanted. "Unseen, it sees. Unknown, it knows.
Unmoved, it moves all things." The oracle closed her eyes and
put her hand on top of Lydia's head. Her lips moved noiselessly.

Lydia felt awkward and exposed. All Thyatira stared at her

as the holy woman held onto her and went on and on with her strange, silent communion. Lydia wished she could at least see Menander, but she dared not try. The priests were standing very close and they would notice. She would be thought impious and ill-omened. All she could see was the oracle's face, clenched in hushed concentration.

Now the old woman began to sway slowly back and forth, a low moan escaping her lips. "Blood," she croaked. "It must have blood." Her eyes snapped open as she flung her hands above her head and staggered backward. "Blood!" she cried with a sudden, ear-splitting shriek. "Blood!" She flung down her cane, and it clattered down the steps of the guildhall.

Lydia could not move. She stared wide-eyed as the oracle careened about like a drunken fool, screaming "Blood!" over and over. She staggered over to the altar and smeared her hands with the spillage from the sacrifices. Then she turned, coming toward Lydia with a crazed look in her eyes, her red-stained hands held in front of her. "The blood will be on you," the oracle said. "It will cover you. The blood will cover you!" The old woman seized Lydia's face between her hands, rubbed the blood on her cheeks, her forehead, down the front of her clothing. Lydia wanted to scream, but her throat was paralyzed by shock and loathing.

Then, just as abruptly as it had started, the oracle's seizure ended. She stood up straight and looked about her. She looked at the guildhall and the altar. She looked at the priests and the other officials. With a final, careful glance at Lydia, she turned and hobbled down the steps. She bent over to retrieve her cane, grunting as she straightened. Then she ambled slowly back the way she had come, the crowd parting silently before her.

he oracle left the forum. Lydia touched her fingers to her cheek; they came away smeared with blood. All around the forum, the crowd stood like a wall of silent faces. Her frantic eyes found her mother on the temple platform near the altar. But even in her mother's face, Lydia saw the reflection of her marking, her separation. Lydia doubled over with a sob and crumpled to the pavement.

She stayed in her room four days. For a while on the first day, her mother tried to convince her to join the family in the dining room. Lydia supposed her father either didn't care or was too disturbed by the omen's possible implications for his civic respectability. When her mother's pleas proved useless, the servants began bringing food to her at mealtimes. They wouldn't come inside her room; they set baskets outside her door, like votive offerings at a shrine.

Eight days after the dedication, she allowed herself to be talked into leaving the house to attend a ceremony at the guildhall. Knots of people in the street stared at her as she approached with her family; conversations halted as she passed. It was easy to imagine their whispers: "She's the one: Threnides' daughter, the girl marked by the priestess." Her singularity angered and frightened her; made her want to run, to drown the hateful whispers in the rushing of the wind past her ears.

Her involuntary celebrity made it impossible to meet Menander without being noticed. Of course, it was entirely possible that Menander wouldn't want to have anything to do with one so tainted by strangeness.

Finally, she could bear the uncertainty no longer. She called Hestia, the slave she mistrusted least, and promised her two silver *drachmae* if she could get a message to Menander without being found out by anyone in either household. Hestia's curiosity was bested only by her yearning for money, so she quickly agreed. Lydia concocted a story for her mother about an ill friend and sent Hestia out the gate with a basket of henbane, garlic, hyssop, and mint. Then she went up to her room and thrust her attention onto a scroll of Euripides to distract her mind.

The midmorning hours trickled into afternoon and still Hestia didn't return. Euripides long forgotten, Lydia paced back and forth between her window and her couch, stopping by the window at each round to peer up the street for any sign of the slave woman. What could have happened? Even if Menander had summarily refused her, why should it be taking so long?

Finally, when the afternoon shadows had crept nearly halfway across the street, Lydia saw Hestia scurrying toward the gate of the house, still carrying her basket of herbs. Her face flashed up toward the window where Lydia waited, and then she was entering the courtyard.

Lydia raced down the stairs to the atrium and rushed up to

the slave. "What took you so long?" she whispered.

"I had to wait for him to leave the *rhētor's* with the other young men, didn't I?"

"Quiet!" Lydia hissed, as her mother rounded the corner from the women's suite, a scroll in her hand and a distracted, studious look on her face.

They watched until Lydia's mother had wandered off in the general direction of the kitchen. Lydia grabbed Hestia's elbow and herded her toward the stairs. As they started up the steps, Hestia gave her an important look.

"Your friend will recover from the illness," the slave said with a smile.

Lydia felt relief loosening the knot in her stomach. When she had gotten Hestia to her room and given her the coins, the slave reached beneath the dried herbs and produced a small roll of parchment. She handed it to Lydia.

"Read this, mistress. You won't be sorry."

"How do you know? You can't read."

"The young master told me what he wrote. I remember everything."

Lydia gave her a quick look. "Then you'd best forget it. You've done your errand and gotten your money. Now you may leave."

Hestia strolled out of the room, aiming a final, sly smile over her shoulder.

Lydia quickly scrabbled the binding off the roll and sat on her couch. She spread the parchment on her lap.

Menander, faithful friend and lifelong admirer, to Lydia, most beautiful daughter of Threnides: Greetings.

My dear Lydia, surely you cannot think that my

thoughts of you and my abiding love for you could be altered by the screams of a half-mad old woman. I am tormented by not being able to see your face and hear the music of your voice.

How much longer will you sit in self-imposed confinement? Will you not speak to your father and advance our cause? I await your answer. Send it by the same messenger; I have given her payment for her discretion. May the gods protect you and speed you to my side.

Farewell.

Lydia's mind raced as she reread Menander's letter. He was still true! Then she thought about what it would be like to speak to her father, and her enthusiasm faltered. Her father was becoming more and more a public man, much concerned with his standing in the city. Would he really let his youngest daughter marry someone not of his choosing, simply because she wanted to? Still, Menander came from a good family....

Then there was Menander's offhand comment about the oracle. Lydia wasn't overly superstitious, but she knew it wasn't wise to speak flippantly about matters of the gods. Menander's studies in philosophy had made him careless, maybe. Was it really prudent to dismiss as foolishness such an obvious prophecy, witnessed by practically the whole population of Thyatira? *The blood will cover you.* Lydia shuddered, remembering the slick, sticky blood on her face, its sour-sweet, sickening smell. She remembered the way everyone's eyes shifted to her when the oracle had gone, the distance she had felt in their silent, staring faces. How could the meaning of the oracle's words be anything good?

Yet Menander still wanted her. Part of her exulted in his

steadfastness; the other part worried about his judgment.

The next morning, when Lydia came down into the atrium, the first person she saw was her father. He was on the other side of the courtyard, sitting by the cistern and pulling hunks from a loaf of bread. He looked as if he hadn't rested well. His face had a drawn, haggard look, and the flesh around his eyes sagged. He chewed his bread and took a sip now and then from a bowl on the bench beside him. Mother was nowhere to be seen.

Just at that moment, he glanced up and saw her standing there. He gave her a smile and beckoned her over. Lydia took a deep breath and went to him. He patted the place beside him on the bench. She sat down. He tore off a piece of bread and offered it to her.

"No, thank you, Father. I'll eat later."

He shrugged and bit a plug from the bread. "You've been resting well?"

"Yes, Father. Well enough. And you?"

He looked at her a moment, then took a drink from his bowl. Lydia could see the crumbs in his beard. She reached over to dust them out. "You're a messy eater."

He smiled and shrugged again. "How are you coming with Euripides?"

Lydia made a face. "He uses five words where one will do."

Her father leaned back and laughed. "Well! A critic, yet! And when may we expect to see one of your plays at the festival?"

"Give me time."

He chuckled, taking another sip of water. "Just don't let your reading take up time that needs to be spent weaving." He took a bite of bread and gestured at her with the half-eaten loaf.

"A husband appreciates a wife who converses well, but he appreciates even more one who keeps him warmly clad."

Lydia began to wish that she had broached the subject of Menander first with Mother. Mother could have advised her how to proceed.

He started to get up.

"Father?"

He paused, looking down at her.

"I want to ask you—tell you something."

He stood, waiting. Lydia wished he would sit down again. She took a deep breath.

"Father, I love someone. I want to marry him. I'm almost sixteen, so I'm old enough. I want you to speak to his father." She said the words in a rush, without looking at him or taking a breath.

For a long time, Father didn't say anything. She couldn't bring herself to look up at his face, but he stood very still, and she could feel his eyes on her.

"Who?"

Lydia forced her eyes up, toward his face. She needed some hint of what to say next. He was looking down at her. The line of his mouth was straight, impassive. But he hadn't shouted at her or stormed off in a rage. Not yet.

"Menander, son of Timon. A good family, Father. I've heard you say so yourself."

"I didn't know at that time I was passing judgment on a future son-in-law."

"I love him, Father."

"So you say. He is—how old? Barely two years older than you? Not yet of marrying age, Lydia."

"Younger men sometimes marry."

"It's not customary for men to wed until they're nearly twice his age. Until they've established themselves and can support—"

She bounded to her feet. "Custom! Why should I care about custom?"

"Lydia. Sit down."

At the sound of his voice, she quickly returned to the bench. Her jaw clenched and unclenched, chewing the words she couldn't say.

"You will not raise your voice to me. Do you understand?"

She nodded, swiping at her angry tears with the heel of her hand.

"I have not forbidden this marriage, Lydia. Not yet. But I have also not agreed to it. Marriage is an important matter, and a prudent man does not permit his daughter's fancies to crowd him into a hasty decision."

Lydia's knuckles clenched white at her sides, but she kept quiet.

"It may be that Menander would be a fine husband. Or it may be that he would not. But you must give me time to carefully consider the situation."

"Yes, Father." A whisper was all she could manage.

"There, now. Don't worry. I have your interest at heart." She felt his hand on her head. His footsteps went away from her, toward the kitchen. Then he halted. When some time had passed without his moving, Lydia raised her face to look at him. He was looking at her, still holding the partially eaten loaf in his hand. There was a strange, faraway look on his face.

"It was Menander you beat that day in the race, wasn't it?"

She nodded.

"Odd I should remember that." He shook his head. "I never imagined you'd win that day. When you did, I knew I'd made a great mistake." He turned and went around the corner into the kitchen.

On the first day of Dios, they began preparations for the Pyanepsion. Lydia objected to being forced, at her age, to participate in a children's celebration, but Father was adamant, and Mother would say nothing to contradict him. Though she dragged it about like a stone chained to her waist, Lydia's sour attitude didn't prevent her from helping her mother form and bake the little pastry-cakes for the *eiresiōnē* which Phillip had cut from a young laurel near the river. The cakes shaped like grape leaves were Lydia's favorites; even in her funk, she took a distracted pleasure in tracing the delicate lines for the veins.

The fruit harvest was bountiful that year; in the markets there was an ample selection of apples, pears, pomegranates, and figs. They passed string through the juicy bodies of the fruits, bound them to the laurel branch, and then hung the cakes from it with lengths of dyed string.

On the third day before the tenth, Lydia and all the other youths who had two living parents gathered in the forum, on and near the steps of the Temple of Apollo. All of them carried their eiresiōnēs; the crowd of chattering children was a waving, shifting sea of decorated laurel wands. There was a slight nip in the early autumn air, and most of the youngsters' faces were flushed with the invigorating chill and eager anticipation of the procession.

The priest of Apollo came out of the temple and raised his arms for quiet. Slowly, the children's voices stilled, as the older ones hushed the younger and directed their attention toward the waiting priest.

"Lord Apollo Tyrimnaios, we invoke thee this day. Attend our celebration and receive the praise of our lips for the bounty which thy strength brings forth from the earth. Inhabit our hearts, which we raise to thee in thanks, and grant that we may enjoy thy protection in the days ahead. Quicken the seed in the ground, and bless it with thy warmth, that we may feast on good things and offer thee the firstfruits."

A group of acolytes began the festival hymn, which the children quickly took up. Even the youngest ones knew it by heart.

> *I will remember and not be unmindful*
> *of Apollo who shoots afar*
> *As he goes through the house of Zeus,*
> *the gods tremble before him*
> *and all spring up from their seats*
> *when he draws near, as he bends his bright bow.*

Led by the acolytes, the children formed a loose procession and made their way out of the forum. They would go through all the streets of Thyatira. Now and then small groups would peel away from the main body, stopping to sing at the homes of friends and family members. Sometimes the occupants of the houses would give the singers small gifts: trinkets, pieces of fruit, or small honey cakes the size of a drachma coin. One of the singers would then make a gift to the household of an eiresiōnē, which would be hung above the main gate for luck.

Lydia found herself walking beside a small child who was having difficulty keeping his eiresiōnē out of the dirt. She took one end of the little boy's wand and walked ahead of him in the procession, trying to choose a less-crowded path for the young celebrant. He appeared to be about the age of Zobia's youngest son. Actimon was his name, she found out. She also learned that he hated girls, liked almond-honey candy more than anything in the world, and had an abounding curiosity about everything and everyone. He peppered her with questions during the entire march, sometimes asking another while she was answering the previous one. "How many figs are on your wand?" "What's the name of the priest of Apollo?" "Why do dogs walk on all fours?" "Who lives in that house over there?" Actimon also had a pleasant little singing voice, as Lydia noticed during the brief interludes between his interrogations. He would catch a stray bit of a hymn and sound it out in a sweet, pure tone, until his mind was sidetracked by the need to know why clouds looked like fleece, or how the ocean became salty, or if Lydia had any toys at her house, or why the route of the procession took so long to finish.

Lydia was wondering much the same herself when she realized they were on her street—and Menander's.

"My house is just ahead," she told Actimon. "You must stop and sing with me."

The boy nodded and they began working their way to the edge of the troupe. By the time they reached her gate, Lydia's parents and a handful of the household slaves were standing in the entry, beaming at the passing children.

"This is Actimon, my new friend," Lydia announced.

Her father had a strange expression on his face as he looked at Actimon, but it faded when the boy began singing.

The eiresiōnē bears rich cakes and figs
and honey in a jar, and olive oil
to sanctify yourself,
and cups of mellow wine
that you may drink and fall asleep.

Their little audience applauded, and one of the servants brought a small basket of candied figs. Actimon handed his eiresiōnē to the slave and peeked in the basket. He looked a bit disappointed that there was no almond-honey candy, but still helped himself to a double handful of the sticky, rich treats.

They rejoined the procession just as it neared the house of Menander. To her surprise, just as Lydia was about to urge Actimon toward the edge of the throng, he grabbed her hand and pointed toward the house.

"This is my cousin's house," he said. "Let's stop and sing to them."

No one was in the entryway to open it for them, so they pounded on the gate. Finally, it swung open and there stood Menander. When he saw Lydia, his eyes widened and a broad grin opened on his face.

"Menander, I brought Lydia here to sing to you," Actimon said. "Do you have a treat for her?"

Menander tousled the young boy's hair. "I could probably find something, Actimon. Where's your older brother?"

"Stephanos said he was too old. Lydia told me she was too old, too, but her father made her anyway. Why didn't Stephanos have to come out, if Lydia did?"

"Different fathers, different rules," Menander said with a laugh.

Lydia blushed at Actimon's words, but when she saw the shape of Menander's mouth as he laughed, her blush deepened into something much warmer and more pleasurable.

"What shall I sing for you?" she asked in a coy voice.

"You have to sing the eiresiōnē song," said Actimon, rolling his eyes. "Everybody knows that."

"No, I think I'd like to sing something else."

Oh, Eros, do you not see me?
Take pity on your poor Psyche.
Long years have I searched high and low,
Longing for you, seeking for you.
Will you forsake my love always?
Will you forever hide your face?
Oh, please forgive my transgression.
Forget not that 'twas love for you
That caused my fault. My holy awe
At your great beauty made me err.
Remember, sweet beloved—Forgive!
I sit among the lilies by the stream,
And mourn for you. My own bloom fades.
Come back to me, beloved Eros.
Come back to your adoring Psyche.
End my woe and quench my thirst
With love. And feast with me once more.

"What kind of song was that?" Actimon wanted to know. "That sounded like some silly love stuff to me."

Lydia looked at Menander. His eyes were wide and staring at something behind her. Lydia turned and saw her father standing in the entry.

hy is your father here?" asked Actimon. "Did he want to hear me sing again?"

"I remember now," Lydia's father said, nodding to himself. "Actimon, the young son of Philonides."

"Yes, he is the son of my mother's sister and her husband," Menander said.

"Father, Actimon said this was his cousin's house. I didn't—"

Her father silenced her with a gesture. "Your reasons for stopping here are obvious to me." Threnides looked carefully at Menander.

The younger man faltered, then braced himself, shouldering broadly into Threnides' scrutiny. "I am an honorable man, sir. I am no seducer."

Threnides' gaze shifted to his daughter. "I'm not worried about that, Menander. And I know your reputation. I've made careful inquiries."

"Then why did you follow me here?" Lydia demanded. "You mistrust me, don't you?"

Actimon's upturned face was round-eyed and still as he

peered from one of them to the other.

Threnides opened his mouth, then closed it. He looked at Lydia, then at Menander. Lydia could see her father's jaw tensing.

Just then, a man came through the gate behind them: Timon, Menander's father. "Hello, Threnides," he said.

"Timon, I beg your forgiveness for intruding on your house," said Threnides. "I thought you might be at home on this festival day."

"I was just at the forum, attending to some business at the Temple of Apollo. I came home as quickly as I could. I had hoped to be here when the procession passed, but I see that...." He looked at them all with a puzzled expression. "I see I've arrived in time for something else. Menander, can you tell me what's happened to bring my friend away from his home on a day of feasting?"

Menander looked first at Threnides, then his father. Finally, he seemed to come to a decision. "I've spoken to you before of my feelings for Lydia, Father. I ask you, here and now, for permission to marry her."

Timon's face dropped open in surprise. "Well, my son, this is hardly—" He looked quickly at Threnides, searching for his reaction.

"I'm ready to establish my own household, Father," Menander went on. "She's the one I desire. I ask you to give me your blessing."

Timon wore a guilty, embarrassed look. "It seems my son is quite smitten." He tried a quick laugh and a dismissing shrug. "Young men."

Lydia's father said nothing. His gaze had left Menander and now wandered back and forth on the ground around their feet.

"Come on, Actimon," Lydia said abruptly, grabbing the little boy's shoulder. "We'd better catch up with the others before they get back to the forum, or we'll miss the blessing and the bean stew."

Lydia half dragged the boy out of the courtyard and up the street.

"Is Menander going to be your husband?" Actimon asked.

"We'd better hurry. They're pretty far ahead of us."

"Why is your father angry?"

She stalked ahead without looking at him.

"You're hurting my arm, Lydia. Why are you crying?"

She released the boy's arm. She realized she couldn't go back to the forum.

"Where are you going, Lydia? Why are you running?"

The wind in her ears was loud, but not loud enough. She needed to go faster.

There was a discreet cough from the doorway. Syntyche swiveled about as Lydia opened her eyes. It was the carpet weaver from the middle shop of the three attached to the front of the house. "Mistress, I'm sorry to intrude. I know you're ill—"

"Come in, Marcus. What is it?"

The weaver ducked his head. "Please, Mistress. I can come back when you don't have guests."

"Nonsense." Lydia tried, and failed, to keep the impatience out of her voice. "Now's a perfectly good time, Marcus."

The man took a shambling step or two into the room. He was bony and short—all joints and knuckles. His legs were bowed, probably from years of squatting in front of his loom. He wouldn't lift his face; he addressed the floor at his feet, and as he spoke his fingers twitched, weaving a carpet of air on an invisible loom.

"Well, the thing is, there hasn't been much trade these last days, Mistress. No one wants to pay what a carpet's worth anymore—at least, not what one of mine is worth. Why, just the other day, a man was in my shop, looked like he could afford what he wanted—good clothes, well-groomed sort of man, you might say. He turns over a few of my pieces, looks at the knotwork, then offers me three obols. Three obols! For *my* goods! Well, what could I do? Word gets around that Marcus is letting his carpets go for three obols, pretty soon my family's starving. Three obols! I can't even buy my thread, keep my looms in repair for that kind of—"

"Marcus."

"Then there's the dyers. Meaning no disrespect, Mistress, but they've gotten completely out of hand. What they're charging nowadays for dyed thread is taking the food from my children's mouths—"

"Marcus, if you'd—"

"So, anyway, Mistress, as I was saying, things are kind of tight right now, with trade being like it is, and all, and I was wondering—"

"If you need more time on the rent, Marcus, it's all right."

"Beg your pardon, Mistress?"

"It's all right."

"What is?"

Syntyche clucked her tongue. "If you'd listen, she's telling you—"

"Please. Syntyche. Let me speak to my tenant. Marcus?"

"Yes?"

"You don't have to bring me the money today. If you need

to wait a bit more, it will be all right."

He looked at her from under his eyebrows. "Mistress, I don't know what to say."

"I doubt that," Lydia murmured.

"Thank you, Mistress. And as soon as I can, I'll get you the money—"

"Yes, of course you will, Marcus."

"As I was telling my wife just the other day, 'I've got to get the mistress her rent,' I said. 'Woman in her condition shouldn't have to worry about—'"

"Marcus."

"Soon as I can find a few folk who appreciate good work—"

"Marcus, you may go now."

"Man shouldn't have to give his goods away, now should he? That's what I say."

Lydia gave Syntyche a helpless look. Syntyche went to the man and gestured him toward the doorway. He was still talking as he went out. Syntyche came back, shaking her head. "What a ridiculous person! Does he always jabber so?"

Lydia smiled and shook her head. "No. Sometimes, it's worse."

"Why do you endure him?"

"Because I doubt anyone else will. And he really does make fine carpets. That's one of his over there."

Syntyche nodded with raised eyebrows.

"Besides, I don't have to listen to him much longer." She drew a sharp breath, then let it out slowly as the spasm ebbed. "I've directed in my will that he be allowed to stay in his shop."

"Your inheritor may not remember you kindly for that."

Lydia smiled again—a small, satisfied smile. "That will be as it may."

Lydia ran until her breath came in ragged gasps, until her legs felt wobbly and almost numb with fatigue. She stopped by the side of the road, leaning over with her hands braced on her knees, and sucked great draughts of air. After a while, she straightened and looked around her.

Thyatira was nowhere in sight. Apparently, she had run up into the hills north of town on the road that led to Pergamum. She stood at the top of a knoll. The soil was thin and chalky. A few juniper bushes and scrub terebinths struggled for life among the loose, flinty stones and rock outcroppings. Lydia walked over to a large, flat rock and sat down.

She looked down at her clothing. Her chiton was wrinkled and sodden with the sweat of her running. It made her think of the way she had continually mussed her garments as a young girl, running over brushy, rocky ground and climbing in trees.

And then she thought of the strange, hide-clad wanderer who had appeared that day, under the plane tree beside the river. "As the One God is my witness," he had said. And what was it that the oracle of the Sybil had invoked? "The Unmade." Who had ever heard of but one god? And wasn't everything made by something else? Even the primordial Titans, the stories said, had sprung from the union of Father Heaven and Mother Earth. Everything came from something, didn't it? *Unseen, it sees…Unknown, it knows…Unmoved, it moves all things….* The words made no sense; they sounded like something from one of the philosophers Menander was always reading, with their questioning and their endless riddles. He told her his rhētor was forever scolding him for filling his head with words that wouldn't help him win his debates. He said he didn't care; he'd keep on reading Socrates, Pyrrho, Aristotle, and all the rest. He said he

wanted to fill his mind with the thoughts of men who had dared
to raise their imaginations beyond the horizon.

Menander. Lydia thought of the bold way he had met her
father's measuring gaze. Had her father given him credit for the
manliness of his bearing and words, or had he only seen a boy
too young to wed his daughter? She tried to imagine what sort
of discussion had taken place in Menander's courtyard after she
left, but there were too many ways it could have gone badly.
Better not to go too far that way.

Lydia stood up from the rock and paced to the crest of the
hill. She peered southwest, toward the lower country that ran
like a ribbon between the ranges of highlands from the sea east
to Thyatira. Somewhere in that direction lay Father's plantation,
where the field slaves tended the madder plants until they were
ready to be harvested, their roots pulped and pressed to squeeze
out the juices that made the Asian purple dye.

A few times, Lydia had visited the rendering plant, where
the root was brought to be processed. The macerated root was
dumped into a huge, stone press. Then slaves trod round and
round, pushing on the long, wooden poles set into the sockets
in the wheel of the press. The great screw twisted slowly down,
squeezing from the roots every last drop of their essence. The
fluid drained down into channels cut into the press floor and
ran into the huge vats beneath. The slaves trod in the liquid as
they turned the press, their feet gradually turning the color of a
king's robe.

She would not marry Menander, she realized; her father
would force her to wed some proper man twice her age who
presented a more advantageous alliance. He would have a house
and slaves and an established trade, and he would not, could
not ever, understand or love her half as well. She sternly shoved

down the sob that wanted to rise up her throat. What use was crying? Her path was set. There was no point in thinking otherwise. She turned away from the crest of the hill and picked her way down the slope toward the road back into Thyatira.

The sun was almost touching the western rim of the world when Lydia let herself through the gate. She crossed the atrium and climbed the stairs to her room. Her stomach was grinding with hunger, but she was in no mood to chance seeing anyone. She sat on her couch for a long time, looking out her window as the sky's blue deepened into the dark of night. She watched as the stars began to show through the last, dim glow of the dying sunset.

After a while, she got up from her couch and went to the small chest where she kept her few personal belongings. She searched in the near-darkness until her fingertips found the bronze shears Father had given her years before as a gift. She went back to her couch. For a time, she held the shears cupped in both palms—out in front of her, like a ceremonial knife. Then, with slow, careful motions, Lydia unbound her hair and let it fall down over her shoulders. She threaded the fingers of her left hand through her hair, letting it slide over her palm and fall back onto her shoulder. She took a final look through her window at the stars. Then she took the shears in her right hand and began to cut.

Her hair fell in long, looping strands around her feet and onto her couch. Lydia cut and cut until there was not enough hair left to grasp in her fingers. She placed the shears back in the chest and gathered up all the hair she could find. She was vaguely surprised at the size of the bundle; she had to grip it in both hands.

Lydia went out of her room and padded softly down the

steps leading to the atrium. She paused every few paces, listening for the sound of voices or footsteps. But tonight, the house was oddly quiet. Father was probably drinking in the andron, and Mother was doubtless pursuing one of her artistic quests in the women's suite. The atrium was still and silent in the darkness. Good.

Lydia crossed the open space quickly and quietly. She went to the household altar and laid on it the dark, curly drifts of her hair. She turned to leave and paused for an instant, looking at the unmoving figures of Vesta and Janus. Then she ran back upstairs to her room.

She started gathering things to take with her, then realized that if she reached her destination, she wouldn't need anything. Lydia took a final, slow look around at her room, lit only by the stars. She tossed a dark, woolen robe over her shoulders and went out. The courtyard was still deserted. She crossed it quickly and went to the gate. She winced as it squealed on its hinges. She stepped through the opening and pulled the gate closed behind her. She paced into the darkness with long strides, making for the eastern gate.

The guard was snoring when Lydia reached the otherwise vacant gateway. She thought briefly of trying to slip through without waking him, but she doubted she could manage to lift the heavy latchpole out of its brackets without disturbing him.

She strode up to the sleeping guard—like most of the night wardens, an old, heavy military pensioner—who sat with his arms crossed in his lap. He had leaned his stool against the wall beside the gate and his head was tilted back; his breath snarled in and wheezed out. Lydia leaned over and shook his shoulder. His head bobbed forward and he made wet, smacking noises with his lips as he tried to force open his eyelids.

"What? Who is it?" He finally managed to peer up at her. Lydia hoped she'd pulled the hood of her robe far enough over her head. But it was dark—he wasn't likely to see her face. "What do you want at this time of the night?" he asked in a slurred, annoyed voice.

"I must make pilgrimage to the shrine of the Sybil," she answered in a low, urgent tone, clutching at the front of her robe. "I'm compelled by an oath."

"Oath? To the Sybil?" He rubbed his face and the back of his neck. "Can't it wait until the light of day?"

"I'm sorry. I must go at night, when there is no moon. So says the oracle."

He grumbled in his beard, something about weird old women and those gullible enough to listen to them. He made no move toward the gate.

"I can always go out by the north gate. The guard there was wide awake when I came by."

He gave her a sharp glance, then shoved himself up from his stool. He mumbled something about stubborn women, but he pulled back the latchpole. After he'd satisfied himself that a marauding army wasn't waiting outside, he moved aside and let her through the opening.

Lydia heard the gate close and the latchpole thump into place behind her. Now that she was this far, a part of her mind suddenly began adding up the improbabilities of her intentions. She whispered a quick prayer to Artemis, took a deep, resolute breath, and began walking east. Soon she had left behind the last, outlying houses and was in the open country that rose gradually toward the foothills, looming as a deeper darkness ahead of her, low in the starry night.

The way to Pergamum was not an Imperial route, only a

provincial one. It was maintained sporadically, when enough citizens had complained of its condition. The road was unevenly paved, as Lydia soon learned by striking her toes against the edges of the poorly seated paving stones. Trying to see precisely where she was stepping was useless. She had to let her eyes sift back and forth in front of her, trying to gather enough light from the stars to separate the dim outlines of the roadway from the rocky, rising terrain.

Lydia began to wish desperately that she had brought a lamp. The sounds of her breathing and her sandals slapping the pavement were loud in her ears. If any brigands were about, they were sure to hear her. At this thought, having a lamp suddenly became less desirable. Then again, what sort of simpleton would go out at night, alone and without a light? Maybe even bandits would not suspect such silliness; maybe her folly would be for her protection.

The grating screech of a night-hunting bird glided down the wind. Moments later, somewhere in the darkness to her right, she heard the shrill squeaking of some small animal; heard its claws scrabbling frantically against stone, then an abrupt silence.

She could smell the sea. The light westerly breeze carried its salty, slightly brackish tang. Lydia had never seen the sea; her only knowledge of it was from descriptions by her father and its faint scent when the wind was right. She stopped walking and turned around. The city, so familiar when she walked among its streets and buildings, was now an unfamiliar clump of shadows. Lydia turned back and resumed her journey.

Just as the road began angling across the face of the first range of foothills, she came to the path she sought, twisting off the main road to the left and diving into a gully, then up the other side before it disappeared behind the lip of another ridge. This was the trail that led to the shrine of the Sybil Sambethe. Lydia picked her way carefully along the path, trying not to listen to the voice in her mind that reminded her she'd never actually been to the shrine. She'd heard plenty of people talk about going there, and she knew she was sure to find the place if she could just stay on this crooked, switchback path. It led nowhere else.

Lydia slid down the slope of a ravine and scrambled up the other side. There were places where the way was so steep she had to go on her hands and feet to keep from tumbling to the bottom of a washed-out cleft. She scraped her arms and legs on the rough edges of rocks; she got gravel and grit in her sandals. How had the crippled old oracle negotiated this path to come into the city on the day of her father's dedication? Lydia wondered how even a wild goat could manage such a difficult course. For long periods, she fought against the panic of wondering if she was still on the path or clambering about aimlessly in the darkness.

She smelled the shrine before she saw it. The odor of incense floated to her along the cool night breeze, faint at first, then deepening as the crooked path dipped down into the hollow where the sanctuary was. The shrine of Sambethe was a stone building, but nothing about its exterior suggested any of the temples Lydia had ever seen: no pillars, no facade, no frieze. Its face was blank except for a few low slits of windows and one small wooden door. Built of a single story on a simple square plan, it squatted at the bottom of the hollow beside a small stream that was fed by a spring somewhere in the hills nearby.

Lydia approached the door. She raised her hand several times, then lowered it to her side. At last, she forced herself to knock. There was no response. She looked about her nervously, then knocked again, louder. Still nothing. She pounded on the door with her fist, feeling the first stirrings of panic in her throat, when the door suddenly opened.

There stood the oracle, looking much as she had that day in the forum. Lydia had thought of some words to say, but in that moment they deserted her mind. The old woman looked at her for a moment, then quickly reached up and pulled back the hood of Lydia's robe. She peered at Lydia's denuded head. She reached out and grabbed Lydia's chin, turning her face this way and that, as if examining a piece of goods in a market. Then she nodded and stood aside, gesturing for Lydia to enter.

Seven

She went in. The air inside the sanctuary was heavy and dense; incense clouded the room like a sweet, heavy fog. Lydia coughed, waving her hands in front of her face. She felt the oracle's hand on her elbow, and then she felt air moving on her face. They were standing by one of the narrow, slitted windows. Lydia could breathe a little here. She felt something bump against the back of her knees—the oracle had slid a stool over to her. She pressed Lydia's shoulders, prompting her to sit. Then she was gone again, into the swirling incense.

Lydia remembered she had eaten nothing since morning, before the beginning of the Pyanepsion. Her belly felt like a clenched fist. She heard shuffling steps approaching, then felt a wooden bowl sliding into her hands. In the bowl were soft cheese and dried fruit. Lydia ate. A cool skin of water was placed in her hands. She drank.

Lydia's breath came easier now; she was feeling a bit drowsy. The thought of lying down was becoming the most alluring image she could form. She set aside the bowl and skin and lowered herself to the floor. The stone was cold against her cheek, but she couldn't summon the energy to care.

She was awakened by someone gently shaking her shoulder. It seemed only moments after she lay down, but as she raised herself on one elbow, she saw a silver wash of moonlight across the floor of the sanctuary. She looked out the slit window. The humpbacked moon, still hidden below the horizon when she had arrived here, was now more than halfway to the zenith. Lydia looked around the room. The clouds of incense were gone; the air inside was clear, scrubbed clean by a cool draft from outside.

This was unlike any temple or shrine Lydia had ever seen. The room was very plain. The stone walls were unpainted; there were no coverings on the floor. No frescoes, no tapestries, nor furnishings of any kind. Almost as if the place were uninhabited. If the oracle had any needs, they must be very sparse, indeed.

A wisp of blue flame curled upward from the middle of a wide-bowled brazier at the far end of the room near the short wall opposite the door where Lydia had entered. The low flame cast a meager, flickering light on a niche in the wall that housed the cult image of the Sybil: the figure of a squatting woman, her hands covering her face. Carved from the native stone of the surrounding foothills, the figure sat atop a section of the trunk of a huge cypress, rubbed shiny over the long years by the hands of pilgrims to the shrine. Mounded on the floor at its base were shards of pottery vessels in which the mendicants brought their prayers, written on scraps of parchment or papyrus. The vessels were shattered on the floor at the base of the image and the prayerscraps burned in the brazier that sat on the floor in front of the image. Mixed into the pile of shards were the leavings of the Sybil's worshippers: husks of fruit and grain, some long-dried, some fresh; charms of silver and bronze and copper; scraps of brightly colored cloth; even locks of hair.

She pulled her robe closer against the chill. A hand was on her elbow. Lydia hadn't heard anyone approaching, but the old woman was there, motioning for Lydia to rise. The oracle helped her to her feet. Lydia was surprised at the strength in the old, bent woman's grip. She put an arm around Lydia's shoulders and walked her toward a doorway between two pilasters set in the middle of the opposite wall.

The door led into a smaller side room. In the middle of the floor a single tallow lamp was burning. There were no other furnishings or occupants in the room. Surely the oracle didn't stay here alone, but Lydia had neither seen nor heard evidence of another living being since she had gotten here.

They reached the lamp. The oracle gestured at the floor on one side, and Lydia sat down cross-legged. The oracle levered herself down on the other side, the lamp between them. She stared at Lydia through the shuddering light. Lydia tried to meet her gaze, but soon turned her face aside.

"I want to become an acolyte of the Sybil," she said, looking at the backs of her own hands. "I've come here to place myself in your service."

The old woman didn't answer; didn't move. She peered at Lydia, as still as the squatting image in the next room.

"Why are you looking at me that way? Why don't you say something?"

The old woman's hooded eyes never moved; her expression never altered. Her face, underlit by the lamp, was a shifting, crevassed terrain of shadows.

"Why did you mark me, that day in the forum? I suffered

under the strangeness—my own family now holds me at arm's length. Why did you do that to me? And why won't you talk to me?"

And still the old woman said nothing.

Before Lydia realized it, she was on her feet. She grabbed the old woman by the shoulders; shoved her down on the stone floor. The oracle of the Sybil lay on her back, staring up at Lydia with an unchanging expression. It was as if nothing had happened.

Lydia stalked away from her to the farthest corner of the small room. She hugged herself and turned her face to the wall. Her eyes were stinging and there was a sharp, expanding ache in her throat. She held her face in her hands and let the moans rise from far away and deep down. For a long time they swelled and fell back, unsatisfied and unanswered.

A hand touched her shoulder, gently patting. It was the old woman.

"Yes, child. Yes. You feel it, don't you?"

"Feel what?"

"The emptiness. The longing. Yes."

"I don't know. Maybe."

"Yes. I see it. I hear it in your voice." She lightly touched Lydia's cropped hair. "You wear it here."

"Will you let me stay? I don't want to go back."

The oracle studied her a moment, then glanced back toward the doorway of the room where the Sybil's image sat on its block of wood. She shook her head sadly. "No. What you're looking for isn't here."

"How would you know what I'm looking for?"

"Because I came here looking for it, too. Long ago. So long ago."

"Why did you stay?"

"By the time I knew, it was too late. I had nowhere else to go."

"Why can't I stay? There's nothing for me back there."

"No. This is not your path." She turned and gripped Lydia's shoulders, a sudden kindling in her manner. "It isn't too late for you. There will be other chances. You may yet discover your way."

Lydia looked down at her bruised, scratched arms and feet. "I wish I'd known that before I started here."

The old woman spun about and hobbled quickly across the side room and through a small, dark doorway. Moments later she came back, carrying a small lidded pot. "Sit."

She squatted beside Lydia and set the pot on the floor. She removed the lid and the sweet, thick smell of spikenard oil plumed out. The oracle dipped her fingertips into the creamy balm. "Hold out your arms," she said. She smoothed the ointment onto Lydia's arms. It eased the burn of the scratches and cuts.

"It won't be easy," the old woman said as she massaged Lydia's feet. "It never is. You will get hurts that will make tonight seem a pleasant memory. You will suffer. Oh, yes. You will have heartache. But there will be chances. Not here. Back there. Back there is where you must begin."

Lydia realized her head was pillowed by a soft roll of perfumed linen. Where had it come from? And she was covered by a warm, thick, woolen blanket. She hadn't noticed the old woman bringing it.

"With the sun, they will come, and you will begin again. Not here—not for you. When the sun comes."

Lydia's mind tipped over the soft edge of sleep.

She was awakened by the pounding of fists on the sanctuary door, and a voice shouting her name. Her father's voice. Why didn't the oracle answer the door? Lydia pulled the blanket over her head and covered her ears with her hands. But the banging and shouting continued.

She sat up and looked around. Pink, early morning light filtered through the doorway of the side chamber. She was alone. She stood up and walked into the main room. Still no one. Her father's blows and cries resounded in the sanctuary like echoes through a cave. Where was the old woman?

"Lydia! I know you must be here! Lydia!"

Lydia stared at the door. She pulled her cloak closer around her, went to the door, and lifted the heavy bar. The door swung open. Her father, frozen in midmotion, looked at her. His eyes widened when he saw her hair. Her brothers stood behind him, peering over his shoulders.

"What have you done to yourself?" Father hissed.

"How did you find me?"

"When I saw the altar, I...we feared...I looked everywhere in the city, among all our relatives and friends."

"When even Menander didn't know your whereabouts, we decided you'd left Thyatira," Philip put in. "Then we started questioning the night wardens."

Her father was still staring at where her hair had been. "You have shamed yourself. Shamed me and your mother."

"I knew something like this would happen with her," Philip said. "Since the day of the guildhall dedication, I've suspected she was hiding things from us."

"You aren't my *kyrios*, Philip. Father is. It was none of your concern."

"You did all this because of Menander?" Father asked. "Because I didn't give easy consent?"

The morning wind was cold. She pulled up the hood of the robe and wrapped her arms around herself. "No, Father. Not because of him. Not even because of you. Because of me."

She walked past them, down the path toward the highway back to Thyatira. How different this place looked in the daylight—much smaller. After a few paces, she turned back. The three of them still stood where they were, half-turned, watching her. Philip's face was unreadable. Andronicus wouldn't meet her eyes; he angled his face to one side. But Father looked at her as if he had never seen her before.

"Well, aren't we going home?" Lydia asked. "I thought that was why you came." She turned again and continued on down the path.

"It was agreeably cool that day, wasn't it? I remember the sun felt good on my arms." Syntyche's fingers felt pleasant, sifting through Lydia's hair as she combed. "And I think one of the young men was reading from the Torah scroll. I remember I liked the way his voice sounded, mixed in with the noise of the river water going over the stones."

"I don't think I quite understand you, dear."

"The first day we met Paul. You remember, don't you? You should. You couldn't keep your eyes off him."

"What on earth are you talking about, Syntyche?"

"Oh, Lydia! Don't pretend you've forgotten. From the first instant, you were fascinated by everything about him. Everyone could tell."

Lydia rolled her eyes and made an annoyed little grunt. People with poor memories were always so sure of their version of events.

"Don't pull so hard, dear. I'd like my hair to stay on my head until I'm gone, if you please."

A titter leaked from one of the servants. Lydia cut her eyes toward them. Probably Clystra.

"Mind what you're doing with that needle, girl. You'll have blood on your linen."

She bent to her work, but not before Lydia saw the smile she tried to swallow. Where did Euodia find such ninnies?

"And I remember how he kissed the scroll before he put it back in the sheath," Syntyche went on, "and how he began telling us about Jesus the Christ. I even remember the story the young man was reading from the scroll: how Father Abraham entertained the three men of God. And then, just like that, there were the three of *them* standing there, the same as the story. It was almost like a vision from God."

"Oh, Syntyche, that's nonsense," Lydia said. "Perfect nonsense. If I didn't know better, I'd say you weren't even there."

"What do you mean?"

"There were four of them, not three. You're confusing the Torah reading with the event."

Syntyche's hands paused. "I don't remember it that way at all."

"I'm telling you, there were four: Paul, Luke the physician, Silas, and young Timothy."

"Was he handsome?" Euterpe wanted to know.

"Who?"

"The young one—Timothy."

"I'm afraid I was rather taken with him," Syntyche admitted.

"What did he look like?"

"Euterpe, you ask too many questions," Clystra said.

"Tall and stately, like one of the pines along the Egnatian

Way between the city wall and the pomerium stone. Oh, he was a sight, I assure you." Syntyche's voice was breathy, like a young girl suffering her first infatuation.

"Syntyche, you just described Luke the physician," Lydia said.

"Timothy *was* tall! You don't know everything, Lydia."

"I know you were too old for Timothy then, and you're too old for him now. But you probably don't remember it that way."

Syntyche flung the comb across the room. It struck high on the wall in the corner and plopped into Clystra's lap. The servant gaped at Syntyche, who was storming toward the courtyard door. She whirled and aimed a glare at Lydia.

"You are such a hateful old woman! No wonder your daughter stays away from you!" And then she was gone.

Lydia turned her face away from the staring servants. "Bring me another blanket, one of you. I'm cold. I want to sleep now."

Lydia went back to Thyatira that day like Odysseus returning to Ithaca. It seemed years since she had left, instead of a single night. Everything she saw was draped with peculiarity: the city walls, the men at the gates, the buildings and temples of the forum. She realized she had never before considered her connection with this place and its people. Now, she was aware of a distance, an oddness—as if, in her absence, the city and all its inhabitants had shifted slightly one direction or the other. Or maybe, more as if the entire town of Thyatira had been disassembled, stone by stone, and rebuilt from imperfect memory. The same, and yet not the same. Maybe part of the Lydia who had left in the dead of the night had not come back here. Maybe she never would.

When they arrived at the house, Mother was standing in the center of the courtyard, one hand at her side and one hand slightly raised, as if she had been interrupted in the middle of a declamation. She made no move toward Lydia; uttered no word. Chloe didn't speak to her husband or her sons; didn't stare questions at them as they came through the gate behind her. Her eyes stayed on Lydia, following her silently across the atrium, past the household altar—still adorned by the dark drifts of her hair—toward the stairs to her room.

Lydia remembered when her mother had moved forward against the current of her life. Even in her quirks and the inconveniences they caused, she had insisted on seeing for herself. What had changed her? Why did she now stare after her youngest child like someone watching the disappearance of her final hope?

Some of the slaves huddled here and there in the courtyard in clumps of two or three, but none of them turned aside to whisper to her companions. Maybe they were all entranced by Lydia's strangeness. Maybe she was, herself.

Two days later, Hestia ducked hesitantly into her room and announced that Menander had come to see her. Lydia turned her head and gave the slave a puzzled look, trying to piece together the words of the message. Had she really said that Menander was here? And who, exactly, was Menander? Who was she, for that matter?

"What answer shall I give the young master?"

Lydia kept looking at Hestia, who blushed, nervously tweaking at the front of her garment.

"My mistress mocks her poor slave." Hestia's eyes twitched toward Lydia, then away. "Please, Mistress. What answer shall I give?"

Lydia's eyes roved out the window. Two cock sparrows sparred on the roof of the next house. Why should she attend to the slave's words rather than the battle of the small birds? What made one event more important than the other?

"Does my father permit this interview?" she asked.

"He says—you may do as you like."

Lydia threw back her head as laughter pealed from her throat. "Is that so? Oh, that is funny!" Abruptly, she stood from her couch. "Then I will come to him."

She moved toward the door. Hestia quickly held up a long, gauzy piece of linen.

"Mistress will want this?"

Lydia looked at the cloth, then at Hestia. "Whatever for?"

Hestia turned her face aside. "To cover your—your hair, Mistress."

Another laugh bubbled up inside her. "Oh, I think not, Hestia. The condition of my hair won't be a secret, I think. Let him see me as I am." She pushed past the slave and out the door.

As she came down the stairs, his feet and legs came into view, framed by the archway into the main atrium. Menander stood in front of the altar, staring at the pile of hair. His hands twitched upward from his sides now and then, as if he wanted to touch the hair, but dared not.

Well, it was on the altar, after all. Best not to meddle with that which was devoted to the gods—wasn't that the conventional wisdom?

She crossed the atrium toward him. Still, he hadn't noticed her approach. "Menander," she called. He turned and saw her.

Eight

ydia watched his face. She could tell that some-how it still wasn't real to Menander, even though he'd been staring at the hair. Only now when she stood in front of him did he comprehend. The shock ran slowly downward over his face and body, like honey on a cold day.

"Menander." She wasn't sure why she said it again or why she inflected it just so—not a question, not a plea. Just his name. A fact.

"Then it's true," he said. He pulled his eyes away from her head and looked down at the hair on the altar. He picked up a handful of it and closed his eyes as he held it to his nose. "It still smells like you. How is that possible, do you suppose?"

She watched him, bracing herself for the emergence of his disgust, even his anger. But he straightened himself and dragged out a smile from somewhere.

"I'm so glad you're back." He reached for her hand. "When they said you were gone, I was afraid for you."

She let him hold her hand and tried to imagine a life where happiness was allowed. "Menander, I wish I knew what to say to you. I wish I could explain."

"Even if you could, do you really imagine it's necessary?" He looked at her, and it was like looking in a mirror or a window into herself. "I will never love anyone else, Lydia. No matter what the oracle may have said, no matter what happens, I will love only you."

The corners of her eyes were stinging and brimming over. Warm, grateful tears spilled down her cheeks. Menander raised the tip of his finger to her face and caught one of the drops.

"This is all the answer I need," he said.

He turned and walked toward the gate. He looked over his shoulder at her for a moment, and then he was gone. For a long time Lydia stood staring at the gate, letting the tears course down her face. Then she turned to go back to her room.

Her father stood by the door to the anteroom of the men's suite, watching her. Lydia had no idea how long he'd been there and realized it didn't matter. She nodded gravely to him and went across the atrium and up the stairs to her room.

The arrangements were concluded within the month. Lydia would bring to the marriage a dowry of four gold talents, all necessary utensils for setting up a household, and ten bolts of good purple cloth. The contract was drawn up and witnessed by Menander and his father and countersigned by Threnides and his oldest son, Philip. The dowry was deposited, along with the marriage contract, in the Temple of Apollo. Auguries were consulted, and the date settled upon for the ceremony was the third day after the first decade of Audynaios.

The day of the wedding was gray, blustery, and cold. A few stray pellets of hard snow spattered down from the sky. Lydia waited in the bath alcove, just off the kitchen, gripping her arms to her sides while the slaves heated the water for the *loutrophoros*. Her mother came in, carrying a small pair of shears to take a lock of her hair for the final offering to Artemis. In those first weeks, it had been a problem to find a place on her cropped scalp where the hair was long enough to clip. Now, though, her thick, dark hair was starting to regain some of its length. Lydia consoled herself with the thought that many women cut their hair for their weddings, anyway. Maybe Menander would not find the sight of her so shocking as it had been in those first days.

The slaves began carrying in urns of warm water, and soon a plume of steam rose from the loutrophoros. It was time for the bridal bath. Lydia removed her himation and chiton, then her shift. The flesh along her arms and thighs prickled with goose bumps as she took off the white linen maiden's girdle she had worn since the time of her first monthly flow. No more would she wear it; she was soon to be a wife. Lydia stepped into the water, very glad of its warmth.

As the slaves poured water over her shoulders and along her arms, her mother recited the formula: "In this nuptial bath is Lydia cleansed of the foolishness of childhood. May the water of this sacred washing purify her of any habits of idleness, gossip, or willfulness." Lydia heard the slight pause in her mother's voice. She kept her face turned away, hoping no one could see the renegade smile she tried, but failed, to contain. "May Artemis look upon her with favor and may her womb be fruitful, bearing sons and daughters to her husband. By the skill of her management, may she bring peace and joy to his household and cover him with honor and the respect of his friends."

One of the women poured perfumed oil into the bath. The mingled scents of musk and lavender rode upward on the rising steam. Lydia lay back in the loutrophoros until her face was the only part of her body above the surface of the water. She could hear the slaves murmuring and giggling as they readied her wedding garments. Her ears were underwater, so the sound of the words was blunted and blurred. It was just as well; she had no desire to listen to their thinly veiled lewdness or their salacious speculations about how she would enjoy her wedding bed.

She stepped out of the loutrophoros onto a thick pad of coarsely woven linen. The slaves brought large sheets of cloth to wrap Lydia and dry the water from her body. She put on a fresh shift, made of the sheerest fabric, and tried to ignore the titters of the slaves. Over the shift went, first, a pleated chiton that fell in graceful folds from her shoulders to the tops of her feet. Next, she donned a woolen himation. The slaves helped her adjust it to drape just so from her left shoulder, down across her chest, to a point just above her right hip. All her garments this day were of the whitest and softest of bleached cloth. Finally, Lydia slipped her feet into new shoes of the supplest calfskin, stitched with good luck symbols rendered in red embroidery. There wasn't much to be done about her hair other than combing it thoroughly; that was one advantage of her short style, at least. She went to the women's quarters to wait until time for the feast.

Lydia hoped that her sisters might, this once, ignore custom and stay away, but when she arrived in the main room of the *gynaikonitis*, there they were, waiting with her mother. When Lydia came in, they looked at her with knowing smiles, suddenly all a-flutter at seeing their little sister adorned in her wedding finery.

To Lydia, the three of them looked like figures on an urn: Lydia's mother stood between her older daughters, with Zobia sitting on a cushion to her left and Thetis standing to her right. Her mother's hand rested on Thetis's shoulder. Something about the tableau gave Lydia a sudden, unaccountable urge to laugh. She managed to pare it down to a broad grin.

"Oh, Mother! Isn't she beautiful?" Zobia leapt up from her cushion and ran to Lydia, embracing her and kissing her youngest sister on both cheeks. She held Lydia at arm's length and gave her a fond look. "I never thought I would see this day."

Lydia masked her discomfort by turning toward Thetis and holding out her arms. Thetis came toward her, all smiles. "Lydia, I'm so happy for you. Menander is a wonderful boy."

"Oh, yes, he seems such a good lad," Zobia agreed. "I know you two children will be perfect for each other."

Lydia clenched her face into a determined smile and marched toward the couch at the back of the room. Across the couch lay her veil, a wispy square of finely woven silk. Lydia felt a tiny stab of guilt at how much this single piece of cloth had cost her father. But it was so beautiful, so rare. In her fingertips it felt scarcely denser than empty air. She could close her eyes and think she only imagined holding it.

"Lydia, dear, why don't you come over here and sit with us?" her mother asked. They still stood together, like the three Fates, watching her, measuring her—maybe comparing her chances with their choices. Lydia didn't want to go to them, didn't want to listen to whatever they wanted to tell her. But it would be ill-omened to insult her mother and her married sisters on her wedding day. She laid aside the veil and went to them. They moved aside and made a place for her on the cushion, then seated themselves around her. Lydia felt hemmed in. She commanded her breathing to remain slow and deep. She carried Menander's image in her mind like a talisman, reminding herself constantly that, no matter what they said to her now, they couldn't keep her from him.

"Lydia," Zobia began, "your life will change after today." There was a pause, and Lydia saw Zobia's eyes flicker toward Mother before going on. "You won't be able to think always about pleasing yourself. From now on, you'll be under the rule of your husband."

"And he'll depend on you," Thetis said. "You'll manage the household, you'll see to the slaves—he does have an adequate number of servants, doesn't he? Good," she said after Lydia's tight nod, "a woman can't keep a proper house without some help. And in all this, you'll be his indispensable helper. You'll bear him children."

"And teach them to behave properly," Zobia put in.

"As you did, Mother?" Lydia's words came through tight lips.

Chloe looked at her daughter, indignation chasing surprise across her features. "Lydia, what do you mean?"

"How long has it been since you did something just because you wanted to? I remember when you would spend an entire day not just reading Euripides, but enacting him. When you would pore over a whole chest full of scrolls for the sake of a single line from Aeschylus that you wanted to remember exactly."

"Lydia, this isn't very—"

"I admit, there were times when you made us dress up like Athenian soldiers or Argonauts, when all I wanted was to talk to you or just be left alone. But at least you were doing something about the questions in your mind."

"I will not have you talk to me—"

"When did you lose that, Mother? When did you stop wondering about things? What made you give up?"

She never saw her sister's hand coming. The slap stung her

face and set her ears to ringing. She gasped in surprise.

"What do you know about giving up?" Zobia said through clenched teeth, her finger in Lydia's face. "The girl who won the boys' footrace. The child who did whatever she wanted."

"Zobia, maybe you shouldn't—"

Zobia shook off Thetis's hand. "When I think of all the times you have brought embarrassment to your family.... Oh, yes, it still touches me, even though I'm in my husband's house now. 'Isn't that your sister?' they want to know. 'The one marked by the oracle? The one who ran away in the night, who cut off all her hair?' Did you ever think about what your headlong actions might mean for someone else? Did you ever stop to think about your family, its reputation? Did you ever consider anyone other than yourself and what you wanted?"

Lydia felt her face stiffening, felt the shock of her sister's animosity run freezing through her body. She looked at her mother. Her expression made Lydia think of someone clinging to a runaway chariot.

"Just remember this, Lydia, after you marry your young husband: Those who defy tradition do so at their own risk. You may think he's the answer to all your problems. But next time, your hair may not be enough."

Hestia came through the doorway and stood with her hands folded, looking at her feet.

"What is it, Hestia?" asked Lydia's mother.

"The guests are arriving, mistress. It's time for the feast."

Lydia could hear the preparatory squeaks and plucks of the musicians from where she stood. She could count on one hand the number of times in her life she had been permitted into the part of the house reserved for the use of the men: at Zobia's and Thetis's wedding feasts, of course, since those were occasions where the presence of the bride's and groom's entire families was expected. And at one of the feasts celebrating the successful dedication of the guildhall, Father had specifically requested the presence of his wife and Lydia, though they had to leave before the beginning of the symposium. The drinking parties were for men only.

So this was what it felt like to be wed. Lydia searched herself for nervousness, apprehension—feelings she had always imagined she would have before such a life-changing event. But she felt none of them. She thought about Menander, about his kind eyes and the gentle way he had with her. If she was anxious, it was only for the feast to conclude quickly so she could get on quietly with her chosen life.

Her mother was making the final adjustments to her veil, which drifted in front of Lydia's face like a gentle mist. Her sisters had gone inside to sit with their husbands.

Mother dismissed the slaves, then turned to Lydia with a purposeful expression. "Try not to feel harshly toward Zobia. And try to forget what she told you." She glanced at the doorway to the andron, then back at Lydia. "You may succeed where I failed. I wish that for you, at least. And now, I think it's time for the bride to join the feast."

The door swung open, and a merry shout greeted her entrance. Father and Timon sat together at one side of the head table, and Menander sat on the other side. Her father wore an expression of good cheer as he talked and laughed with Timon. Lydia admired him for that, at least.

The room blazed with light; there must have been forty or fifty lamps on and around the triclinium, besides the braziers at

the four corners of the room. All of the officials of the fuller's and
dyer's guild were here, with their wives. One of the city magistrates was even in attendance. And wasn't that the priest of
Artemis? His presence was a good omen. Father must be very
pleased. The lamplight made the frescoes on the andron's four
walls seem alive; the eyes of the figures blinked and shifted, as
if they, too, were eyeing the bounty of the wedding feast, trying
to decide which food to sample first.

Menander stood and beckoned Lydia to join him. He was
wearing a *chitōniskos* and himation of white linen, and he already
wore the garland of dried laurel leaves. She went to him
between the triclinium and the low table, laden with delicacies
of every imaginable kind. She reached her place and Menander
gently raised her veil. At the uncovering of her face, the musicians struck up the traditional chorus in honor of the god of the
marriage bed. Quickly the guests joined in:

> *You shall have a fine house,*
> *No cares, and the best of the figs.*
> *Oh! Hymen! Oh! Hymenaeus....*

Menander put her laurel wreath on her head and she joined him
on the couch.

The slaves began serving the guests, starting with the
fathers, then the bride and groom, and finally reaching the
women and lesser relations at the far ends of the triclinium.
Lydia tried to count the different kinds of foods: pig, of course,
roasted whole; venison, hunted only days ago in the hills
nearby; rich, grain-fed beef, probably from the meat market at
the temple of Apollo; and numerous platters of roasted coney,
fish, and mussels. There were huge bowls of dried figs, dates,

raisins, and walnuts. There were pots of honey, candied almonds, and four different kinds of cheese. There were casks of olives, packed in oil since last summer's harvest. There were steaming bowls of boiled lentils and beans, stewed with onions, leeks, and garlic. There were dried figs and apricots and quinces; dates and pistachios. There were mounds and mounds of freshly baked bread in large, round baskets scattered here and there on the table. Not to mention the ewers of wine sitting within the easy reach of each guest. The andron was crowded, but even with all those in attendance, Lydia didn't see how they could possibly consume all this food.

The room blazed with talk and laughter, and the servants kept the lamps filled and the braziers stoked. Every little while the musicians would strike up another tune, and the guests would drop their food, quickly wipe their hands, and join arms around the room in a back-and-forth, shuffling ring dance. As the evening progressed and the wine ewers emptied, the singing became less and less melodious, the dancing more and more bedraggled.

Finally, the time drew near for the procession to their new house, secured by Menander only a week ago. It stood nearer the forum. Much smaller than this house, yet still ample for their needs, it had formerly belonged to one of Timon's clients, a wool trader named Archanthus, who had kept it for the use of his parents in their old age. The house had been vacant since the deaths of the trader's parents the previous winter. Archanthus, only too happy to place the house at the disposal of his patron's son and his new wife, had required a nominal lease.

The celebrants heaved themselves up from the couches of the triclinium, giggling and weaving as they tossed on robes against the chill outside. Some of the men resumed the wedding chorus, albeit in voices markedly less clear than those with which they had saluted the bride's entry much earlier in the evening.

> *Let's put the handsome groom*
> *Up on our shoulders*
> *And carry him to his house.*
> *Oh! Hymen! Oh! Hymenaeus!*
> *What shall he do with his new wife?*
> *He'll steal her kisses, one by one.*
> *Kisses sweeter than honeyed wine.*
> *Oh! Hymen! Oh! Hymenaeus!*

The verses became progressively bawdier as the wedding party spilled through the gate and onto the street. There were cries of surprise when they came outside into a thick shower of fat snowflakes. The hissing of the flakes in the revelers' torches soon became almost as loud as the singing.

A chariot waited in the street, its handsome roan gelding fretting between the traces. Lydia's father took the horse's lead from the shivering slave who had held it, and the newlyweds climbed aboard. With a chorus of *Oh! Hymenaeus!* the procession swayed forward. Lydia pulled her thick cloak as close about her as she could, then leaned into Menander's protective arm as they went off, surrounded by singing, staggering well-wishers.

When they reached the house, the celebrants formed a gauntlet from the chariot to the gate of the house. They sang and clapped as Menander escorted his wife to the entry. Lydia's father handed the horse's lead to another man and strode ahead of the couple to the gate. He opened it and beckoned them to enter. Menander, following the Roman fashion, scooped Lydia up in his arms and carried her over the threshold of their home. The crowd cheered and belted out one last stanza of *Oh! Hymen! Oh! Hymenaeus!*

Threnides leaned close to his daughter as her husband took her inside. "You have him now. I pray he is truly what you want." Then he closed the gates behind them.

They stood in the small courtyard of their new home. To the left was the kitchen and storeroom. Straight ahead was the main hall, which they would use for dining and almost everything else. To the right was their private chamber. There was no well or cistern, but the house's proximity to the forum and its public wells and fountains mitigated the lack of a private water source.

An old man stepped into the doorway of the kitchen and bowed. "Your room is prepared, master," he said in a high-pitched voice.

"Thank you, Felix," replied Menander. He looked down at Lydia and smiled. With his arm around her shoulders and her arm around his waist, they walked together toward their bedroom. Outside, they could hear the wedding guests going their separate ways. Some of them were still singing, but the falling snow soon muffled the sound.

Inside, two large braziers stood on either side of a wide *klinē* on a low frame fashioned of mahogany. The bed was piled high with woolen blankets. The scent of myrrh bathed the room; old Felix had thought of everything.

Menander took her shoulders and turned her to face him. "Do you find everything to your liking?"

She smiled and nodded. "Except this," she said, removing the soggy wreath from his head. "And you?"

"Almost perfect," her husband replied.

"Almost?"

His face bent toward hers, and words quickly gave place to touch, to the quickening of flesh against flesh. No words were needed after that.

ydia studied the young man seated at the foot of her couch. Again she marveled at how much he looked like his father—very nearly the image of Stratius. Other than some broadness about the bridge of his nose and the un-Roman thickness of his lips, few of his mother's Thracian features were in evidence. Yes, in every way his father's son.

"How is your father these days, Gaius?"

"Well enough, Mother Lydia. He and Mother send their greeting."

"I'm glad to have it, though why they'd subject a healthy young man like yourself to the drudgery of attending an old woman's sickbed, I don't understand."

He smiled at her. His teeth were strong and white; they reminded Lydia of her beloved Menander so long ago.

"I was glad to come, Mother Lydia. Besides, my father is pre-occupied with public matters just now."

"Oh?"

"Domitian has just decreed a reduction in the silver denarius, and the *duumvirī* have charged Father with setting the exchange rates for the old coinage. Also, there's an imperial quaestor making the rounds in the province, asking questions and demanding to see tax and expenditure records."

Lydia sighed and shook her head. "Your poor father. I remember when all he had to worry about was the nose count of his prisoners."

"I've heard him tell the stories many times."

"The reward of diligence. From centurion to provincial *prōquaestor*. I'm so proud of him."

"I think he'd gladly go back to being a jail keeper, right now. He says the emperor meddles too much. He says he spends all his time sending posts to Rome instead of overseeing the district's business."

It was a fine day, and Lydia was glad she'd had them move her couch into the atrium. It felt good to be out in the fresh air for a change. Euterpe came into the atrium, mincing toward them in that annoying way she had. Lydia scowled at her, but the silly girl's eyes were fastened on the handsome young male form at the foot of the couch, and she never saw Lydia's look of disapproval. She asked if Lydia needed anything, but she stared at Gaius the entire time she spoke. Thankfully, his back was to her, and he didn't see the unmannerly display. Lydia dismissed her curtly and Euterpe retreated back toward the doorway of the kitchen. Lydia saw Clystra's head poke out, saw Euterpe cover her mouth against the giggle that escaped anyway. She really ought to say something to Euodia about these two.

"He doesn't say that anywhere but at home," Gaius added hastily. "Father is a loyal subject."

"As if I needed to be reminded of that. I think there are no official spies in this house, Gaius. Not yet, at least."

He grinned and ducked his head. "I forget myself some-times."

She made a little hiss as a sudden pain lanced her abdomen.

"Are you all right, Mother Lydia? Can I do something for you? Get you something?" He half-stood, leaning over her.

"No, thank you, Gaius. It'll pass." Such a polite boy. So kind and thoughtful.

"Shall I send in one of the servants?"

"No!" She patted her hand toward the foot of the couch, where he had been seated. "No, just sit here with me and talk to me. That's all I want right now."

A scattering of sparrows bounced and chattered in the far corner of the atrium, near the colonnade enclosing the well. Lydia watched them skip back and forth, pecking at the minis-cule crumbs mingled with the grit coating the flagstone paving.

"I brought you some figs," Gaius said, holding up the bas-ket he had brought. "Mother said figs were your favorites."

"So they are. But my fig-eating days are past, I'm afraid."

He set the basket down. His face was downturned, sad-dened.

"What's the matter, Gaius?"

He wouldn't look at her. "I don't like to think about your—your leaving."

Lydia watched him, watched the curve of his back as he slumped in the place where he sat. "Gaius, it's the way of things." Her voice was gentle, careful.

He pressed his lips together, still looking down.

"I don't expect you to understand this," she went on, "but my death doesn't frighten me. In the first place, I'm too old and tired to run from it any more, even in my own mind. There comes a time, Gaius, when what's chiefly wanted is rest."

From the corner of her eye, she saw a movement close to the ground in the archway that opened onto the atrium from the entry yard. It was Lachesis, one of the cats. She crouched in the entry, her eyes fixed with a quivering intensity on the sparrows across the atrium. Only the tip of her tail moved—a nervous, barely bridled twitch—as she watched the unsuspecting birds. Lydia could see the tendons and muscles of her hind legs bunching beneath her as she readied herself for the charge.

"Find something to throw at that cat," she said, pointing toward the archway.

Gaius swiveled around and looked where she pointed. He searched the ground at his feet, then reached into the basket and grabbed one of the figs. He lobbed it at the cat and it hit the pavement with a ripe-sounding splat an arm's length away from her. Lachesis sprang straight up, then bounded away, retreating into the entry yard. The sparrows swirled above the courtyard for a moment, then alighted and resumed their noisy foraging.

Gaius turned back toward her. "Your house was the first place my parents brought me after I was born. I remember First Day gatherings here, waking up in my mother's lap from the singing. Playing with my friends in the torchlight. Dropping pebbles into your well and listening for the splash. Sneaking hot bread and honey from your kitchen while we waited for the meal to start."

"You think I didn't know who was getting into my honey?"

He smiled then, looking away down the atrium toward the colonnade. "This house holds so much of my life, Mother Lydia. But when you're not in it anymore…."

Lydia wished she could reach him—pat his shoulder or even kiss the top of his head. She closed her eyes and tried to imagine the smell of his hair: the strong, disorderly, mingled scent of sweat and grass and outdoors and movement that enveloped a boy, or even a young man like Gaius.

It was what she remembered best about Parmenes: that sweet, unruly boy-smell. He would have been—what?—nearly sixty years old by now, had he lived. Could that be? She tried to imagine Parmenes as a man, gray of hair and beard, with an overhanging paunch and jowls, maybe. Impossible. The only picture she could form was of the laughing, shouting, scurrying, tinkering, curious boy, the one with boundless energy and no discretion whatever, the constant object of her harried attention. Gone, now. Gone for a long, long time.

"Tell me again—the story," Gaius said.

"What story, Gaius?"

"The one at the beginning. You know—the earthquake, the stocks coming loose."

"Why? Surely you've heard your father tell of that night more times than you can count."

"Yes, but he doesn't tell it the way you do. He can't see it from the outside—not the way you can."

Lydia plucked an imaginary piece of lint from the blanket across her knees. "What did you say? 'The one at the beginning.' Is that how you think of it?"

"That's how Father always starts it. 'When it all began,' he says. And then he tells it. But I want to hear it from you. Again."

"You mean, 'one last time.'"

"Please. Just tell it, Mother Lydia."

She smiled and leaned back against her cushions. The song, always the song: Silas's rumbling, low voice and Paul's high-pitched, raspy warble. And neither of them able to tell a tune from a horse whinny. Time and again she had imagined the darkness of the underground cell, the dank smell of mildewed straw and unwashed bodies, the sour odor of fear. And then, through the blackness and the tilting uncertainty, the sound of the two voices, raw and untrained and brimming with belief—the ancient Hebrew hymn rising from their throats in the midnight dungeon.

I love you, O LORD, my strength.
The LORD is my rock, my fortress and my deliverer;
my God is my rock, in whom I take refuge.
He is my shield and the horn of my salvation,
my stronghold.

She realized later she should have noticed the animals; they'd been acting peculiar all day. The cats in her yard minced back and forth, calling out in the most forlorn, piteous voices, turning away from food and water. When she visited the market stalls near the forum, Lydia had to walk around a donkey that had lain down in the middle of the street, scattering its load. The beast would not budge for all its master's blows and curses. Even the birds seemed subdued; they clung in clumps on the edges and peaks of roofs, fluttering up nervously, then perching again.

I call to the LORD, who is worthy of praise,
and I am saved from my enemies. . . .
In my distress I called to the LORD;
I cried to my God for help.

One of Euodia's girls came rushing in at midafternoon to tell her the tale. The men who kept the inn just outside the northwest gate—if you could dignify the place by calling it an inn—had dragged Paul and Silas into the forum and accused them before the duumvirī of advocating customs harmful to the peace of the empire. They were in the public prison, the girl said, bound hand and foot in stocks.

From his temple he heard my voice;
my cry came before him, into his ears.

Only later did the full story come out; how the poor, haunted drudge had followed Paul all over Philippi, crowing in her strange, cracking voice about the power that made a home in Paul. She was a familiar sight in the forum: her unwashed, uncombed hair and filthy clothing, her face smeared with ashes. She had a distant, vacant stare and her mouth hung open most of the time. They would put her in a stall in the forum and people would line up. They'd pay four obols a throw to hear the strange, rhyming couplet the girl would pronounce—always a couplet, always in rhyme. She spoke in a flat, straight line of a voice and sounded as if she really wanted to be saying something else, people said. Some folk thought they could trace the future in her verse; others claimed her words had helped them recover lost objects or avoid illness. Lydia had heard hints that the innkeepers offered her for other services to those desperate enough to want them. For that, they asked a higher price than four obols. One of the men always stood behind her shoulder in the forum to take the money and hurry the customers away. The girl never touched any coin herself.

The cords of death entangled me;
the torrents of destruction overwhelmed me.

It wasn't difficult for the innkeepers to convince the duumvirī of Paul's culpability; the memory of Claudius's banment of the Jews from Rome was still fresh. Lydia could easily imagine the scene in the forum: the curious, the concerned, and the idle, gathered around the bema; the angry shouting of the innkeepers; Marcus Quintus's fat, sweaty face and Tullius Rufus beside him—cold, aloof, and suspicious of everything and everyone. Quintus would do almost anything to avoid making a difficult decision and Rufus could be counted on to insulate himself as quickly as possible from anything that might jeopardize his standing in the provincial government.

Epaphroditus saw the whole affair from the back of the crowd that gathered quickly to observe the proceedings. The innkeepers were indignant in their denunciations, he said. They played to the crowd; they shouted and waved their arms and wagged angry fingers at Paul and Silas. If the two accused men had any words to offer in their own defense, they were lost in the torrent of invective loosed by the angry innkeepers. Tullius Rufus quickly heard enough, Epaphroditus said. He cut off the innkeepers' tirade in midsentence and made a curt pronouncement. He made quick, jabbing motions at the commander of the city militia and the two men were quickly surrounded by soldiers.

Their coats and tunics were torn roughly from them and they were tied with leather straps to some nearby posts. Two big-chested fellows with thick, muscled arms beat them with supple wooden rods as long as a man's leg and about the thickness of a finger. The rods whistled through the air and made a dull, meaty thwack when they struck. By the time the lictors were finished, the naked backs, buttocks, and legs of Paul and Silas were crisscrossed with bloody, purpling welts. The guards picked up the prisoners' clothing from the ground and tossed it at the two, then hustled them off toward the public jail in the

Upper City. Marcus Quintus looked after them with a grateful, relieved expression, mopping his face with a silk kerchief.

The cords of the grave coiled around me;
the snares of death confronted me.

Lydia rushed up the hill to the prison as soon as Euodia's girl finished the telling. The jail was beyond the citadel, in the fortified section of the Upper City, far around the eastern shoulder of Mount Orbelos—almost halfway to the amphitheater. It was a low, rambling, unadorned building of rough-finished stone. It had small windows, high up, spanned by iron bars set in sockets in the stone. She was about to pound on the ironclad oak door when she felt a touch. Lydia looked down. Sitting cross-legged on the ground beside the gate was the fortune-teller. Her face was different: still smeared with ash and grime, but not vacant now. Her eyes looked at Lydia and really saw her.

"You're here about the good men," the girl said. "The ones they arrested." Her voice was changed, also. It had inflection; it rose and fell with the meaning of her words.

Lydia nodded.

"I didn't hear the voice when I said that," the girl said in a wondering voice. "I guessed it from your face. I decided to say it myself." She looked up at Lydia with a faint smile. "I can pick my own words now. I don't have to do what the voice says anymore. I don't even have to listen to it."

"Why are you here?" Lydia asked her.

The girl shrugged. "They made me leave. Without the voice, I'm no good to them, they said. I heard the good men were here, so I came, too. The soldiers wouldn't let me inside, so I'm waiting here. Will the good men come out soon?"

Just then, a burly, rough-looking man passed in the street, giving them a long look as he went by. Lydia knelt beside the girl. "I'm a friend of the good men. You must come to my house to wait for them."

The girl gave her a wary look. "I want to see the good men."

Lydia nodded. "You will. They're staying at my house. That's where they'll come when the soldiers let them go."

The girl's expression brightened. Even through the grime, Lydia could see that she had a simple, pleasant face. Why had she never looked at this child before? The girl nodded and got to her feet. Lydia hurried her away, looking over her shoulder. She prayed silently that she hadn't just lied to the poor thing. On the way home, Lydia found out what the girl called herself— Persephone. In a moment of cruel irony, someone had named this pitiful creature for the unwilling bride of Hades.

*In my distress I called to the L*ORD*;*
I cried to my God for help.
From his temple he heard my voice;
my cry came before him, into his ears.

By the time she got back to her house, Luke and Timothy were there. They met her in the entry yard with widened eyes and fear-blanched faces. "Is it true? Are Paul and Silas taken?"

"Yes. I went to the prison to try to see them, but—"

"Are you friends of the good men?" Persephone wanted to know. "When will the good men be here?"

Lydia gestured impatiently to one of her servants. "Take her and bathe her. Give her one of my daughter's old robes; they're about the same size." The servant led Persephone away.

"Who is that young woman?" Luke asked.

"She's the one who was following us around," Timothy said. "Don't you remember? She kept shouting."

Luke looked at his young companion, then at the archway to the main atrium, through which the servant had just ushered the girl. "Are you sure? This girl seems to be in possession of her mind, at least."

"Never mind that," said Lydia. "We must do something, and quickly. Paul and Silas are in stocks in the underground cell, and the guards aren't letting anyone in to see them. They'll be lucky if they're only—"

"Have you heard anything else?" It was Euodia, hurrying toward them from the gate. Syntyche followed close behind her. "I went to the prison, but they're not letting anyone see them."

"I heard someone say the duumvirī gave the guards special orders about them," Syntyche said. She was wringing her hands and her voice had a quavering sound.

"Get a grip on yourself, Syntyche," said Euodia. "You won't do them any good by getting overwrought."

Syntyche tucked her hands under her crossed arms and pressed her lips together.

"Perhaps I should go to the jail and try to speak to the centurion," Luke said.

"No! Their accusers poisoned the forum crowd against them," Euodia said. "You've been seen with them all around Philippi. You'd just end up in the same cell with them if you went up there."

"Then what can we do?" asked Syntyche.

"We can wait," said Lydia. "Who knows what will happen? Maybe the duumvirī will release them. Or maybe they'll only make them leave Philippi." Lydia felt herself losing the battle to keep what she felt out of her voice and off her face. "We might as well eat and try to get some rest. Tomorrow will be another day." She called for one of her servants and sent her to the kitchen to begin getting the food ready.

The earth trembled and quaked,
and the foundations of the mountains shook;
they trembled because he was angry.

Lydia woke in the pitch dark, her stomach yawing uneasily. The air seemed unnaturally still; even the night insects were silent. Then the shaking started, and she knew.

She vaulted from her couch and dashed into the atrium, yelling as loud as her groggy voice would permit. "Earthquake! Earthquake! Everyone outside, quickly!"

The flagstones of the courtyard buckled and heaved as if they floated atop a huge, boiling pot. Lydia saw the stone pillars of the colonnade sway back and forth as the wooden supporting beams across the top of the course creaked and groaned. She heard the sound of pots crashing in the kitchen. Some of the scullery girls came weaving through the doorway, rubbing their faces and trying to keep their balance on the swaying ground.

Lydia dashed across the atrium, giving the doorway of the hall a wary look before ducking inside. "Persephone! Come outside quickly, child!" She went to the far corner, where the servants had made up a pallet for the girl. Persephone was sleeping amid the din as soundly as an infant. Lydia bent over her, with many a frightened look at the groaning ceiling beams. "Get up, dear! We must go outside." Lydia reached out to jostle the girl's shoulder, and a chip of plaster from the ceiling fell on her arm.

"Are the good men here?" asked the sleepy girl as she sat up. A larger chunk of plaster, the size of a big serving bowl, smashed to the floor behind them.

"No, they're not here. Come on." Lydia hauled her up by her armpits. "We have to get out of here." They hurried out the doorway and across the portico toward the main courtyard. Most of the household was gathered there, in a frightened little knot at the center. Luke and Timothy were trying to calm them and keep them together. And then, as quickly as it had started, the earthquake ended. The only sounds were the whimpers of her servant girls and the shouts of people in the night, some near and some far, calling to each other and announcing the damage done by the quake.

Lydia's eyes met Luke's. Paul and Silas were in an underground cell when the quake hit.

Ten

They hurried toward the street, when suddenly Lydia remembered they would need brands. She ducked back inside and sent one of the girls to scrabble in the storeroom and find some pine knots smeared with pitch. Plenty of live coals remained in the ash bed of the kitchen hearth, and soon Lydia, Luke, and Timothy held aloft burning torches. They were nearly to the gate when they heard running steps slapping across the atrium. "Wait for me," Persephone called. "I want to go with you."

Lydia looked at Luke. He shrugged. "Let her come. What can it harm?"

They picked their way carefully through the streets. Paving stones were thrust up from the roadbed at crazy angles. They came to the forum. Though none of the buildings or temples had sustained major damage in the brief quake, many of the smaller memorial plinths were toppled, and here and there small fissures had opened in the ground, inviting unwary feet. Lydia held her torch high, straining forward in the darkness as she led the way. They passed the Temple of Zeus at the northeast corner of the forum. Lydia noticed a large crack running nearly the entire length of one of the fluted, Corinthian columns supporting the front portico. They crossed the Via Egnatia and started the climb through the switchback streets crisscrossing the slope that led to the Upper City.

Parties of half-dressed citizens roamed here and there: merchants hurrying toward their shops and bankers rushing to their countinghouses. Now and then they passed patrols of soldiers moving quickly from place to place.

They arrived at the public prison. Lydia was relieved to see that the building was still standing, at least. In the flickering light of their torches, it was impossible to tell whether the structure was damaged.

Luke pounded on the door. There was no answer. He put his ear to the massive oak door and listened. "I can't hear anything, but this door looks to be pretty thick." His fist thumped again on the door. "We have friends inside. Please let us in."

After several moments, the huge door swung open slightly, and a man's head appeared from inside. Wide-eyed and cautious, he peered around the door at them. "What do you want?"

"We have friends inside," Luke said. "We were worried for them, after the earthquake."

"Everyone in here is all right," the fellow said. "You can go back home." He started to pull his head back inside.

"Can't we at least see our friends?" Lydia asked, stepping forward.

The man stuck his head back out. "I said we're all right. None of us are hurt."

"Our friends—they're prisoners," Lydia said. "In the underground cell. We were afraid—"

"Prisoners? I can't let anyone go talk to the prisoners. You think I want a flogging? Go away."

He started to pull the door to, but Timothy wedged his foot between the door and the jamb. "Paul and Silas, two men of Antioch. They were brought here just today. We have to know if they were hurt in the earthquake."

The fellow released the door and staggered back, making the sign against the evil eye. "Those two," he hissed. "Sorcerers. Singing songs to bring the earthquake. Stratius may be taken in by them, but not me."

Luke strode forward to tower over the guard. "Where are they? Take me to Paul and Silas, I tell you."

"They're not here! They did some witchery on Stratius, and he took them away. To his house, maybe."

"Where does he live?" Lydia asked.

"On the Street of Figs, where it runs into the main road."

"I know the place," Lydia told her friends. They turned to leave.

"Jewish sorcerers!" the guard shouted after them. "Bad luck! A plague on the lot of you!"

The Street of Figs lay beyond the western end of the forum. To get there, they had to tramp back across the breadth of the upper city, then down the winding, narrow streets once again, until they reached the flatter ground near the Via Egnatia. The Street of Figs was a short street, and they had to knock at only one wrong gate to get directions to the house of Stratius, the centurion in command of the prison guards. When they reached the centurion's house, they could see the yellow flickering of lamplight above the wall that faced the street. They could hear the sound of singing drifting into the night air.

You, O LORD, keep my lamp burning;
my God turns my darkness into light.

With your help I can advance against a troop;
with my God I can scale a wall.

Lydia peered in wonder at Luke and Timothy. The words were Hebrew and the singing was awful. "Who else can that be but Paul and Silas?" she asked.

Luke shook his head and shrugged. Persephone was smiling and bouncing on the balls of her feet. "The good men! They're here! They're here!"

They all turned toward the gate and began knocking and calling. Soon the door opened and a man stood there. He was of medium height and build, and his hair—wet, Lydia noticed—was cut in a Roman tonsure. He was smiling.

"Yes, friends. How may I help you?" he asked.

"Are you Stratius, the commander of the jail guards?"

His smile drew down at the corners. "I am. Who are you?"

"We're friends of Paul and Silas," Luke began.

"If you're friends of Paul and Silas, then you're welcome here." He stepped aside and beckoned them. "Come into my house."

The courtyard was small, barely bigger than Lydia's entry yard, and unpaved, but it was very clean. Just to the right of the entrance, a lararium sat in a small niche in the wall. Lydia looked at the pictures of the dancing lares that decorated the small, wooden cupola. They were rendered as gaily dressed youths holding wreaths above the head of a staid, draped figure that probably represented the genius of Stratius's household. On the ground below the cupola was a shattered clay image. Lydia guessed the figure of Stratius's household god must have fallen from the cupola's shelf during the quake. The torso section was still mostly intact; one of the god's hands was raised in a gesture of blessing.

Two small rooms, their front walls perpendicular to each other, opened onto the courtyard. Persephone ran to the doorway of the first, calling out for the "good men." Paul and Silas came through the doorway of the other room, followed by an older man Lydia didn't recognize, presumably Stratius's slave. Persephone ran to the two men and, just as she reached them, prostrated herself on the packed earth at their feet.

"No, child," Paul said. He reached down and took hold of her shoulders, raising her to her feet. "You must not worship us. Worship the true God. He's the one who healed you, not me."

Lydia felt the warmth rising in her: the same disturbing eagerness that enveloped her anytime she observed Paul acting from his finest, truest self. He cupped Persephone's cheek in his palm and gave her one of his flickering, thin-lipped smiles. Lydia tried to take her eyes away from him, but after the upset and dread of his imprisonment and the earthquake, the relief of seeing him safe and sound was too strong. She watched him and soon his eyes found her. Their gazes locked for an instant, then he pulled his attention elsewhere. "Luke!" he called, hobbling toward the physician on his wounded, bandy legs. Lydia went to Persephone and dusted the front of her garment where she had lain in the dirt in front of Paul.

What was it about this wiry, round-shouldered, balding little man? Lydia wondered. She could hardly imagine anyone more opposite to her beloved Menander. And yet, much like the thought of her husband's death, the thought of never again seeing Paul caused a place in her to wilt and darken.

It was comical the next day when Stratius sent word to the duumvirī that they had ordered the public beating of a Roman citizen without giving him the benefit of a trial. Marcus Quintus himself came up to the prison, huffing and sweating behind his worried deputies. Later, gathered at Lydia's house, Silas gave an amused report of Paul's interview with the fat magistrate. "He couldn't apologize enough," Silas said. "When he saw Paul's writing kit and stylus, I think he thought we were just then composing a complaint to Caesar. He nearly started crying, I think." By that time, they were able to laugh.

"It was not long after that," Lydia said, "that your father became an aedile for the provincial prōquaestor. He was still fairly young for such a post. We were all very pleased for him."

Gaius beamed. "Now he is provincial prōquaestor himself."

"And when my business made it impossible for me to continue to care for Persephone, he took her into his home. That was no small thing. He had just married your mother, in those days."

"I still remember Persephone," Gaius said. "She was always smiling."

"Yes. A simple mind, but a happy one. She took care of your brothers and sisters, and then you. She was a great help to your mother."

"And to the rest of us. I still miss her."

Lydia closed her eyes and leaned her head against the cushions beneath her head. "Like so many, she died too young."

"I remember there was no one who would play with me, after she was gone."

"You were only a little fellow. Maybe eight years old."

His back was curved again under the burden of the memory and the other thoughts it birthed. Looking at him, Lydia felt tears welling into her eyes—not for herself, but for the sadness of this young man who already knew too much about partings and was bound to learn more.

Lydia woke to the sound of water sloshing into an urn in the courtyard. She yawned and stretched. Felix was commendably discreet and always respectful, but Lydia thought he had his opinions about how late people should sleep in the mornings— even his newlywed master and mistress. Sometimes he would cough quietly outside their door; other times he would mutter softly to himself as he paced back and forth on his errands from the main hall to the storeroom, where he also slept. Today he was pouring the water he'd carried from the well in the forum— a little louder than was strictly necessary, Lydia suspected.

She rolled onto her side and looked at Menander. It was still deliciously new to her, this business of waking up next to him. She ran a hand softly along the contour of his shoulder, where the bedclothes had fallen away. She didn't want to wake him; her touch was evanescent, barely there. His shoulder rose and fell, evenly and slowly, with the cadence of his sleeping breaths. He slept on his side, his back turned slightly toward her, and she studied the fine, sculpted line of his backbone, from the cleft between his shoulder blades to the place where the blankets hid it from her view.

He sighed and rolled onto his back. His arm fell across her belly. Lydia put her hand in his, and his fingers closed over hers. Lydia felt in the center of her an infilling that was rich and warm. She wanted to stroke his face and twine her fingers in his hair, but she didn't want to wake him. She wanted to savor this moment and remember everything: the dim light of morning seeping through the window above their bed; the sound of Felix's footsteps as he went back and forth in the courtyard; the smell of Menander's skin; the warmth of him next to her; the soft, hushing sound of the air going in and out of him. Even the chill of the morning air on her exposed arms and shoulders was welcome since it made more enjoyable the cozy comfort of the rest of her, tucked beneath the bedclothes. Lydia tried to hold herself perfectly still and capture it all, to hold it within her as a motionless pool holds the reflection of the sky.

But Menander stirred and his eyes fluttered open. His face turned toward hers. "Hello, wife," he smiled, sleepily.

"Hello, husband. Felix is getting impatient. I think it's time for one of us to get up."

"Which one, I wonder?" he said as he reached for her with a lazy motion.

"Now, now. None of that. You drank your fill last night, as I recall."

"And you didn't mind my thirst one bit, as I recall."

They laughed together the low, easy laugh of young lovers who have all the time in the world. She touched his face and he turned toward her hand, kissing it.

"Ah, well," Menander said, yawning and stretching, "if you won't have me, then I'll find other employment."

"Best you do. At the rate Felix is filling the water jugs, he's working up an appetite. And I could do with some breakfast, myself."

"Eaten out of house and home." Menander sat up on the edge of the bed and reached for his chitoniskos. Luxuriating beneath the covers, Lydia watched him dress.

Most mornings, Menander left for the forum just as the sun was clearing the roofline of the Temple of Zeus. He would go to the portico on the northeast side, the favored gathering place for the buyers and sellers of wool, linen, hides, and other such commodities. Menander's father had lucrative agreements with procurers for the imperial army, but maintaining a steady supply of the needed goods required large volumes of materials obtained at the best possible price.

Buying was a big responsibility, but Menander sometimes wore it ill. His older brother would chide him over every unnecessary lepton he allowed into the offer price, he said, and his father would question him about every lot of product that went to one of their competitors. Menander sometimes told her he wearied of attempting to do business, knowing that mistakes would be found in his decisions no matter what he did.

Her husband's real passions were rhetoric and philosophy. In the evenings when he returned home, he would eat a light supper, then spend hours poring over his growing collection of the writings of the great thinkers. Menander used every drachma he could spare to buy or trade for more scrolls. With his work, he wasn't able to go to instruction at the rhetor's anymore, but his former teacher was a regular guest at their table, and such was old Sosipater's delight in Menander that he often wound up staying late into the night, giving impromptu lessons in argument and logic or discussing philosophy.

Lydia liked Sosipater. The aging rhetor had views that differed in many particulars from those Lydia had been accustomed to in her earlier years. For example, Sosipater thought nothing of Lydia's presence at the table and in their discussions. Though he didn't entirely approve of his former student's wide-ranging reading habits, the instructor clearly enjoyed Menander, and his enjoyment of Menander seemed to spill over onto his young wife. He would talk to Lydia as freely as to her husband, posing questions and listening to her responses as if they really mattered to him. Lydia adored the feeling of being heard; even of giving as good as she got in the long, evening talks. She found herself fascinated by the ideas and teachings of Socrates, Plato,

Aristotle, and all the rest. She sometimes had difficulty keeping proper lines of division between the place where one left off and the other started, but the swirl of thought, the sweep and grandeur of the ideas was a heady draught to her. And she sensed that as her appreciation and understanding deepened, Menander's trust and confidence in her deepened, as well. Under Sosipater's enthusiastic sponsorship, their minds were twining together as intimately as their hearts already had.

"But if Aratus can say we are the offspring of the gods, how can it also be said the gods dwell in us?" Lydia wanted to know. It was a fine, spring day. She and Menander walked together in the countryside west of Thyatira. The rounded flanks of the hills greened under the warm sun; the whole landscape seemed to preen and stretch like a just-awakened cat after the long drowse of winter. Clusters of small wildflowers, growing close to the ground, splashed patches of color here and there across the terrain. It was the midspring festival, and the trading house was inactive, as was nearly every other shop and business in Thyatira. She and Menander had watched the beginning of the young girls' Artemisiad in the forum, but the day had beckoned and their feet had led them out of the town to wander among the easy slopes of the foothills.

"It isn't precisely 'the gods' who dwell in us," Menander said, reaching down to pluck a long grass stem and stick it between his teeth. "It is the spirit, the pneuma that permeates us—and everything else. The stuff of the gods, but not them, strictly speaking."

"That makes no sense. If it is the stuff of the gods, why isn't it them? And if it is them and it's in us, why aren't we gods?"

Menander chuckled and shook his head. "Little Lydia, if you once grab an argument, you hold till death, don't you?"

"You didn't answer my objection, O worthy opponent."

"All right, then." He ran his fingers through his hair as he gathered his thoughts. "The entire cosmos—everything we can see, and even that which we can't—is held together, just as our bodies are held together by the union of flesh and spirit. And, just as our thinking directs our bodies, so there is a leading part of the universe—its mind, you might say. And since we are a part of the universe, we are also a part of that mind which directs and orders everything for our good."

"And that is Zeus?"

"Well…not exactly."

"Why not?"

"Well…because Zeus is a part of the universe-mind—a picture of it, maybe—but not the thing itself."

"What's the difference?"

He made an exasperated snort. "You're trying to wear me down with your questions. I feel like an accused man on trial in the forum."

"Oh, you poor thing," she said, pinching his cheek. "Tell you what. I propose another, quicker way of settling this argument."

"And what might that be?"

"You see that patch of windflowers over there? Halfway up the next rise—about a javelin throw away."

"Yes…."

"I'll race you to it. I will be the champion of the gods, and you can be the advocate of your strange, foggy philosophy. If I get there first, then Zeus is seated firmly on his throne on top of Olympus, all in one piece and eating ambrosia at this very moment. If you make it first, he's just as you say: a wise vapor diffused throughout the universe, floating in and out of people's noses with or without their permission."

"Lydia, that is hardly—"

"What's the matter? Afraid I'll beat you again?" She wore the taunting grin that she knew always reached into him, touched the tender sources of his warmth. She twisted her chiton between her legs, tucking it up high into the waistband of her garment. "I'm ready. What do you say?"

He wheeled and broke for the flower patch.

"Cheater!" she screamed, and dashed after him.

Laughing like children, they kited down the grassy slope. Menander was slightly ahead, but Lydia gained steadily. At the bottom there was a small, muddy gully, left by the last spring downpour. Menander tried to vault it, but his foot slipped and he fell to his hands and knees. Lydia vaulted over him and started up the slope toward the windflower patch.

"Zeus punishes your hubris!" she called over her shoulder.

"Better save your breath!" he replied as he tore after her.

She pushed herself through the burning in her calves, all the while hearing his footfalls closing on her. But the flower patch was just ahead and he hadn't passed her yet. Getting closer…closer….

With a shout that was half a grunt, he flung himself past her and dived into the patch of anemones, a bare half-stride ahead.

"Vindicated! I'm vindicated!" he shouted. "The champion of philosophy defeats the shadows of superstition."

She leaned over, her hands braced against her knees, catching her breath. "You…started…unfairly."

"Did I?" He crawled over to her and raised himself to stand in front of her. He took her hands and pulled her upright, then into him. He kissed her. She tasted his breath in her mouth, warm and urgent from the run—from something else. Her arms went around him and they kneeled together, then lay down in the middle of the windflowers.

Eleven

s spring broadened into summer, Lydia began to notice she frequently felt fatigued and faintly ill, for no reason she could discover. The summer drew on and she realized her waist was thickening, though she was eating no more than her habit—maybe less. By the end of summer, there was little doubt. Menander called for the old slave woman of his father's household, the midwife who had delivered him and his brothers. She ran a hand over Lydia's stomach and looked at her a few moments, then nodded. "Next winter, probably sometime around the middle of *Peritios.*" Lydia began savoring the secret warmth of the life growing inside her, life that belonged to her and Menander.

For Lydia, the fag end of summer was a dreary, endless corridor of heat and lethargy. During the hottest part of the day, all she could do was lie against the cool earth in the small courtyard, shifting herself heavily as she followed the shadows around the perimeter of the walls. Most evenings, she slept on the roof, dreaming of autumn. Felix brought her damp cloths and cool water. He handed them to her without saying anything, without looking at her. Lydia guessed the old slave considered her lazy. Let him carry this baby, she thought.

Lydia watched Felix as he went about his duties. While he swept the loose dirt from the courtyard or stacked cakes of dried dung for the kitchen fire, she could sometimes see his lips moving. Once, as she was coming down from the roof in the morning, she saw him kneeling in the middle of the courtyard, doing an obeisance toward the southeast. He heard her footfalls on the stair and quickly got up, dusting off his knees. He sent a guilty glance her way and avoided her as much as possible the rest of the day.

She found herself wondering about him. He didn't look like he was native to Thyatira, or even Asia Minor. In the forum she had seen Galatians with their strange, pale skin and hair. Felix wasn't like them. His coloring was dark, his eyes a deep, chestnut brown. The fringe of hair ringing his bald scalp was kinky and grizzled. The skin of his face was as smooth as a young boy's; from this and his high voice Lydia knew he was a eunuch. He had full, almost purple lips and a heavy, prominent nose. And there was a soft accent to his Greek that Lydia couldn't place. He sometimes rolled his words on the back of his tongue, like someone trying to keep from swallowing.

"Felix," she asked him one day, "how did you come to the household of my husband's father?"

His dark eyes flickered at her as he handed her the cup of water. "I belonged to him, and to his father before him. The master's grandfather was a commander in the army of the Roman general Pompey, and he brought me back with him from his last campaign."

"Where was that?"

"Judea, Mistress. It's a small land; you've probably never heard of the place."

Lydia frowned down at the cup before taking a drink. "No, I haven't. Where is it?"

"It lies to the south and east, Mistress. Far from here."

"How did your people come to be slaves?"

He hesitated. "My family found itself on the wrong side of a conflict." He turned to go.

"Felix, do you remember much of Judea?"

He half-turned toward her, but kept his eyes away. "No, Mistress. I was very young. Do you need anything else?"

"No, Felix. That's all for now."

"Yes, Mistress." She watched him thoughtfully as he padded across the courtyard toward the storeroom.

Two days later, Lydia had a sudden craving for pistachios. She laid aside her small loom and looked around for Felix. He was nowhere in sight, and her head was starting to hurt, so she didn't want to raise her voice enough to summon the old eunuch. She couldn't be sure, but she sometimes suspected him of sudden deafness when she called without being able to see him. Sighing, she levered herself to her feet and ambled toward the storeroom, idly rubbing a hand across her belly.

When she reached the doorway of the storeroom, she heard Felix's voice from inside. He was singing. Lydia was surprised to realize that it was quite pleasant to hear. The slave spoke so little, she would never have expected him to be able to sing. She stood very still and listened. She didn't recognize the language at all. The melody rose and fell in plaintive, searching loops. Even without knowing the words of the song, the tune made Lydia think of loss, of open, barren places—of someone crying into emptiness and hoping upon hope for an answer.

Her shadow must have fallen across the threshold, because the singing stopped suddenly. A little embarrassed at being caught eavesdropping, Lydia stepped into the opening. "I think there's a basket of pistachios over there. Get it for me, Felix."

"Yes, Mistress." He turned in the direction she pointed and rustled among the shelves in the corner. "Here it is." He brought it to her and offered the basket, his face turned away.

She took the basket and reached inside to gather a handful of nuts. She turned to go, then turned back. "I heard you singing, Felix. Your voice is very pleasing."

He stood as still as if he'd heard nothing.

"Was that the Judean language?"

After a moment, he nodded.

"Would you sing for me, Felix? Not now, of course…but some other time, maybe?" She wondered at her shyness. He was her slave, after all. But Lydia had the sense he hid a precious, intensely private treasure behind his silence. She was loath to intrude—and yet she had an unaccountably strong desire to hear again the melody that made her want to weep and pray at the same time.

As her belly grew, so did her ennui. More and more she looked forward to Menander's return in the evenings, longed to let him gentle her with sweet words and careful, thoughtful touch. But business conditions had been more difficult lately; success in the forum and at the trading house was harder to come by. There were days when he was distracted, when his eyes didn't meet hers with delight or even interest. Lydia thought her husband must surely be disgusted by her bloated figure. She lectured herself: Menander was a good, kind man who loved her. Besides, the baby distending her middle was his child. Surely he was not so unfair as to forget the part he had played in creating her misshapen condition.

"The drought has hurt the herds and crops," he said one

evening while they ate. "There just isn't much of a supply out there. And it doesn't help that I'm the youngest buyer in the forum. 'Boy,' they call me." He shook his head as he scooped up a dollop of cheese.

Lydia's back hurt and her ankles were swollen and she desperately wanted Menander to ask her how she felt, how many times the baby moved, if there was anything he could bring home from the trading house that would ease her or lend some small spot of pleasure to her long day. But what she said was, "You know as much as any of them, though, don't you?"

He shrugged as he added some water to his winecup. "I don't know. Maybe. But you couldn't get Father or my brother to say I do."

She shifted to her other side, trying to find a position that eased her back. She made a little wince and grunted under her breath.

"What's the matter?" Menander asked.

"Oh, it's all right. Just my back—a little sore."

He nodded and took a sip of his wine. She wanted him to ask if he could get her another cushion, or if he could send Felix for something, or if she wouldn't like him to just stay here and keep her company tomorrow instead of going to the forum and the trading house, where no one appreciated him anyway. But she could tell by the furrows in his forehead that any tiny space cleared for her in his thoughts had already been crowded out by the drought and the scarcity of goods and the difficulties of being the youngest merchant in the forum and the impossibility of doing anything to earn his father's and brother's respect.

"I'm going up to bed," she said, rolling onto her side so she could stand up. Menander's eyes flickered toward her, then back down, into his cup. He nodded. His head hung low. If Lydia weren't so miserable herself, she would have felt sorry for him. She climbed the stairs to the roof and looked up at the stars. She hoped there was a cool breeze tonight, at least.

Lydia's water broke on the seventh after the tenth of Peritios, true to the midwife's prediction. Fortunately, it happened early in the morning before Menander left for the forum, so the only place they had to send Felix was to the house of Menander's father to bring the midwife. The old woman arrived, grumbling sleepily, and commanded Menander to bring her clean water, clean linen, and a loaf of bread.

"What's the bread for?" he asked.

"Because I haven't eaten yet. Now go, young Master, I don't have time for any more questions!"

The old slave spoke harshly to the young, worried father and to Felix, but with Lydia she was comforting and gentle. From just before sunup until the middle of the afternoon she talked to Lydia and daubed her forehead and face with cool cloths and gave her twists of persimmon twigs to grip between her teeth when the pains came. She deftly probed and pushed on her abdomen to judge the position and progress of the baby, and when it was time, she crouched between Lydia's thighs to chant and shout and urge and finally to hold up a small, squirming, squealing thing and announce that Menander's oldest child was a girl. She reached into the bag she had brought with her and produced a knife and a roll of clean, woolen twine and made quick business of cutting the cord that still bound Lydia to her daughter. She laid the baby on Lydia's heaving, sweaty bosom.

"Here. Hold your baby, Mistress. She needs to smell you and feel your hands on her and look into your face."

As exhausted as she was, Lydia felt enchantment as she

looked into her daughter's blue-black eyes. She made such a small handful, Lydia thought; she could easily span the baby's tiny back with the palm of one hand.

"She's slippery," Lydia said.

"Oh, yes. We'll clean you both up in a bit. But you won't drop her—don't worry. See? She's looking at you." The old woman smiled, then went back to her work.

The baby began rooting on Lydia's chest. "She wants to eat," the woman said. She helped Lydia ease her garment to one side and move the baby close to her breast. The tiny girl found the nipple and began busily pulling at it with her gums.

"This one knows her business," the old woman chuckled. "Better watch out for her!"

The midwife busied herself wiping off Lydia's sweat- and blood-slick thighs, then gently cleaned the baby girl. Once or twice, she had to pull the greedy little mouth away from Lydia to wipe her cheeks, and the baby let out a quick, loud squawk of protest each time. Lydia and the midwife laughed together.

"Has he chosen a name for her?" she asked Lydia.

"I don't know. We haven't had time to talk much lately."

The old woman nodded knowingly. "Well, let's call him in to see this fine girl and we'll find out." She wrapped a piece of clean linen around the baby and tucked it in at the edges, then went to the door of the bedchamber. "All right, young Master. Come in."

Menander edged into the room, his eyes flinching toward Lydia, then away, as if he wasn't sure he wanted to see the tableau in the bed. But when he saw the blood was mostly out of sight, he came over to her. He touched her cheek, then slowly stroked the baby's as he looked at her feeding. "Is it—what is it?" He looked at Lydia, then at the midwife.

"It's a 'she,'" the slave woman said. "You have a daughter."

Lydia saw the quick twinge of disappointment in Menander's face, which he just as quickly covered with a game smile. "Her name shall be Hermeia," he announced in a firm voice.

Lydia breathed a sigh of relief. Menander had recognized his daughter; she wouldn't be exposed. Lydia had believed him unlikely to do such a thing, but her mind was more at rest, now that the child's naming was formally done.

Menander gave her another smile and turned toward the door. As he passed the midwife, Lydia heard the clink of silver. The old woman nodded her thanks.

Peering around the doorway was Felix. Lydia's eyes caught those of the old man, and she would have sworn, for an instant, she saw tenderness there.

"Lydia? Look who's come to see you, dear. Lydia? Is she awake? Has she gotten so bad she can't hear us?"

It was Euodia's voice. Lydia wondered how long she could prolong her friend's consternation. She kept her face still, her eyes closed. She tried to slow her breathing to a bare minimum.

"Lydia. Wake up, dear, won't you? How long has she been like this, Clystra?"

Lydia felt Euodia touching her shoulder, gently at first, then more insistently.

"Lydia! Wake up. Clystra, why didn't you tell me she was getting worse, you foolish girl? She's slipping away from us."

"If you're trying to break my shoulder, you're going about it the right way," Lydia said without opening her eyes. "What must a dying old woman do to be treated with respect?" She smiled up at Euodia.

"Oh, you cruel thing!" Euodia stood with her hands on her hips. "Why must you tease me so? And here I've brought Xerxes to see you. You've probably frightened him."

"No harm, no harm," said the old, bald man. "Just old Xerxes, no harm."

"Hello, Xerxes. I'm glad you're here."

Xerxes' once-chubby face and neck now hung with translucent folds of flesh as wrinkled as a rooster's wattle. She had never known his age, nor had anyone else, as far as Lydia knew. He lived no particular place; these days he sheltered most often at Euodia's. He had stayed with Lydia frequently through the years. He was no trouble. He came in just before lamplighting, usually. He would never ask for anything, but he would eat if food was offered. He would sleep in any out-of-the-way corner, and he was always gone before sunrise the next morning. Various households among the community of believers took him in from time to time. Before that, no one really knew how he had managed. He especially loved children—loved to tell them nonsense stories and make them laugh with his comic facial expressions.

Euodia must have found some clothes for him; his garments were better matched and in better repair than his usual lot. His eyes were cloudy; Lydia guessed he must be nearly blind by this time. But it didn't seem to matter much to Xerxes. Maybe he had wandered the streets of Philippi for so many years that he didn't need to see to know where he was.

He reached out to touch Lydia's hand, and she took his fingers in hers and squeezed.

"No harm," he said, softly. The corners of his eyes were moist.

"He's been pestering me for days to bring him over here," Euodia said.

"Xerxes, you didn't need to wait. You're welcome in my house any time, you know that." Lydia patted his hand.

"Xerxes wanted to come," he said. "Wanted to see Lydia. And the little ones."

"What? What little ones, Xerxes?"

"The boy and his sister. Xerxes has a story for them." He pulled away from her then and began tottering toward the doorway from Lydia's room to the atrium. "Boy! Girl! Come here! Xerxes has a story."

"What's he talking about?" Lydia asked.

Euodia shook her head and opened her hands. "I have no idea. This is the first I've heard of it."

They could hear him calling as his slow steps shuffled back and forth in the courtyard. "Boy! Girl! Come here. Xerxes has a story. No harm. Make you smile and laugh. Come out."

"Go after him," Euodia told two of her women in a low voice. "Bring him back in here. Gently." She sent a worried look after them as they left. Soon they returned, slowly escorting the old man between them.

"Can't find them," he said, shaking his head. "They should be here. Mother needs a drink."

"Sit down, now, dear," Euodia said, trying to soothe him with her voice. "Get him some blankets," she said to her servants. "Tell Euodia who you're searching for, won't you?" She rubbed his hand solicitously between hers as she knelt in front of him.

"Xerxes keeps them safe," he said in a breaking, dejected voice. "Tells them stories while their mother gets water."

Lydia felt her heart dropping out from beneath her. Of course. "He means my children. He's looking for Hermeia and Parmenes."

Euodia looked at Lydia, chewing her lip as she turned back to the feeble old man. "Xerxes, be still, now. There aren't any children here. You understand what I'm saying, don't you?"

"Boy. Girl. Come out. Xerxes is here. No harm." Lydia could hear his soft sobbing. The poor, sweet fool. Memory had such sharp edges.

"A story for them. A good one, too. About the Christ. Not a silly story."

"Maybe I should take him back," Euodia began.

"No. Not yet." Lydia said the next words quickly, before she could convince herself not to. "Xerxes, why don't you tell the story to us? Then I can tell the children—later. After you've gone."

He raised his head to look at her. He daubed at his eyes with his knuckles. "Tell Lydia the story? Tell Euodia?"

"Yes, Xerxes," Lydia urged. "Tell us. You will tell us, won't you?"

Twelve

Xerxes pulled into himself. He folded his hands in his lap and pressed his knees together; to Lydia, he looked almost like a nervous little boy at his lessons. His eyes were closed.

"The Christ came to Philippi one day in the summer. It was hot. He had walked all the way from his home in the faraway place at the eastern end of the sea. He was thirsty, and no one would give him a drink. He tried to go to the fountain in the forum, but the people would not let him near. Every time he tried to get up and drink, they would crowd in front of the fountain and keep him away. 'You can't drink here,' they said to him. 'You don't belong.'

"He started to leave since the people didn't want him, but then he began to watch them. He thought they were just trying to keep him away because he was from the faraway place, but he saw that they were keeping each other away, too. They were fighting with each other and taking away each other's water jugs and spilling the water on the ground instead of drinking it or taking it to their homes.

"While the Christ was watching all this, Zeus came up to him. 'If you were as strong as I am, you would turn yourself into a bull and shove the people out of your way so you could drink.'

"'I cannot become a bull,' the Christ answered.

"Zeus laughed at him and sprang into the air, flying away on a beam of sunlight.

"Then Hades came up to him. 'If you were as fearsome as I am, you would frighten them away so you could drink.'

"'I cannot frighten them,' the Christ said.

"Hades laughed at him and vanished into a crack in the earth.

"Then Socrates came up to him. 'If you were as wise as I am, you could reason with them, so they would let you drink.'

"'I have no wisdom to give them,' the Christ replied.

"Socrates laughed at him and called him a fool, then went away with a group of students.

"Finally, Hermes spoke to him. 'If you were as fast as I am,' he said, 'you could dodge past them and get a drink.'

"'I am a runner,' the Christ answered, 'but speed is not important for my sort of race.'

"The wings on Hermes' sandals fluttered as he paced back and forth in front of the Christ. 'What do you mean?' he asked. 'Who ever heard of a race that wasn't won with speed?'

"'In my sort of race, it matters more how far you can go than how fast,' the Christ answered. 'But that won't get me a drink at this fountain.'

"Hermes laughed at his sad-looking face. 'I'll make you a wager,' he said. 'I'll race you to Thessalonica and back. If you beat me, I'll give you my serpent staff. With it, you can force a path through these people and get to the fountain to drink.'

"'And if you win?'

"'Then you must worship me.'

"The Christ took another long look at the people around the fountain. They were still fighting each other and spilling the water, but when he tried to move toward the fountain, they blocked him and threatened him with their fists. He turned back to the place where Hermes waited. 'I'll race you,' he said.

"Hermes looked at how the Christ's shoulders slumped and laughed again. 'I'll beat you easily,' he said, and took off running down the Via Egnatia toward Thessalonica. With a sigh, the Christ started after him—at a much slower pace."

As Xerxes kept speaking, his voice grew stronger. Soon, his hands were unclasped from his lap and waving about, punctuating his story with gestures. His eyes opened wide and his face unhinged as he acted the parts: now the cheerful, vain Hermes; now the unruly mob surrounding the fountain; now the tired, resigned Christ. The years fell away from him as Lydia watched. Except for the more sedate pattern of his clothing, he might have almost been the chuckling, joking, rotund buffoon her children had found in the forum that day when Lydia had just entered Philippi for the first time in her life.

"When Hermes reached the gates of Amphipolis, he came upon someone running slowly down the side of the road. As he passed him and looked back, he realized it was the Christ. He was so surprised he stopped running and watched the Christ as he struggled forward. 'How did you get here ahead of me?' Hermes asked. 'There is only one road from Philippi to Amphipolis, and I left you behind when we started.'

"The Christ made no answer, but just kept on running with his head down. 'Just see if you can trick me again,' said Hermes, and he dashed off down the road from Amphipolis to Apollonia.

"Hermes ran faster than the wind to Apollonia. But when he

reached the city gate, there was the same, worn-out figure, clop-clopping down the side of the road, looking as if he could barely move one foot past the other. 'Are you more than one?' he asked the Christ, whose breath wheezed in and out of his heaving chest. 'You must be, for that is the only way you could have come here ahead of me.'

"The Christ stopped running and looked at Hermes. When he could catch his breath, he said, 'I am one, and alone. There is no other.'

"'Well, you won't get past me this time,' said Hermes, and he started toward Thessalonica, his heels flashing like summer lightning.

"He reached Thessalonica without seeing any sign of his strange, worn-out opponent. 'Now,' he thought to himself, 'I've left him behind for good.' But when he started back from Thessalonica on the road to Apollonia, whom should he soon see ahead of him but the same, dusty, laboring figure?

"'Now I know you are a trickster,' Hermes said when he drew abreast. 'I just ran down this very same road into Thessalonica, and you were nowhere to be seen. Yet when I turn back toward Philippi, here you are, where you cannot be. Admit you are cheating me with some kind of sorcery.'

"The Christ leaned over, propping his hands on his knees. To Hermes, every breath he took sounded like it would be his last. He shook his head. 'No sorcery,' he gasped.

"With an angry curse, Hermes was off like a bowshot toward Phillippi. He went through Apollonia like a whirlwind, and the speed of his passing tossed the boughs of the trees in Amphipolis. He never stopped for an instant until he was back in Philippi.

"He ran into the forum and saw a crowd gathered near the

fountain. They were looking at something on the ground. Hermes pushed his way to the center of the crowd, and there was the Christ, lying on the pavement. His chest was motionless; his eyes were dull and glazed. He was dead.

"Hermes screamed and tore his robe. 'Cheated! He cheated me of my victory, and now he has cheated me by dying before I could make him confess his treachery!' But he had made a bargain, and he was bound. He flung his serpent staff at the Christ's corpse and stalked away.

"Hermes felt a touch on his shoulder. He whirled around, and there stood the Christ, alive again and holding out to him his serpent staff. 'I don't need this now,' he said with a smile. 'You can keep it.'

"'How is it possible?' Hermes asked. 'Everywhere I went, you were there ahead of me, though you were weak and slow. And you are alive, though I saw you lying dead, just over there.'

"The Christ smiled even wider. 'I cannot tell you. But I will tell them,' he said, pointing at the quiet crowd. 'Maybe they can explain it to you.' And he turned and walked back toward the fountain. As he neared the crowd, they opened a path for him. The Christ knelt beside the fountain and drank."

For a while, no one moved or spoke. When Lydia looked up at Xerxes, he was sitting quietly, his hands folded in his lap, his eyes closed—as he had been before he started the story. Euodia stared at a spot just beneath the ceiling of the room and her face had an unreadable expression.

"Thank you for telling it, Xerxes," Lydia said. "I know it would make the children happy."

"Just a simple story. No harm." He didn't open his eyes.

"We should leave now," Euodia said, standing abruptly. "Come, Xerxes. I'll take you home."

He didn't move. "Xerxes will stay here."

Euodia's lips tightened into a thin, pinched line. She stared at him for a few moments. "Xerxes, Lydia is ill. You don't need to stay here. You need to come home with me. We can come back and see Lydia again—soon."

"Xerxes will stay. No harm."

"He's welcome, Euodia," Lydia said. "You know he isn't any trouble. And Clystra or Euterpe can get him something to eat. I really don't mind."

Euodia drew herself up in that commanding way she had, her eyes flashing, her face hard with disapproval. "Very well, if that's what you want. Come, Beryl and Sophia. We must leave." She strode into the atrium and turned sharply on her heel toward the entry court, her two women scurrying after her. The second one, Beryl, gave Lydia a guilty backward glance as she scampered through the doorway. Their steps crunched away across the courtyard. Lydia heard the gate open, then close.

Lydia closed her eyes and drew a slow breath. Poor Euodia. Ah, well. No harm.

Even amid her wonder and absorption with her new daughter, Lydia could not help noticing the change in Felix. At first, as she healed from the birthing, she spent most of her days sitting on the klinē, holding Hermeia and cooing to her. As the Jewish slave would walk past her doorway, he would glance in at them. The sight would hold his eyes, even as his feet carried him past, so that he appeared to lean backwards, trying to see for as long as possible without seeming to break his stride. Lydia lost count of how many times he stood in her entrance, eyes toward the ground, and asked in his soft, high voice if she required anything to eat or drink. Raising her voice in a vain attempt to summon him from some far corner of the house was a thing of the past. He found ways to cause his household duties to carry him past her room more and more often.

One morning, after about the fifth such pass within a short time, Lydia called him. He came into the room, his head bowed and his eyes lowered.

"Felix, please hold the baby for a little while. I feel strong enough to walk around a bit, and my back could use the rest." She held the wrapped bundle toward him.

His eyes were round and white. "The baby, Mistress?"

"Here. Take her."

His arms bent slightly and his fingers twitched, but he still made no move toward her.

Lydia stifled a laugh. "Yes, Felix." She smiled at him. "Please."

He shuffled closer. Giving her a final, wary look, he leaned over and held out his arms.

"Just hold her like this. Yes. Let her head rest in the crook of your—yes, that's it."

He let out a long, soft breath through rounded lips and looked into the tiny, sleeping face of the baby girl. Something warm and grateful rose in Lydia as she saw the gentle, rapt expression on the old slave's face.

"I think you've got the way of it, Felix."

He beamed at her, then turned his eyes back on Hermeia. She squirmed briefly and opened her eyes, and he sent Lydia a panicked look. But then the baby closed her eyes and sighed—a sound as soft and quick as the wing beat of a sparrow. She was asleep.

"I'll stretch my legs a bit," Lydia said. "Don't worry. I won't go far." Felix never took his eyes off the baby's face.

Lydia strolled across the courtyard, flexing her stiff shoulders and kneading the small of her back with her balled fists. She leaned back to look up into the blue of the clear, unseasonably warm day. And then she heard a sound coming from her room.

Felix was singing.

She moved quietly back across the courtyard, careful to keep herself out of his view. She sidled along the wall beside the doorway and stopped just outside to listen. It wasn't the same song he had been singing that day in the storeroom, the melody so burdened with heartache and longing. No, the song today lilted and swayed; it was full of trills and lifts. It made Lydia think of enfolding warmth and soft light. It sounded like turtledoves soothing their young.

Lydia peered slowly and cautiously around the door. Felix was holding Hermeia up, close to his face. His eyes were closed as he sang over her; he looked as if he were breathing her in and breathing the song out. Lydia stepped quietly inside and stood as still as a shadow, willing the moment to go on, willing the sound of Felix's voice to continue, to wrap Hermeia and herself in its gladdening, comforting glow.

He opened his eyes and saw her. He faltered; Lydia felt her heart sag. But then his voice resumed. And now he was looking at her as he sang. When the song ended, Lydia went to Felix and took the baby from him.

"Thank you, Felix."

His eyes held the tiny girl for an instant longer, then shifted quickly away as his face angled down in his usual deferential pose.

"I should thank you," he said in a voice barely more than a whisper. He started to walk away.

"Felix, wait….Please."

He stopped, but didn't turn around.

"Felix—that song. It was the Jewish language, wasn't it?"

His head half-turned toward her, then pulled the rest of him with it. "Yes, Mistress. It's an old Hebrew song."

"Hebrew? That's your people, or your language?"

"Both, Mistress. A language and a people."

"What do…rather…would you tell me what the words mean?"

He thought for a moment. "Some of them have no exact Greek equal, but it would be something like, 'Hush, my child, hush. Close your eyes and sleep. The pillar of fire leads on; the pillar of smoke leads on. We shall soon be there. Hush my child, hush.'" As he said the words, his face changed, softened.

"What does it mean by 'pillar of fire,' 'pillar of smoke?'"

Felix stood there, halfway between the klinē and the door, his elbows cupped in his palms, looking down at the floor and pondering. Lydia held her breath, hoping he would trust her enough to answer. She sat down on the edge of the bed and waited.

"It is a very old song, Mistress. It goes back to a time when, they say, my people wandered from one place to another, looking for a homeland. Mothers used to sing it to their babies as they carried them on the journey."

"The fire? The smoke?"

"Our God led us on the journey, Mistress. In fire by night and smoke by day. Or so we believe. Will there be anything else?"

She cupped her daughter's soft, downy head in her hand. The baby was still asleep. "No, Felix." She heard his footsteps going away.

"Felix?"

The steps paused.

"I thank you."

"Yes, Mistress."

Lydia began asking Felix to help her with the baby more and more often, and nothing in his manner or words told her he minded the duty. She loved watching the eunuch with her daughter: the way his face bloomed when he held Hermeia; the way he murmured to her in a gentle tumble of Greek and Hebrew words; the way his fingers touched her tiny body—as if she were an ampoule of the most delicate blown glass. And yet he wasn't timid with her; he never shrank back when Lydia asked him to tend her daughter. In fact, Lydia thought he finished his other duties more efficiently to give himself more time to spend with the baby.

There were times when Hermeia seemed to prefer the eunuch's touch to her mother's. And, to Lydia's surprise, she didn't mind. She realized she needed space from her daughter sometimes, an interval when she could be to herself and not have to think about the unending needs of the growing child. Watching Felix with her baby gave her a sort of guilty pleasure, as if she had chanced upon some choice thing she really ought to give back, but decided to keep.

And as the eunuch cared for her child, he began to talk to Lydia. He pretended to speak to Hermeia, allowing her to overhear. Or it might have been that he really intended the baby to receive his telling—that he was planting the words in her mind against the day she could understand. But at least Lydia could listen, and Felix didn't seem to mind.

"Lovely child," he might say, while changing the linen bindings on Hermeia's tiny body. "As lovely as Rachel on the day

Father Jacob first saw her by the well in Haran." Lydia might ask Felix the meaning of the strange Hebrew names. He would continue with what he was doing for the baby—changing her wrappings, maybe, or rubbing her cheeks and the top of her head with oil, or perhaps just playing finger games to try to tease out one of her increasingly frequent smiles.

Lydia would think he was ignoring her or hadn't heard. And then, he would tell a story, aiming the words toward the grinning, wriggling baby. A story about ancient people wandering to and fro across an ancient, savage landscape. Of ancestors blown by hot, dry winds and stung by driven sand, tossed back and forth between the stark biddings and long silences of a strange god with no name or face. Stories of tents and flocks and droughts and skirmishes fought with clubs and shearing knives and fists over the few wells strung like rare jewels across endless stretches of rock and scrub—skirmishes that became battles, then wars, then epic campaigns with the passage of time and the handling of generations of tellers. Of strange errands, of signs in unexpected places, of promises made and broken, of lies between kin and lies between strangers. Of doubt and belief and failure, of endurance. Of victories that should never have happened and of defeats that became greater and better than the victories. Of outsiders coming in and of insiders turned out. Of deliverance coming beyond hope or reason, arriving on the heels of disaster like a song of healing in a house of death.

Unlike the tales from her childhood—the shimmering, astonishing goings and comings of shape-shifting gods and audacious heroes—these stories explained almost nothing. They simply were. They waited in her with the patience of stones. They set out a space within her where she could bide, and watch, and sometimes, in surprising ways, start to understand.

There were moments when Lydia wondered who Felix was caring for the most—the baby or his mistress.

Thirteen

Menander loved his daughter; Lydia knew it in her soul. When he came back from the forum in the evening, she watched the way his eyes lingered on Hermeia, the way his face changed when she made one of her little cries of delight. He loved her, and yet he wrestled with himself over showing it. The shadow of his father—even more, Lydia thought, his older brother—would fall across Menander's mind and he would retreat from the tenderness he might have shown, retreat to the genial distance considered proper for respectable fathers of a proper age for the responsibilities of manhood and citizenship.

Lydia hated the men in the forum who called him "boy," hated Menander's older brother for his constant derision. "Hey, Menander, draw up a contract for Philomenes, here, unless you're too lovestruck for useful work…." "This is my younger brother, and he'll discuss the terms with you; he doesn't look too addled today…."

Menander would have denied all of it, she was sure. Even if she asked him, he would pass it off with a shrug and a quick smile and immediately begin talking about other things. But she saw the defeat grow a little longer in his face, a little heavier on his shoulders each day when he came home. He couldn't help but measure himself by their opinions.

Lydia knew her husband was meant for other things. She knew the keenness of his mind, his hunger for new ideas. He could become as great a rhetorician and advocate as any of the elders in Thyatira, she was certain. But all they saw was his youth and inexperience—that, and their persistent doubts about his early marriage. Their ignorance of his true gifts reinforced the scorn of his brother, the detachment of his father. Menander wanted to become, to surpass—but he wasn't strong enough to overmaster the gathered weight of indifference and custom. He had the soul of a philosopher; how could he be expected to summon any passion about buying and selling wool?

Lydia tried to give more of herself—to be enough to him. She left Hermeia with Felix for long periods of time during the day to read his scrolls of philosophy. In the evenings, she tried to ask him questions that might occupy his mind with something besides his own discouragement. She posed him problems in logic. She sent for Menander's old teacher, Sosipater, and plied him with meals, arranged evenings of discussion and argument. In bed, she tried to enfold her husband so completely that he could not possibly imagine he was less a man than anyone of any age or station in Thyatira.

For a time, it seemed to help him. Sometimes, when she lay in his arms or when he would win a concession from Sosipater, she saw the old quickening ripple through him; saw the flash and sparkle of his former enthusiasm. But as day after day went by she could tell he knew it all for a ruse—well intentioned, but still a ruse. He tried to keep up his end, but time and sameness wore at him, dragged him down until the time came when Lydia would greet him with an affectionate embrace and mention the latest thing she had noticed in a passage of Chrysippus, and he would give her only a tired smile and a diverted glance, maybe a nod. He was too tired to pretend.

Lydia felt him slipping away from her and had no idea what she could do about it. And she knew she couldn't keep it up, in any case. There wasn't enough of her to give life to her husband, to her daughter, and to herself.

The words came on a day in early spring when the sky hung with tattered clouds.

"Lydia, I'm going into the army."

She knew he was watching for her reaction, and she knew she probably ought to say something, but everything in her mind was scattered by Menander's announcement.

"The legate of Syria is raising three new cohorts of auxiliaries to support the legions along the Parthian frontier. Father knows one of the military aediles. I can go in as a prefect in the quartermaster corps. I'll be supplying the troops, not really doing any fighting, and when my service is complete, I'm virtually assured of promotion to the equestrian order." He grabbed her hands in a rush of eagerness. "We'll be equites, Lydia! Not just Roman citizens, but nobility!"

She looked into his eyes and tried her best to smile, to summon something to her face other than the blankness of shock and apprehension.

"How long must you serve?"

He turned his face to the side, and she felt an empty place opening in her chest.

"Twenty-five years," he said, without looking at her.

"Twenty-five—"

"But listen, Lydia! I'll send for you. You and Hermeia—and even Felix. Once I get my final posting, I'll send my wages, every bit of it except what I need to buy my rations. And as soon as it's enough, Father will help you book passage with one of the caravans. We won't be apart very long, Lydia. And who knows? We may decide we like Syria so much we don't want to leave!"

It was her turn to avert her face.

"Lydia, you know there's nothing for me here." His voice was low, pleading. "This is a chance to make something of myself—a chance for our daughter to be something other than the child of a minor trader of the forum at Thyatira."

"Or fatherless." She made herself look at him. "Menander, we aren't exactly destitute. I brought a dowry of four gold talents to this marriage, and we've scarcely dipped into it at all. We can go away from here, to someplace where you don't have to listen to your brother's ridicule. We can do that and stay together."

He looked away from her, speaking in a quiet voice. "A few days ago in the trading house, I was standing behind a column, and I heard two of the men from the forum. They were talking about me, Lydia. Do you want to know what one of them said? 'A man can marry more wealth in one day than he can earn in a lifetime.'" He gave a harsh bark of a laugh. "They're all watching me, Lydia. Expecting me to content myself with pretending the man's part while squandering my wife's money. They don't think I can make a go of it on my own.

"I'm twenty-one years old, and you're not yet nineteen. When I get out of the army, I'll be forty-six and you'll be forty-four. Not exactly young, but still with enough of life ahead to expect some good times. We'll be respected, not just tolerated.

We'll have a pension. I'll wear the purple stripe on my robe, and you'll be a lady of standing. Our daughter will have opportunities to meet other young men of good families.

"You know what awaits us in Thyatira. As long as I live, I'll be the softhearted little brother, the boy who runs and fetches for the men who really know things—"

"And have the good sense to marry at a proper age?"

"Those are your words."

"But aren't they your feelings?"

"You know better, Lydia. Only your fear makes you say such things." He looked at her, and into her, and she couldn't hold his gaze. "This is for us. Please try to think of it that way."

Menander was to leave the next month, when spring had well opened the shipping lanes. He planned to board a coastal trader at Ephesus that would take him around the bends of Lycia and Cilicia before docking at Seleucia, the port city of the Syrian capital, Antioch. He would carry letters from his father to the military aedile and his tribune. There was a spring in his step these days and a look of determination in his eye Lydia hadn't seen since that day in his father's courtyard when he had asked for her hand. He had a plan, a goal. He was doing something of his own choosing.

Lydia wished she could doubt his motives, or even bring herself to anger. That would have made it easier, she thought. She could see his resolve as obstinacy, as simple, willful selfishness, and use it to stoke her ire; she could feed on and draw strength from it.

But it wouldn't do. Lydia knew as well as she knew herself that her husband had chosen this path because he thought it was the only way out of the rut carved for him in the terrain of Thyatira. It had been the same with her uncle, Menippus. Like

Menander, he was the younger brother. That was why Menippus left for Philippi—to try and find something that was his own.

No, if Menander stayed here, he risked becoming a person Lydia could not respect, and they both knew it. He was just more willing than she to admit it. Agreeing with him in her mind was the hardest, most necessary thing she could possibly do.

And so she caromed back and forth between fear and sadness, between frustration and apprehension. Did he really understand how long twenty-five years was? Did she? How long would it be before she could go to him? How would she preserve his memory in the mind of their baby daughter? When they were so far apart, how would they still understand what it meant to be a family?

On the night before his leaving, Lydia asked Felix to put Hermeia to sleep on a pallet near his own bed. By now the two of them were fastest friends; Hermeia toddled happily off with the old eunuch as carefree as if she were in her mother's arms. Lydia watched them go, then went to the bedchamber, where Menander waited. She embraced him in an embrace that lasted far into the night, until every ounce of passion was wrung from them both, and they slept, having spent themselves to exhaustion in saying to each other with their bodies what words could only approximate.

Xerxes sat on the floor at the foot of Lydia's couch, sucking on the seeds of a pomegranate.

"Xerxes, why doesn't God go ahead and take me?" Lydia asked. "My insides don't work anymore. I've lived long enough.

I have no reason to stay. Why doesn't he just let me die?"

Xerxes noisily licked pomegranate juice off his fingers.

"I don't know why I'm asking you, old friend," she went on. "Your precious mind isn't troubled by such trivial things as sickness and death. You tell us your stories, you eat our food, and you sleep on our floors. And none of it seems to matter to you, one way or the other. I think you'd be quite as happy, right now, sitting in Euodia's atrium and eating a piece of bread from her larder."

"No harm. Xerxes will stay here with Lydia." He pulled a piece of rind from between his teeth. "Xerxes must see the children."

"There you go with that again. No children live here, Xerxes. What children are you talking about?"

"The little boy will see Xerxes, and his sister will follow. Xerxes keeps them safe while their mother drinks."

"No, Xerxes. The little boy is gone, and his sister—" *His sister can't abide her mother's presence. Oh, Hermeia, I tried so hard! But for all the wrong things, though I couldn't see it at the time. How I wish you could find it in your heart to forgive me.* "His sister isn't coming, Xerxes. You mustn't wait for them."

"Xerxes will stay here with Lydia."

Always around the circle to arrive at the same place. Not that she minded him being here, but it hurt her to have him so set on seeing them. Not to mention the freshening of her own wounds each time he insisted on waiting for them.

How old was Hermeia these days? She must be more than sixty. How strange, to think she and her daughter had grown old at the same time. All those years.

Lydia was so doggedly determined in those days. Never again would she be forced to depend on the good graces of a

man, however well meaning. She would take Menippus's opening, she would snatch it up like a dare, and she would make it
into something. She would prove her tenacity to them all—and
to herself. Uncle Menippus had made no mistake in his bequest,
and by the time she was finished, everyone in Philippi would
know it for a certainty.

What was the price of proving herself right?

"Lost."

"What did you say, Xerxes?"

"Xerxes is lost, lost, lost."

"What are you talking about, dear?"

"Lost. Coming from the forum to the house of friend
Euodia. Knows the way, knows it well, no harm. But there is a
turning, then another, and Xerxes takes the turning too soon.
Wrong turning. He is lost."

"I've told you many times, Xerxes, you ought to let someone help—"

"Knows the sound of the streets, he does. Knows the smell.
Xerxes can see with inside eyes. But now he is lost, lost, lost.
Wandering. Cannot find the way to friend Euodia. Are there any
more pomegranates? Xerxes likes pomegranates best of all."

Lydia motioned to Euterpe, who ambled off toward the
storeroom. "When was this, Xerxes? When did you get lost?"

"Turned too soon. Xerxes listened to himself, instead of the
sound of the street. Now he is lost. It is the day of the gathering,
the day of the Sun. Xerxes wants to be with the friends of the
Christ, but he cannot find the way. He tells himself a story, but
he is still lost. He is starting to cry because he doesn't know
which way to turn." The old man put his face in his hands and
rocked back and forth.

"Now, then, dear. You aren't lost again. You're still here, at

Lydia's house. No need to make yourself upset, all over."

"Lost, lost, lost," Xerxes moaned. "Doesn't know which way to go." Euterpe walked up to him and held out a pomegranate. Xerxes raised his face, sniffed at the reddish yellow fruit, and gave the servant a beaming smile. He set happily to work, tearing off the rind.

Lydia watched him for several moments. He was sucking at the round seed-globules, sorting the pits from the juicy pulp with his tongue, smiling like a child with a new toy.

"Well," Lydia said when she could hold the words no longer, "What happened? How did you find your way to Euodia's?"

"No harm. Xerxes didn't find his way." He sucked at the pomegranate.

"Xerxes, you're being cruel, and I think you're enjoying it."

He slid his cloudy eyes toward her and gave her a crafty smile. "Lydia asks. She wonders. That is good."

"You horrible thing! I ought to have Euterpe toss you into the street!"

The servant girl chuckled, shaking her head.

"No harm, no harm. Now Xerxes will tell." He gave the pomegranate a final, careful sniff and an exploratory lick or two, then tossed aside the empty rind. He crawled over to Lydia's couch and put his lips close to her ear. "Xerxes didn't find his way," he said in a rough whisper. "He learned to be found."

Lydia pulled back her head to give him a confused look. "You what?"

"There are places we can't go until we are found. And we can't be found until it is time. Xerxes stood still, and when it was time, one of Xerxes' friends found him. But only when it was time. And only after Xerxes stopped listening to himself and started listening to everything else." He got up and dusted off his clothing. "Xerxes will go now to look for the children. Friend Lydia has been very kind to Xerxes." He began walking toward the door into the courtyard. When he was about halfway across the room, he stopped and once more turned his nearly blind eyes on Lydia.

"Friend Lydia needs to wait and listen. Then someone will find her."

Menander, prefect of the Tenth Quartermaster's Corps of the Syrian Auxiliaries, to Lydia, his beloved wife: Grace to you and to our daughter.

Do not fret yourself about me, my dear wife. The journey was good and the aedile of the Syrian legate was well disposed to my request to serve. We are encamped at Damascus, a pretty large city to the south of Syrian Antioch. When the provisioning is completed, we are under orders to march east and north, to Palmyra, then east again, into the country west of the Euphrates River. No trouble is expected.

The land hereabout is flat and dry. Water is scarce, and they say on our long marches we'll use camels. I wish you could see a camel, Lydia. Ill-smelling brutes with long necks and leathery lips that wriggle this way and that. They're as tall at the shoulder as a man's chest on horseback, and they have a bulbous hump on their backs. They can go for days without water, and they can eat branches off the thorn bushes that grow in the desert. And they spit at you when they don't like you, like some of the new recruits we've got.

They have some good wines in Syria, but we won't be having any of that while we're on patrol. The food is better than I expected it to be. One of the men in my unit has read some Euripedes. That reminded me of you.

*I received my first wages, and I am sending to you
twelve drachmae. This is all I can spare after buying my
provisions, my armor, and two extra pairs of boots. The
rocks in this land are especially hard on boots. Even the pack
animals step gingerly by the end of a day's march.*

*Say my name often to our daughter. When the day
comes—and it will be soon, I hope—that you join me here,
I do not want her to think of me as a stranger.*

*Be well, my dear wife. Ask Felix to remember me
kindly. I will write again when the next pay packet comes.*

Farewell.

Lydia folded the parchment and laid it on the table at the
foot of her bed. Later, she would roll it tightly and place it in her
chest, beside the other two letters Menander had sent since his
leaving. But right now she was too exhausted to think of doing
anything. This was the second month her flow had not come.
She was pregnant again, she guessed—an enduring reminder of
her last night with her husband, most likely. She had not yet
written Menander to tell him.

Felix came in, Hermeia's little hand in his. "I shouldn't mention any names," the old eunuch said with a smile, "but someone here is hungry and not very patient."

"Well, then, I suppose we need to see what's available.
Hermeia, come here and sit with me while Felix gets us something to eat."

The little girl ran to her mother's bed and clambered up into
her lap, jabbering happily all the while.

"Thank you, Felix," Lydia said over the din of the child's
chatter. "You can just bring the food in here."

He bowed himself out the door and crossed the courtyard

toward the storeroom. Not long after, he returned, carrying a wooden tray with bowls of cheese, raisins and dried pears, filberts, and fresh spears of asparagus. Stacked to one side were three loaves of flat bread.

"Oh, asparagus! Where did you find it, Felix?"

"I heard some of the women in the food stalls talking about it. There was a patch down by the river, near a grove of plane trees. There wasn't much, but I thought it would be a good change from boiled beans and lentils."

He set the tray down on the corner of the couch and went back to the storeroom for a ewer of wine and some water. He set the drink vessels down and was turning to leave.

"Felix, won't you stay and eat with me—and Hermeia?"

"Feeks," said the child. She was holding out her arms to him, giving him her most beseeching look.

He smiled and seated himself at the foot of the couch. "Well, then…by your leave, Mistress."

"Please. By all means. Have some bread."

"Feeks." Hermeia clapped her hands and laughed.

ydia, of Thyatira, to her husband, Menander, of the Tenth Quartermaster's Corps of the Syrian Auxiliaries: I greet you with great longing and deep affection.

It is with much joy that I inform you of the birth of your son, on the fourth after the twentieth of Xanthicos. Since you, my dear husband, could not be here to name him, I called upon your father to act in your place, and he has chosen for him the name Parmenes. He is a fine, healthy boy with a good appetite. My dearest wish is that you could see him and give him the blessing of a father's approval.

I received your last letter, and the twelve drachmae with it, the seventh letter I have received since your leaving. It was good to know that you are well and that your duty has so far been quiet.

I thought of you yesterday when Felix brought home from the wine seller a jug of Syrian wine. As you said, it is quite good. I shouldn't tell you this, but I drank a small bit without water right when Felix came back with it. As I *drank, I tried to imagine I was tasting the place where you are, bringing a bit of Syria into myself. A foolish notion, I know, but for a moment or two it made me feel closer to you. And it was very fine wine, besides all that.*

I long to see you again, my husband. I long to embrace you and shower you with kisses. I long to set your son and daughter upon your knees and be gladdened by your enjoyment of them and theirs of you. With the last money you sent, we have now almost two minas of silver. I hope that soon you will say it is time for us to come to be with you.

Felix sends his greetings. He is a great comfort to me. I speak your name each day to our daughter and son, and whisper your name in their ears when they sleep at night.

Farewell.

Lydia looked at the letter one last time before rolling it and slipping it into its leather sleeve. She glanced over at the small bundle in the middle of her bed that held her sleeping son. A fitful sleeper, this one. Not at all like his older sister, who, even at this age, once her belly was full, would sleep soundly—often until nearly dawn. No, Parmenes fought sleep like a bitter enemy, held it off by any means possible and never seemed fully vanquished; an uneasy truce was as much as his weary mother could generally hope for.

Lydia called Felix and gave him the letter. "In the morning, take this to one of the military quaestors and tell the dispatcher it's for the Syrian Auxiliary. And send Hermeia to me."

A few moments later, she heard the scuff of tiny feet. Hermeia stood in the doorway, her chubby fist stuck in her mouth. She looked at her mother, and her eyes were wide and beautiful and dark—glossy with the constant fascination of her unmarred childhood. Lydia smiled at her. "Come here, Hermeia." She knelt down and held out her arms. With an instant grin, Hermeia ran to her and buried herself in her mother's embrace. Lydia held her and stood up. She walked over to the couch, to stand over the sleeping boy.

"Hermeia. Do you see your little brother? Parmenes?"

The little girl nodded, shoving her fist back in her mouth.

"He's little, isn't he? He's asleep."

"Meniss," Hermeia mumbled around her fist.

"Yes, that's his name. Parmenes. And you're his big sister, aren't you?"

Hermeia nodded soberly. She patted her chest with her free hand, still looking down at the tiny boy. "Big."

"Yes, you are. Such a big girl. Will you always help Mother take care of Parmenes?"

Hermeia looked at her mother, pulled her hand from her mouth and gave her a sudden, exaggerated grin. "Big."

"Yes, you're big. So much bigger than your brother. We have to take care of him, don't we?"

"Big," she said again, looking at her younger brother. "Meniss." She pushed away from Lydia then, began wriggling in her grasp.

"Do you want to get down?"

Hermeia nodded. Lydia set her on the floor, and she immediately went to the couch and climbed up beside Parmenes.

"No, Hermeia! You mustn't wake him."

But Hermeia moved gently beside the sleeping infant. She laid a hand softly on the blankets wrapped around him. Carefully she patted the bundle. "Big," she whispered.

Naturally, Lydia would pick a day when the forum was most crowded. But she desperately needed to see something besides the walls surrounding the courtyard of her house, and despite Felix's obvious disapproval, she was glad she had insisted on going to the food stalls herself today. The children would be as well tended in the eunuch's care as in her own, and it would probably be nearly midday before Parmenes would want to nurse again.

Her biggest concern was to be certain she avoided Menander's older brother, if he was here today. She had no stomach for tolerating the look on his face if he saw her. Lydia doubted there was much chance of running into her mother or sisters; they were far too correct to venture into the forum unless they were in attendance with their husbands on ceremonial business. Now and then, from the corner of her eye she caught a curious glance following her as she made her way across the bustling square. Let them wonder. She needed the fresh air more than she needed to meet their expectations.

Just ahead was her father's guildhall. Probably better to give the place a wide berth. Since her marriage, her father hadn't had much to do either with her or with Menander. If he saw her on a festival day, he might give her as much as a gravely polite nod, which she would return. He paid infrequent visits to his grandchildren, and when he did come the occasions seemed to Lydia more like official business than family calls. He was no more than a polite stranger to Hermeia. He might possibly be more involved with Parmenes as he grew older, but Lydia couldn't honestly say it mattered to her much, one way or the other. She was determined to raise her children alone as long as her husband's absence made it necessary, and she would sooner leave

Thyatira than ask any of them for help.

A group of ragamuffin boys played a stick-and-hoop game near the steps of the Temple of Apollo. Lydia stopped to watch them. Most of them looked eight or nine years old; had they been from better families they would have been at gymnasium. They had bent a green withe into a ring about the diameter of one of their waists. They were formed in two rough lines, and they took turns standing the withe on its edge and batting it back and forth at each other with their sticks. There was much bantering and arguing back and forth about whether the withe had crossed some imaginary line between the players of the other side. Lydia couldn't imagine how they could ever arrive at any agreement on such a boundary, since the lines constantly snaked back and forth. Now and then, the boys would argue, but they quickly settled their disputes, or ignored them. They were there to play, not to debate. The pursuit was all that mattered.

Lydia felt an upsurge, a sudden, buoying sense of expansiveness and ability so sharp it was almost painful. Almost. She pulled in a chestful of the day's air, threw her head back, and stared up into the clear, blue dome of the late summer sky. At that moment, she wished to launch herself forward, like a green, springy withe, batted by the stick of her restless aspiration past the loose, shifting, opposing line of her limitations. She walked past the boys and their game, briefly wondering if she might join them.

Lydia stretched out her hand to pull open the gate of the house, when it suddenly flung open from inside. A man wearing the insignia of the imperial army gave her a troubled glance, then nodded at her and paced quickly away. Lydia stared after him a moment, then rushed inside, closing and bolting the gate behind her.

"Felix! Where are you? Is everything all right? Where are the children?"

The slave came out of the main chamber, cradling Parmenes in one arm and holding Hermeia's hand in his other. He had a stricken look on his face.

"What's the matter, Felix? That man—who was he?"

"There is a message, Mistress. A letter. Perhaps you'd better read it for yourself."

"What? A letter? From Menander? Where?"

He shook his head and gestured with his chin toward the chamber. He wouldn't say anything else. Lydia rushed into the chamber and found the leather-wrapped packet lying on her bed, still unopened. Hurriedly she unwrapped it and pulled the papyrus roll from inside.

> *Claudius Tertius, commander of the Tenth Quartermaster's Corps of the Syrian Auxiliary, greets you. He regrets to inform you....*

The words tumbled from the page into Lydia's mind, piling into a tangled confusion as she read. There was a march northward, into the remote country north of Babylon.... The supply train became detached from the main units.... Nomads, mainly interested in foodstuffs and gear...in the dead of night...chance raid, unforeseeable...such a great loss...raiders caught and killed without mercy.... Menander was respected by his men...sorely missed....

There were a few tetradrachmae at the bottom of the packet,

the remainder of Menander's wages, the letter explained. That was the end of the message.

Lydia looked at the floor beside the couch. She realized she had carried the market basket in with her; the vegetables and fruit from her morning expedition still looked undisturbed, unchanged. She thought that she should get up and take it to the storeroom, or ask Felix to take it for her. She formed his name in her mind, as if to call him, even opened her mouth to speak, but no sound came out. She wanted to see her children. She stood, and there was a sudden roaring in her ears, then blackness.

When she woke, she was lying across her couch, and Felix was wiping her forehead with a cool sponge. She turned her head and saw Hermeia sitting on the floor beside her baby brother, tickling him and trying to make him laugh.

"Lucky thing you fell toward your couch," the eunuch was saying. "You could have hit your head on the floor."

She looked at him, and the sudden memory of the letter rushed at her like a thief from an alley. She drew a sharp breath and locked her teeth against the wail that beat against the inside of her chest.

"He's dead, Felix. He isn't coming back."

The slave's hand slowed, then resumed its gentle motion across her forehead, her cheeks. He swallowed several times. He averted his eyes.

She sat up. "You may leave me now, Felix."

He gave her a questioning look.

"I said leave. I wish to be alone with my children."

Hermeia glanced up at the sharp tone in her voice, then turned her attention back to her brother when she realized her mother wasn't speaking to her.

Felix got up and bowed as he backed out of the room.

Lydia watched Hermeia playing with Parmenes, trying to focus, trying to rein her mind back from racing over the edge of the cliff into the darkness below. How was it possible? How could Menander be dead, and she still be able to draw breath? How had she failed to sense, to know that he had died? How could that soul nearest to her own pass from life without her knowing, without pulling some part of her with it? Had he gotten her letter? Did he know about his son before meeting his death? Lydia tried to imagine the rest of her life with no possibility of seeing him again, of holding him and matching her mind, her heart, with his. No image would form. Why go on? Why keep trying, when hope lay dead, somewhere in the bleak wilderness of the Parthian frontier?

Parmenes gave a tiny cackle of delight. Hermeia clapped her hands and looked up at her mother, an expression of distilled joy on her little face. "Laugh! Meniss laugh!" She turned her attention back to the infant boy.

Lydia got down from the couch and scooped Parmenes up in her arms. She brought him to her face and inhaled his smell, felt the warmth and softness of his cheek against hers. She sat on the floor and held him, looking down into his round face, framed by the thick, dark ringlets he had had since birth.

Hermeia stood at her shoulder, peering down at the baby boy. She patted her chest. "Big," she said.

"Yes, you're big," Lydia whispered.

She saw something fall onto Parmenes' wrap. It was a tear—her tear. Tears were draining steadily from her eyes, and she hadn't realized it. She felt a tiny finger brush her cheek. Hermeia looked at the teardrop glistening on her fingertip. She looked at her mother, her forehead wrinkling in confusion.

"It's all right, dear," Lydia said, forcing a smile. "Mother is sad, that's all."

Then she felt her daughter's hand on her shoulder, patting slowly and gently.

"Big."

That night, when the children were sleeping, Lydia went out into the courtyard. She paced back and forth for a moment or two, gripping her elbows to her sides. Then she noticed a sliver of yellow light coming from a crack in the storeroom door. She went to the door and opened it. Felix was kneeling on the floor, in front of a tallow lamp. He was holding his face in his hands, rocking back and forth, singing softly in Hebrew.

Lydia went in and sat down, her back against the wall. Felix paused when she came in, but resumed singing. The sound reached into Lydia, loosening the tightly gripped cords of her control, inviting her to permit her grief to flow along the contours of the tune and the words. When his voice was still, Lydia asked quietly, "What song was that?"

"It is an old song of my people. One that we—that they sometimes sing when troubles are heavy."

"Will you tell me what the words mean?"

There was a silence. "'Hear my prayer, O LORD,'" he said then; "'let my cry for help come to you. Do not hide your face from me when I am in distress. Turn your ear to me; when I call, answer me quickly. For my days vanish like smoke; my bones burn like glowing embers. My heart is blighted and withered like grass; I forget to eat my food. Because of my loud groaning, I am reduced to skin and bones.'"

Lydia allowed the sob to reach the surface, followed by another, then another. She felt the black anguish welling up, made irresistible by the power of Felix's song. Lydia wept for her husband, for her children, and for herself. She lay down on the floor of the storeroom, cradled her head in her arms and keened, long and low and far into the night.

The next few days were a blur in Lydia's mind. She sent Felix with the news to Menander's father; she made arrangements for the obligatory sacrifices at the temples of Apollo and Artemis; she formally received the representative of the wool traders' guild, who came bearing the small funerary stipend the guild provided. During all of it, she went somewhere else in her mind, somewhere away from her grieving heart. It was the only way she thought she could manage.

The inevitable day came when she received her family. They all came at once: Mother, Father, her brothers, even Zobia and Thetis and their husbands. It was a large gathering, and it required preparation Lydia hadn't expected to need. Discreetly, she sent Felix to the food stalls in the forum to purchase the extra supplies.

"Lydia, I stand with you in this time of grief," her father intoned, "and I am ready to receive you and your children back into the household of your youth, in consideration of your straitened circumstances."

He wouldn't look at her while he was speaking, of course. He delivered the announcement in the same tone of voice he might have used for a civic ceremony in the forum.

Lydia looked at them, ranged before her in the courtyard of her house. Zobia continually fussed with her clothing and her complicated coiffure, her eyes flitting here and there—probably calculating the value of Lydia's home and comparing it unfavorably to her own. Thetis's look continually shifted between her husband, Lydia, and her father. Mother stood a little apart from the rest of them, her face still, her thoughts somewhere deep within herself. Philip stood at Father's right shoulder, his arms crossed on his chest, his face a scowling mask of impatience and disapproval. Andronicus was behind him, his face toward the ground. Who were these people? What, precisely, had they to do with her?

"Father, I thank you for your love and your kindness," she said. "It is a great comfort in this difficult time."

She held Parmenes and now she knelt down to Hermeia, standing beside her, and picked up her daughter with her other arm. She stood again and faced them all.

"But I will keep this household in honor of my husband and raise his children here, in the place where they were born."

Her father stared at her a moment before recomposing his face. "Child, I know the dowry you brought to this marriage. Surely you don't believe you can—"

"Your concern for my welfare is precious to me, and while I have great respect for your wisdom, Father, I will stay here."

She held his eyes as she spoke, and she was pleased to hear that the sound of her voice was firm, decided. Just as she finished, and while they were all looking at each other, trying to digest this unexpected development, Felix came through the gate with a full market basket.

"And now, won't you all please come to the table? My servant will bring food." She turned and walked ahead of them, a composed matron in charge of her own affairs.

It was a strange meal, eaten in silence broken only by her unsuspecting children. No one looked at anyone else, and Lydia had the thought that she could have had Felix bring them vinegar water and unbaked flour and it would have tasted much the same to her—maybe to them, also. Father was too astonished by her refusal to say anything, and too bound by form to refuse her ceremonial hospitality; Mother and the rest of them were too nonplussed by his consternation to break the awkward silence.

At last they took their leave. Lydia closed the gate behind her father, then slumped against it, rubbing her temples with her fingertips. She walked across to the main hall and found Felix there, picking up the baskets and bowls left from the meal.

"Where are the children?" she asked.

"Sleeping in the storeroom."

Lydia gave a tired nod. She sank heavily on one of the cushions of the triclinium and watched him. His lips were pinched together as he worked, and the way he kneaded his jaws told Lydia he chewed on words he didn't know how to say.

"What is it, Felix?"

He glanced at her, then quickly back to his task.

"You want to tell me something. What is it?"

He hunched his shoulders, almost like someone receiving a blow. "It isn't my place to say, Mistress." He picked up two more baskets, his face half-turned toward her. "But your father made a generous offer."

Lydia sighed and looked out the doorway, across the courtyard toward the storeroom, where her children slept. "Yes. But I can't afford his generosity."

He carried a stack of baskets to the doorway and shook the crumbs from them, out into the courtyard. He came back inside and hung them on their pegs in the ceiling beams. "You should think more about your future. You can't mourn forever."

"I can't go back there, Felix. Leaving cost me too much."

He began stacking bowls, one within the other. When he had a fair armload, he went out the door and across to the storeroom. In a few moments, he came back, shaking his head as he crossed the threshold.

"Four gold talents won't feed the lot of us more than a year or two," he muttered, just loud enough for her to hear.

The grief was coming. She'd held it at bay all day in front of her family, but it was coming again, with reinforcements.

"Will you sing for me, Felix? One of the songs of your people."

He turned around and looked at her for a long moment. She held his eyes. "Please, Felix."

He slowly set down the cup he had just picked up. He walked over near her, knelt, and sang.

he bark of the plane tree peeled loose in long, papery strips. Lydia dropped them to the ground, watching them twist and tumble as they fell. She shifted uneasily, trying to find a comfortable way to sit on the limb. She reached out and plucked a cluster of the bristly, round seedpods. She pulled them from the stem and rolled them back and forth in her palm as she looked around her. She had no idea how she had gotten up here. How could a dying old woman climb a plane tree, when she had to be carried to her own latrine?

"Ah! The girl who runs with the boys. I've finally found you again."

Without looking, Lydia knew what she would see when she turned her head. In her mind, she could already visualize the wild hair, the tangled, thick beard, the tall, gaunt form clad in the skin robe. She leaned over and looked. Yes. But why was he unchanged, while she had grown old?

"Are you going to come down and talk to me, or must I come up there?" the man asked. Lydia could see the light glinting on his straight, white teeth. He was smiling up at her.

"I can't climb as nimbly as the last time," she said. "Why can't you just talk to me from there?"

"No, no. That would never do." He moved toward the tree, and then he was beside her on the overhanging limb. "This is much better, don't you think?"

"Will you finally tell me who you are?"

"After all these years, that's still your first question?"

"Why shouldn't it be?"

He laughed and shrugged. "Fair enough. But isn't there a more important question you should be asking?"

She gave him a puzzled look.

He leaned in close. "Who are you?" he said in a half-whisper.

The clatter of a bowl against a tray woke her. Euterpe was gathering the vessels from the table, cleaning up after the guests who had left quietly while Lydia slept. Lydia was slightly abashed to realize she had fallen asleep in front of them all. In a way, though, it was appropriate, she guessed. The meal reminded Lydia of a *refrigerium,* except that the one being memorialized by the feasters was still breathing—barely.

She supposed Syntyche intended the meal as a peace offering. Truth to tell, Lydia wasn't sure it was Syntyche's place to apologize. But when she arrived here earlier, servants and food baskets in tow, it just seemed easier to let her do as she wished. Syntyche said nothing about the harsh words with which she had last left Lydia, and there was surely no need for Lydia to mention them. No doubt, Euterpe and Clystra wished that all those who came calling would bring their own victuals.

Lydia wondered what Syntyche was telling her friends right now. What was she saying about the strange old woman on the couch who was so weak she dozed off in the middle of a conversation? How would people remember her? As the sick old woman, maybe? The strange young widow who came among them with little more than two children and her own determination? The shrewd, self-reliant merchant? The running woman, the one with such odd habits and unlikely companions?

What caused one person to be remembered and another to be forgotten? What were the chances of life and circumstance that etched one life in memory and allowed another to slip into the indistinct mists of the past? Memory was an odd thing; it both preserved the past and reconstructed it. And sometimes, in the rebuilding, things were lost and new things created. Where did the lost things go?

Lydia found herself thinking about the funeral games for the emperor's son, Drusus. She and Menander had not been married long; Hermeia would not be born for over a year. She begged and pleaded with him to take her to Ephesus to watch at least some of the races, and finally he gave in. They made the four-day walk, arriving in the huge seaport city with a crowd of other sightseers from Thyatira, Sardis, and Smyrna.

Going through the festival market was itself a good enough excuse to make the trip. There were exotic foods and spices, people speaking all sorts of strange languages, acrobats and menageries and jugglers and sleight-of-hand performers. They spent their first night in Ephesus in an open field with hundreds of other travelers, curled up together beneath the heavy woolen blankets they had brought with them. They ate fresh bread for breakfast, still warm from the baking stones, bought from an old woman who sold them a palmful of soft cheese for an extra lepton. They slathered the cheese on the bread, then washed down the meal with cold water from a well on the outskirts of the forum.

They skirted the amphitheater in the center of town, where the poetic and dramatic competitions were taking place, and made for the athletic grounds, at the city's northeastern end. They climbed to the highest levels of the slopes overlooking the contest field. There were a few spaces left and they squeezed in among the shouting, gesturing, wagering onlookers. Lydia could turn her head to the left and see, around the shoulder of Mount Pion, the huge roof of the Temple of Artemis. In the light of the clear morning the white marble tiles of the roof were so brilliant they were almost blinding. Lydia could hardly believe human hands had fashioned a building so large.

The runners for the next race approached the starting line. Lydia heard someone in the crowd say this was to be one of the longer footraces, eight complete circuits of the track. Lydia was glad; she much preferred the longer races. The sprints were over so quickly it was difficult to see what happened.

The runners toed the line. Lydia could see the sunlight glistening on their oiled bodies as they strained forward into the moments preceding the starter's signal. The contestants wore only brightly colored armbands, which identified them to their partisans. Blue seemed to have the most supporters, but Yellow had a small, quite vocal section clumped just below, on the same slope Lydia and Menander occupied. Red, Green, and White also had enthusiastic backers scattered through the throng.

Lydia wished they were close enough to see the men's faces, but it was easy enough to imagine: eyes focusing down the track as if it were a lamplit tunnel through a pitch black hillside, jaws slack with concentration, ears that sensed the crowd as an undifferentiated sheet of sound as they waited for the word from the starter.

The starter's arm flashed down and the runners sprang forward. The crowd roared, then there was a collective groan from the Yellow faction; their man had stumbled on the start. Yellow was a tall, lanky Nubian or Ethiopian. He righted himself and set off after the others.

The runners stayed tightly bunched for the first three circuits, with Yellow hanging just behind. On the fourth circuit, spaces began to open up between them. Still, Yellow hung back—not losing any ground, but not gaining any, either.

At the beginning of the sixth circuit, the leader was Blue, followed by no more than a half-stride by Green. And now Yellow was third, maybe two strides behind. The others had fallen back. On the backstretch, Yellow overtook Green, and the Yellow partisans began chanting their man's name: "*Claud*-i-us, *Claud*-i-us, *Claud*-i-us...." The noise of the crowd rose steadily as the distance shrank between Yellow and Blue. The Blues began urging their runner. Even the boxers and wrestlers on the infield stopped their contests to watch the duel on the track.

Blue and Yellow came down the straightaway nearly shoulder to shoulder. The starter flung both arms into the air to signal the final lap. The noise of the crowd, already deafening, rose another level. Lydia was screaming at the top of her voice, "*Claud*-i-us, *Claud*-i-us!" The runners made the first turn, still in a dead heat. Coming out of the turn, they appeared to jostle each other. Claudius faltered and the Yellows below screamed at Blue. Claudius regained his stride and pressed after Blue, now maybe a full pace ahead. Into the final turn they went, Claudius steadily narrowing the gap. They came into the final stretch, and every fist in the place was clenched and pumping in the air. Lydia felt her heart banging away at her breastbone. Claudius had pulled even with Blue and challenged him stride for stride.

They pushed each other forward, each straining against the other runner and his own exhaustion. They blurred across the finish line so close together it was impossible to tell who had won.

And then Claudius stumbled and pitched headlong on the track. Several yellow-garbed attendants rushed up to him. Even from her distant position, Lydia could see the blood coming from his mouth when they rolled him over. There was a stunned silence. In a few moments, one of the judges detached himself from the officials' huddle. Walking slowly, glancing frequently at Claudius's inert form, he went over to the Blue runner. With a hesitant motion, he placed a wreath on Blue's head. The Blue faction made not a sound of acknowledgment.

Blue took the wreath from his head. He looked at it briefly, then raised it high, saluting first the watchers on Lydia's side, then those on the other side. He walked over to Claudius, still surrounded by his handlers. He knelt down and placed the wreath carefully on the still chest. Then he walked away.

The games may have been organized to revere the memory of the oldest son of Tiberius Caesar, but the only name on Lydia's mind, for that day and many days afterward, was that of the yellow-clad African whose heart was too strong to accept defeat and too weak to survive victory. Who received the most honor that day? Did it make any difference, in the long run?

A little more than a year passed after Menander's death. The four talents became three-and-a-half, then three, then less. Lydia sold the purple cloth of her dowry for a fair price through some of her father's contacts, but she knew the money couldn't last forever.

Lydia realized she might have to sell Felix. She alternately toyed with and shied away from the idea. She loved him, and he and the children were inseparable. But every time she watched him carrying Hermeia around the courtyard on his back, or listened to him sing a Hebrew lullaby over a drowsing Parmenes, she had the gnawing sense that she couldn't afford him and ought to do something about it.

Her son had finally fallen asleep. Lydia gingerly pulled her arm from beneath Parmenes, holding her breath as she tried to ease away without waking him. Hermeia was breathing slowly and softly on her pallet in the corner. Lydia left her room, softly closing the door. She paced the perimeter of the courtyard: six steps to the corner where the street walls met—five to the center of the front gate, then five more to the corner—six along the storeroom wall—ten back to her doorway. The evening was warm, but still Lydia hugged herself as she made round after round, watching her right foot, then her left. She counted her steps carefully, one after the other, right then left. She kept a steady pace and a constant count; she needed to keep her distance from the encroaching riot of her thoughts. Maybe if she walked long enough, the drab burden of consciousness would fade.

Lydia sometimes thought of getting out Menander's scrolls and reading herself to sleep with Socrates, Aristotle, Pyrrho, and the others. But the feel and the smell of the papyrus and vellum would summon to her mind the evenings with her husband and Sosipater: the food, the talk, the laughter, the argument. And afterward, when Sosipater had left, the lovemaking. Philosophy was supposed to liberate people's minds from the enslavement of superstition, but Menander's death lay across the threshold of philosophy's temple. For Lydia, that way was barred.

So she walked. Maybe some god or demon would permit her to simply collapse into unknowing sleep without having to face the fearsome trial of dark, quiet, and solitude.

Right, left, right…One, two, three, four…She was passing the storeroom entry when she realized Felix stood in the opening, looking at her.

"What is it, Felix?"

He turned his face aside. "I wondered what you were counting." His eyes flickered furtively toward her in the torchlight, then away.

She was glad for the night; in the daylight he could have seen the red in her cheeks. Had she really been counting out loud?

"How long have you been watching me?"

He wouldn't look at her.

Lydia felt the riot coming closer. She felt her breath getting faster, felt her eyes widening like a frightened animal's. She looked up at the night sky, at the stars, so high above, so far out of reach. Where was the way out? Where was the escape from this ceaseless hurt?

"When I was a young boy," Felix said in a low voice, "my mother once told me the story of how our people returned from exile in a foreign land. They were taken as captives by the king of Babylon and sent away from their land for seventy years.

"Finally, as the prophets of our God had promised, they were allowed to return. They had to travel for many days, back to a land most of them had never seen. And when they got to Jerusalem, the city of their kings and the city of the temple of God, everything was in ruins."

Lydia latched onto the eunuch's narrative, pulled herself hand-over-hand along the line of the story. Maybe Felix's words could deliver her from the tangle of her inner darkness.

"But even though the city of their ancestors was not much more than a pile of burned rubble, my people gave thanks to our God because at last they were back in their own land. And the first thing they began to rebuild was the great altar of sacrifice, so that they could make offerings to our God in thanks for his deliverance.

"When my people began re-laying the foundations of the city, some others from the surrounding country started making trouble for them with the king. They accused them of harboring sedition and rebellion. They told the king that when Jerusalem was rebuilt, my people would set themselves up as rulers, that they would stop paying tribute and take away the king's territory for their own.

"But the prophets of our God told the people to keep working. They told them that our God was watching over them and that he had put it on the king's heart to allow them to return and rebuild the city of his name. So the people kept working. And our God enabled them not only to lay the foundations for the city, but to rebuild his temple—though it was not nearly as grand as the ancient temple of Solomon, the great king of our people. And the people kept working until the walls of Jerusalem were rebuilt, according to the promises of our God."

There was a long silence.

"Your people have done a lot of wandering, haven't they?"

"Yes, Mistress. And a lot of rebuilding."

She hugged her knees to her chest. When had they sat down?

"You know I can't keep you, Felix."

"Yes, Mistress." He turned his face toward her. "And you can't stay here."

"Why do you say that?"

"Because I've been watching you. This place, these people are not right for you."

"Thyatira is my home, Felix. I was born here."

"But you will not die here, I think."

She gave him a long, thoughtful look. She realized the idea of leaving Thyatira was already working inside her mind, stirring things about, rearranging what she thought she knew—maybe even dusting off some abandoned hopes. How did he know? How could he look at her blasted, stricken surface and sense beneath it the tilled plot, waiting for the seeds of his surprising words to fall and take such quick root? Or was it just a lucky guess?

She lay awake most of that night, restless with anticipation, with a vague yet compelling sense that there might still be purpose and direction and something to attempt.

Surely Felix was right. In the morning, she would begin making plans to leave. It would take time—maybe a year or two to make an orderly disposition at the most favorable prices. She knew enough about the ways of the forum not to expect any clemency for a widow who was desperate to sell. So, she would not be desperate. She would take her time, but she would sell everything she couldn't carry with her to—where?

It didn't matter. That would come to her in due course. Once she freed herself from Thyatira, wiped the slate clean with distance and change, things would be better. She would breathe easier. She would make another try.

PART TWO

The Race

ydia, there is no need. You can stay where you are."

"Nonsense. These boys are young and strong. Surely the four of them can carry a bony, sick old woman on her couch into the atrium. I won't have everyone crowding in here and stepping on each other when there's plenty of room outside."

Euodia blew an exasperated breath through her nose. "You are the most impossible old woman I've ever known."

"Thank you, dear. Now, if each of them will get at a corner of the couch, I think we can manage this fairly quickly."

"Oh, do as she says," Euodia flung over her shoulder as she stalked toward the doorway.

Gaius and his three young friends took hold of Lydia's couch and moved it carefully through the doorway and into the atrium. They were going to set her down just outside the entry to her room, but Lydia pointed across the way, toward the colonnade that separated the main atrium from the alcove where the well was.

"No, over there. The breeze is better."

The youths dutifully carried her across the atrium and set her down, angling the couch so she would be able to easily see the president, whose usual place was at the west end of the courtyard.

The moon had set a good while before, but the stars leaned close and bright. Lydia could see the shoulders of the Great Bear and the two stars that pointed to the bright bauble in the tail of her cub, hanging motionless in the northernmost sky. There were already a good number of people here and more were coming through the doorway each moment. Lydia was pleased to see them. Of course she would come into the atrium to assemble with her fellow believers. How foolish to try and cram everyone into her room.

Syntyche was here; Lydia saw her speaking to the people around her, smiling and nodding. It was a bit unusual for her to be this early to the assembly. Normally, she came in breathless and disheveled, just as the first hymn was concluding.

Crescens was presiding today. Good. Lydia liked the sound of the old leatherworker's voice. He stood in front of the western wall of the atrium, and the people began shuffling toward that end of the courtyard, seating themselves on the ground in groupings of families and friends. Lydia noticed that some of the slaves of the new magistrate were here; their well-made livery contrasted starkly with the shabbier clothing of the other servants they sat with. What was the magistrate's name? Marcus Gaius Something-or-other. Lydia hadn't heard whether his servants had learned of the faith in Achaia, where their master had been living, or whether they had been taught after arriving in Philippi. She was glad to see them at the assembly.

"Awake, O sleeper, and rise from the dead," sang Crescens.

"And Christ will shine on you," the congregation answered.

Create in me a clean heart, O God.
And renew a right spirit within me.
Let the LORD's children praise him,
And let us take unto ourselves the truth of his faith.
He shall know his children.
Therefore we sing in his love....

Crescens led them through parts of several hymns. Lydia watched the magistrate's slaves; they seemed unfamiliar with some of the choruses.

"Brothers and sisters, greet each other in the name of the Lord Jesus Christ," announced Crescens.

Those in the gathering turned to each other, offering smiles and a kiss of welcome. Epaphroditus, assisted by a young boy, hobbled over to Lydia's couch. The old man bent low, and Lydia felt his dry, thin lips brush against her cheek. She took his hand.

"Welcome, old friend," she said. "I don't see Theon here today."

Epaphroditus shrugged. "My master didn't feel well enough to come to the assembly. He hopes to be better in time for tonight's *agapē*. He asked me to give you his greetings and assure you of his love and continued thoughts."

"They are gratefully received," she said. "And tell him I pray for his health."

The old slave bowed himself away from her and went back to his place. The assembly quieted as Crescens resumed speaking.

"Friends, today we have a guest among us, a fellow believer from the church in Smyrna." He gestured toward the far wall of the atrium. "Polycarp, please come and read to us the admonition."

A young man stood and walked toward the front of the gathering. In the lamplight, Lydia could barely trace the wispy beginnings of his beard as he passed her place. He had a high forehead and a clear, bright expression.

One of Lydia's girls brought her the chest with the scrolls. Lydia gave young Polycarp a final, thoughtful look, then dug through the leather-wrapped bundles. She pulled one out and handed it to the girl, who carried it to the front and gave it to Crescens. With a shy smile, Polycarp took the scroll from the president and slipped it from its sheath. He shifted beneath the wall sconce until the light from the lamp was right for reading.

"'Paul and Timothy, servants of Christ Jesus, to all the saints in Christ Jesus at Philippi, together with the overseers and deacons: Grace and peace to you from God our Father and the Lord Jesus Christ....'"

Lydia heard the slight hesitation in Polycarp's voice when he read Paul's name; she saw the quick, wide-eyed glance he sent toward Crescens. The young man's awe commended him to her. The writings of Paul and the other apostles were still rare enough that the reading of one of their scrolls—especially, perhaps, for someone in the more remote Asian churches—was an occasion.

It also pleased Lydia to see the immediate smiles of recognition from most of the hearers. This letter from the hand of the apostle was one of their most treasured possessions. Indeed, young Polycarp held not the actual document sent by Paul, but one of the copies they had scrupulously made through the years. The original was hidden in a place known only to Lydia and two of the elders. Though the imperial officials had left them unmolested for a while now, one never knew when their suspicions of the Christians' gatherings might rekindle. That such a precious article as Paul's letter might fall into their hands was unthinkable.

The first time they had heard Paul's letter, the gathering was much smaller and more fearful. The little community of believers came under severe scrutiny in the aftermath of Claudius's edict. They were harried in the forum, sometimes prevented from pursuing their livelihoods. The magisterial militia had even harassed some of Lydia's agents, until the landowners and imperial pensioners began feeling the pinch on their precious purple goods.

And so, the words Polycarp was reading just now held for them in those days an austere, yet precious, assurance: "'I will know that you stand firm in one spirit, contending as one man for the faith of the gospel without being frightened in any way by those who oppose you...for it has been granted to you on behalf of Christ not only to believe on him, but also to suffer for him, since you are going through the same struggle you saw I had.'"

Closing her eyes, Lydia could listen as young Polycarp read and hear the echoes of Paul's voice. She could easily imagine him huddled over a piece of papyrus, scratching away with a pen until the ink skipped and blotched, then turning away with a grunt of impatience to rub the stylus on the moistened ink block. Almost every evening, he would toil until the cramping of his back and neck muscles forced him to stand, digging the heels of his hands into his bleary eyes. Then he would call for one of his companions or one of Lydia's learned slaves to be his amanuensis. He would pace back and forth and dictate correspondence until fatigue bested him.

He was a prickly companion, this Jew who called himself Paul. He was as fearless as a lion, but he could also be as irritable as a she-goat with bad digestion. Speaking to Crescens or one of the other truthseekers, his manner was as patient as a mother teaching her baby to walk. And that very evening he might snap at Luke or Silas for doing no more than blocking his light.

Lydia sometimes wondered why they loved him—but love him they did. All of them. His influence over those who knew him was as broad and unquestioned as the dome of the sky. The pure determination of his will enthralled them, drew them in. Or had her, at least. The force of his belief fascinated her; it reminded her of Menander's single-minded pursuit of his beloved philosophers. But this was something more, much more. There was a depth and breadth to Paul's mind that pulled her in, impelled her forward. If his outer appearance was a bit off-putting, the strength of his spirit and the ceaseless energy of his intellect were powerfully engaging.

Coming up out of the water that day, Lydia remembered, she felt renewed, changed. Her skin burned with the icy fire of new beginning. She could not let this man out of her sight—this man who said words that kindled within her a hope she thought long buried. Lydia was accustomed to the ways of the forum and the trading house. She knew how to ask for what she wanted.

"Come to my house, sir," she said. "There are many things I want to know. If you consider me truly a believer in this Jesus, you must come to my house and tell me more."

He looked at her, and a smile creased the corners of his eyes. Of course she didn't know, then, how rare a thing that smile was.

"We will come," Paul said in his chalky voice, and that was that.

The other women stared at her as they left the riverside. Euodia's and Syntyche's faces had displayed plainly both their shock at such forwardness and their secret envy at not having extended the invitation first. Lydia smiled at the memory. Looking back, she supposed it was rather reckless of her. But she had shed so many things along the path to that river's edge—some of them things she had never thought to count as lost. If this Jesus could show her a surer way, she had to know as much as she could about him. There was too little time left to spend any more of it in waiting—or losing.

Hermeia didn't stop crying for Felix until they reached the port at Smyrna. Lydia wanted to hold her and comfort her, but she couldn't do that and keep up with Parmenes at the same time. It was hard enough to keep pace with the other travelers while carrying her son. But he fretted against her, wanting always to be free on the ground.

The other travelers were mostly merchants and tradesmen, on their way to one of the towns further south. Lydia could tell they tried to distance themselves from the wailing girl and the rambunctious little boy; she walked in a space cleared for her by her children.

"I want Felix," Hermeia wailed, over and over. "Why couldn't Felix come with us?"

"We couldn't keep Felix, child. Mother doesn't have enough money to feed you, your brother, herself, and a slave." She tried to cradle the weeping girl's head against her with a free hand, but Hermeia pulled away, giving her a reproachful look.

"Felix isn't a slave. He's my friend."

They spent that night in Sardis. Fortunately, Lydia was able to find them a sleeping place in a guesthouse attached to one of the temples. She didn't know how she would be able to manage the walk to Smyrna the next day, but she was far too tired to care.

By morning, the traveling band picked up a few more members, and one of the men had a donkey. Lydia traded him two obols for the privilege of balancing her small children atop the beast's load. It was a fair amount of money, but she would have paid twice that much. Even better, Parmenes was fascinated enough by the novelty of riding that he didn't start trying to clamber down until they were nearly to Smyrna.

Lydia found passage on a two-masted coaster that would take them up to Troas, then make the run across the Aegean to the port city of Neapolis. The ship's captain was a jovial fellow, old enough to be her father and very much in love with the sound of his own voice. Lydia found out he had spent some time during his youth serving in the Syrian Legion. She mentioned her fallen husband, and the captain fell over himself. He told her he would charge her only half the usual rate, and he would let them sleep in his own quarters, just above the rear cargo hold. Lydia had no idea whether he was telling the truth about the normal cost of passage, but she was grateful for the gesture, at least. Furthermore, the thought of sleeping on the open deck with a child as busy as Parmenes wasn't very appealing.

The ship left port as the sun was setting, and it didn't take long for Lydia to realize that though the captain's offer was generous, it wasn't going to be too helpful. The rolling of the coaster and the groaning of the timbers prevented anything approaching sleep. The children were uneasy, too, fretting and fussing in the hammock slung from the cabin's ceiling beams. Before long, Lydia felt her stomach buckling with each drop into the trough of the next wave. She scooped up Hermeia and Parmenes and flung open the cabin door, rushing up the stairs to the main deck.

It was a little better aboveboard; the breeze allayed some of her queasiness, at least. She kept a death-grip on the children's hands. If one of them tumbled overboard, she doubted she would even hear the splash.

The captain got up from a little knot of men seated near the aft mast. "Little too rough for you down there, eh? Well, sorry about that. But when we get Chios behind us and the crosscurrents lay a bit, she ought to smooth out some.

"Say, you want to curl up here, in the lee of this cargo?" He jerked his thumb toward several large casks amidships, lashed to the railings on either side. "Taking this oil to Neapolis for some rich so-and-so; he won't mind if it keeps the spray off you and the babies, hey?

"You boys, there!" he shouted, wheeling toward the men sitting by the mast, "have a mind for this good woman and her two little ones. Her husband died an honest soldier's death in the Syrian Legion, same outfit as mine. Anything happens to them, I'll gut every mother's son of you and use your insides for bait. Understand?"

Lydia shuddered, but forced a quick smile onto her face when the captain turned back. "Thank you, sir. You're very kind to us."

Lydia woke at first light and quickly realized Parmenes wasn't beside her. She sat bolt upright, staring about her. Nowhere to be seen. She glanced at the still-sleeping Hermeia and staggered to her feet. "Parmenes! Where are you?"

She walked forward as quickly as the gently tilting deck and her stiff back muscles would allow. The captain was standing in the bow.

"Sir? Captain? My son is gone. Have you—"

"This what you're looking for?" the captain asked, wheeling about. Parmenes was in his arms, laughing and pointing at the waves breaking over the ship's bow. The captain chuckled and ruffled the small boy's hair. "Saw him stirring about just before dawn. Thought he might not ought to be walking the deck by himself, so I kept him with me. We've been sailing the ship together, haven't we, boy?" He laughed again, chucking Parmenes under the ribs.

Her son cackled aloud in the captain's arms, then twisted himself this way and that, trying to get a better view of the water sliding past below them. To Lydia, it looked as if he would have jumped into the sea if given the chance.

"Thank you again, sir," she said, trying to calm the racing of her pulse. "Thank you for keeping him safe."

"Ah, this boy's born for the water, I say. That's plain. Here. Go to your mother, you little scamp."

He set Parmenes down and Lydia quickly grabbed his hand. The child pulled toward the railing, trying to regain the view he'd had in the captain's arms.

"Yes, born for the water," the captain laughed. "Keeps you busy, though, I guess."

They took on more cargo at Troas and another handful of passengers. As soon as there was a full tide, they set sail up the coast. They beat up past the Dardanelles Strait, then across toward the small island of Imbros. From there, they tacked northwest to round Samothrace. Then came the longest leg: the westward run to the island of Thasos, just off the Macedonian coast.

The crossing to Thasos was at night. Parmenes was tethered to Lydia by a length of linen cord, tied securely from his ankle to her wrist. Hermeia slept fitfully, curled into a ball beside her. Every so often her daughter would whimper in her sleep, calling feebly for Felix.

Lydia lay on the deck, sheltered from the wind and spray by the rich man's oil casks, and looked up at the stars, framed and crisscrossed by the dark lines of the rigging. They were the same stars she would have seen from the courtyard of her house back in Thyatira. But in this moment, as she lay on the gently rocking deck and listened to the hiss of the ship's bow cutting through the dark waters of the Aegean, the snap and pop of the sails and lines, all was transformed, reshaped. The stars wheeled above her in a mysterious dance; they sang in words Lydia couldn't quite catch. A streak of light marked the sky. Which one of the stars had fallen? Maybe it was better not to try to guess.

Would her uncle Menippus be easy to find, once they reached Philippi? Would he be favorably disposed to her coming? She would show her uncle that she wasn't a helpless widow; that she could fend for herself and her children without burdening his household with three more mouths to feed. All she needed was a start, a fair chance.

She drifted into a light sleep, but in her sleep it seemed her eyes were still open, still staring up at the night sky. Near the zenith she could see the Swan, soaring among the light-clustered heavens. And then she was there, flying with wings outstretched, gliding easily toward a new place, another try at hope.

But she couldn't go as high or as fast as she wanted. She always had to be doubling back to tend Parmenes and Hermeia, who straggled behind. Again and again, she swooped down from the broad, easy winds of the uppermost heavens—to bear up her daughter, who kept looking backward toward the place they had left, or veering beneath Parmenes to prevent him from flying too close to the crashing waves. Each time it was harder to mount again to the heights from which she had come. She cried aloud to the stars for help, but it was always the same. The stars continued their dance, kept singing their song—but not to her. She was banned from hoarding her effort for herself alone; no star, no god could change that.

Lydia woke as the night grayed toward dawn, troubled by the images in her sleeping mind. Was she really so selfish? Did she really wish to fly away and leave all encumbrances behind—even her own children? She watched them as they slept, wondering what could protect them from their mother's dreams.

They were rounding Thasos by the time the sun was a hand's breadth above the horizon. From there it was only a short haul into Neapolis. Lydia walked down the ramp from the ship to the dock, tugging her children close as they narrowly avoided the swinging, heavy bales and crates, winched into the air by the grunting, cursing longshoremen. They started the dusty, overland trek toward Philippi.

Seventeen

Xerxes was light on his feet for such a corpulent man; he bobbed through the busy streets, dancing on his toes and spinning around to grin and wiggle his fingers at the children, making them giggle with the faces he made. The people they passed seemed accustomed to the bizarre figure he cut. They either ignored him completely or passed him with a smile and a shake of the head. And, just as he promised, he took them directly to the trading house of Menippus.

The building stood on one of the streets that climbed toward the Upper City from the forum; its back half was dug into the hillside. Her uncle's trading house was built of large, gray stones, square-cut and fit together with joints so tight a fingernail could not fit between. There were ornate pilasters on either side of the brass-sheathed main gate. Above the courtyard wall, Lydia could see a large upper story built on the main structure. While Lydia watched, dozens of prosperous-looking men went in and out. With her children's hands gripped firmly, she stepped into the courtyard of her uncle's enterprise.

The courtyard was paved with large, uncut stones. A colonnade of painted stone columns with Doric capitals ran around its perimeter. A cistern stood in the middle of the open space, surrounded by benches of carved wood. Men sat talking or stood in small groups about the courtyard. Some of them were holding cloth close to their faces, examining it. Most of the cloth was of the same reddish purple as the dye that came from the roots of the madder grown on her father's plantation near Thyatira. Slaves bustled to and fro across the courtyard, some carrying bolts of cloth, some guiding important-looking men. Framed by an archway in the colonnade and surmounted by a frieze of carved stone, the doorway into the main hall was as tall as a man standing on another man's shoulders. Both of the double doors were open against the wall. They were made of some kind of dark wood—almost black—and as she stepped nearer Lydia could see the floral and geometric figures that decorated each of the twelve panels on either side.

Her father's younger brother looked almost the same as Lydia remembered him: a bit more gray in his beard and around his temples, a few more crow's-feet at the corners of his eyes, but the same man, with the same quick smile and quiet manner. She was so glad to see a familiar face after the long journey from Thyatira, she completely forgot herself and raced up to him where he stood, in the center of a group of traders. She fell at his feet, hugging his knees.

"Well, Menippus," said one of the men into the awkward silence, "looks like you've been trading in something besides dyed wool." The others laughed.

Her uncle was looking down at her with a confused expression.

"Uncle! I'm Lydia, daughter of your brother, Threnides."

"Lydia? Little Lydia? But—"

"I had to come, Uncle. There was no place for me in Thyatira, no place for my children—" She broke off, standing quickly and peering toward the doorway.

Hermeia and Parmenes stood there, fingers in their mouths, looking about with big eyes at the many strangers who had stopped their usual bustle and now stared at the strange woman and her children who had burst in among them.

"Children?" Menippus's eyes moved from Lydia to the two little ones, then back to her. "My brother's daughter?"

She went back to her children and took their hands. She forced her breathing to slow and walked slowly back toward him.

"Uncle, this is my daughter, Hermeia, and my son, Parmenes. Their father—Menander, son of Timon of Thyatira, whom I think you will remember—died bravely in the Emperor's Syrian Legion. I have come here to humbly ask for your sponsorship until I can make a proper place and home for myself and my children, here in Philippi."

"But, child, why did you—" He suddenly remembered himself, glancing around the circle of curious merchants with an apologetic grin. "Sorry, gentlemen. This is hardly the place to discuss family matters, is it?" He turned to a distinguished-looking older man, standing just behind his right shoulder. "Septimus, will you continue for me, please?" The slave nodded and moved toward the traders. "Come, then, Lydia," said Menippus, indicating the doorway, "let's go up to my house, and you and your children can refresh yourselves. Then, you can help me catch up on all the news from Thyatira."

"I'm so sorry to interrupt your commerce," Lydia said as they climbed the steps up the outside wall of the trading house.

"Septimus has managed the trading house for me for several years now. He knows as much as I do of the business, if not more. He'll do fine." Menippus stopped climbing, and laid a hand on her shoulder. "But now I must ask. Why did you leave the city of your father and your husband's family? Surely it would have been better for your children to grow up in the presence of their grandparents?"

Lydia took a deep breath. "I couldn't stay there. They could never fathom what matters to me."

He looked at her for a long time. He began nodding slowly. "I think I understand, Lydia. I'm still not sure I think your coming was wise, but I think I can see why you had to try." He gave her a quick smile. "And now, let's get you and your children out of this hot sun. I'll have my women prepare a bath. Later, we'll talk."

Within a few days, over her uncle's protests, Lydia found a place to live, not too far away. The owner of the place let her rent one of the small rooms on the roof for two drachmae each month.

Menippus started her in the countingroom. It was tedious, adding up the value of the contracts and calculating the sales, first in Macedonian drachmae, then in Imperial *dēnariī*. But one fact became clear to Lydia early on: the amount of money that flowed through her uncle's hands was impressive. Even allowing for the generous payments he sent back to his older brother in Thyatira, he made a handsome living from the constant demand for purple goods.

Lydia soon began to understand why: though Tyrian purple was more stable and somewhat richer in hue than the dyes made from the madder root of her homeland, it was also much more expensive to import, coming from faraway Syria. The newly created nobility of the Roman colony of Philippi were anxious to display their social status, but could ill afford such costly wardrobes. And so, the Asian purple provided the answer.

Over time, she won the grudging respect of the counting-room slaves. For all their initial distrust of the strangeness of having a woman in their midst, they could see that their master's niece was both determined and eager to understand everything possible about the enterprise.

Lydia started to notice a pattern in the contracts. In the late summer and autumn, when the madder was harvested and supplies of purple were plentiful, the prices offered by the traders went down. But in midwinter and early spring, when the previous season's crop had been largely used up, the prices rose. Lydia also noticed the concurrent increase in the number of side agreements her uncle's agents made to sell dried, unprocessed madder root to other merchants.

One day, she found Septimus in the main trading room. She touched the slave's elbow. "Yes, Mistress?"

Lydia forced herself to ignore the poorly veiled disapproval on his face. "Septimus, I know how well you serve my uncle, and I also know you genuinely have his best interest at heart. He is truly fortunate to have a manager of your experience and skill."

He batted his eyes at the compliments, but his expression was otherwise unaltered.

"Since you are so well schooled in my uncle's trade, I hesitate to bring this matter to your attention. Doubtless you've noticed it yourself, it being so obvious." She forced herself to wait until he said something.

"Well?"

"It seems to me that if we made agreements to sell purple to the merchants at an agreed-upon price for the entire winter—at prices very favorable to them—we could better regulate the income of the trading house and take some of the uncertainty out of the winter and early spring months."

"But, Mistress, how can we know what the supply will be? Weather is uncertain, and the following summer's madder crop may be poor. Yet we will be obligated to sell purple at a lower price than any of the other houses, if we do as you suggest."

He gave her a tiny smile of triumph. She nodded gravely.

"What you say is very true. And yet, loyal friend of my uncle, don't forget that each winter, we sell a large part of our stored root to other dyers—the very ones who would undercut our prices. Suppose we kept larger stores through the winter, hedging against a short season. Let the other dyers find root where they can. Would we not then be in a better position to maintain our agreements with the buyers? And with the increased winter and spring trade sure to follow our favorable prices, we wouldn't have to worry so much about the size of the next summer's crop."

He said nothing.

"My father's fields are the largest in the province of Asia Minor, and our storerooms, both here and in Thyatira, hold more than any other three merchants' combined. My uncle has less uncertainty about his supply than anyone in Philippi. Why not take advantage of that fact?"

His eyes flickered from side to side as he ran the calculations in his mind. She cautioned herself not to smile.

"I will speak to my master," he said, finally. "We shall see."

He walked away abruptly, his back as straight as the staff of a javelin. Lydia permitted herself a grin as she watched him leave.

It was cold, and Lydia's vision blurred with fatigue. When the servants finally walked through, announcing the closing of the doors, she put down her stylus with a deep sigh and rubbed her temples with her fingertips. She dreaded the climb up the stairs to where her children waited. She wanted only to go home, eat a handful of dried apricots and pistachios, and sleep soundly until morning.

But it wouldn't do, of course. She pushed herself up from her small worktable and pulled her cloak tighter around her shoulders. She paused a moment at the brazier by the doorway to warm her hands, then shuffled slowly toward the outside stairway.

Her strategy was working well. Since Septimus had advised Menippus to implement the changes she had suggested, the number of contracts for purple goods showed steady increase. This was the most profitable winter season in anyone's memory. Menippus, who before was rarely seen anywhere but in the main trading room huddling with his buyers and sellers, had lately taken to strolling contentedly through the counting room, the weighing area—even in the backyards, where the root was crushed and rendered. Most telling of all to Lydia, Septimus had begun greeting her openly—sometimes with a smile.

But Lydia was so tired. She leaned against the door at the top of the stairs and went inside. There was a shout, a blur of motion, and Parmenes slammed into her, grappling her at the knees and nearly bowling her over.

"Son, what are you—"

"Hermie say bad me!"

"I did not!" said Hermeia, stamping her foot.

Parmenes held his mother's legs with one arm, pointed at

his sister with the other, and looked up at Lydia with a wide-eyed, imploring expression.

"Hermie say pig me."

"You little liar!"

"Hermeia!"

"All I said was if he didn't quit playing in the ashes, he'd get dirty as a pig."

"Hermie say pig me."

Lydia sent a helpless look toward the slave who was bringing the children's wraps. The woman shrugged. "They've been at each other most of the afternoon," she said. "Nothing I could say or do seemed to count for much."

Lydia shook her head. "Come on, children. Bundle yourselves well; it's getting colder outside. Let's go home."

Their breath puffed white in the near dark as they walked down the alley that led to the small, hired room on the roof. Lydia hoped there was still a live coal somewhere in her hearth. As cold as her fingers were already, she didn't think she could manage a fresh fire.

They turned the final corner and Lydia halted in surprise. The room beside hers, which had been unoccupied all during the time she had lived here, now glowed with lamplight. On the sheets of linen covering the windows she could see the shadows of people stirring about inside.

"Who's up there, Mother?"

"I don't know, Hermeia. I suppose our landlord rented the other room."

"But it was piled with his empty amphorae and barrels, just this morning when we left."

"Well, it isn't anymore."

The wall between the two rooms was not very thick. What

if these new neighbors were noisy? What if they were gamblers, or drunkards, or quarrelsome? A long, tired breath went out of her. She took a tighter hold of her children's hands and started up the steps.

She did manage to find a coal, glowing a dull, brownish red, hiding at the bottom of the ashes on her small hearth. "Hermeia, get some fruit and nuts for yourself and your brother while I build up the fire."

"Don't we have anything besides apricots?"

She ignored the complaint, bending low over the coal and blowing softly as she placed her tinder.

"Want that one!"

"Stop it, Parmenes!"

"No, that one!"

Lydia spun around and shook the shoulders of both children. "Be quiet! Both of you! I'm sick to death of your noise."

Parmenes began whimpering, while Hermeia just gave her a sullen look. She realized she'd probably grabbed them a little harder than she intended, but at this moment she didn't care. She turned back to her fire.

"As soon as you eat, you're both going to sleep," she announced, jabbing small twigs and scraps of bark at the smoking, reddening coal. "I won't listen to any more of your bickering tonight."

And then, Lydia heard the sound coming through the wall. People in the other room—at least one man and woman, maybe others—were singing. And though the words were indistinct and muffled by the wall, the rising and falling ache of the melody was unmistakable. Though she had never heard it before, Lydia knew with certainty that the tune was one Felix might have sung.

Hermeia heard it too. Her face was still, angled slightly as she listened. Even Parmenes quieted.

The sound both warmed Lydia and brought a pang of sadness to her throat. She thought of Felix, holding one of her babies on his lap, singing in his high, strong voice. She thought of the stories he used to tell her, the way his words could soothe her fears and at the same time kindle indistinct, faraway longings. She wondered how he was faring since his return to the household of Menander's father. She remembered how much she missed him.

Hermeia was looking at her. The girl clenched her jaw and her eyes were hard in the dim, smoky glow of the kindling hearth fire. Lydia met her gaze for a moment, then stood and walked quickly to the storage urns.

"Come and get something to eat." Lydia scooped out a handful of pistachios and held them toward her daughter, but Hermeia kept her face turned away.

"'Therefore God exalted him to the highest place,'" sang Crescens.

"'And gave him the name that is above every name,'" responded the gathering.

"'That at the name of Jesus every knee should bow,'"

"'In heaven and on earth and under the earth,'"

"'And every tongue confess that Jesus Christ is Lord,'"

"'To the glory of God the Father.' Amen."

"Amen." Crescens held out his hands toward Polycarp, and the younger man gave the president the scroll. He gave Crescens a small bow and weaved his way through the assembly toward the place he had been sitting. Crescens carefully returned the scroll to its sleeve and handed it to one of the young boys near the front.

"My brothers and sisters," said Crescens in a round, rolling voice, "the words of the blessed Paul remind us of the superiority of the name of Jesus our Lord: that he has received from the hand of his Father all glory and honor; that he who was willing that his own life not be spared has become the source of all life and joy. And how is it that the Christ came to such a place of honor? Did he not come to it, as Paul's letter reminds us, by emptying himself of all desire for the very splendor to which he was entitled?"

As Crescens went on with the homily, Lydia again searched out Euodia and Syntyche, seated in their separate places. No doubt, they were both as relieved as she that the reading had ended where it did. She realized she had been thinking more of young Polycarp than the two women when she selected the scroll. Today, especially, it would have been most awkward had Crescens not had the presence of mind to end at Paul's hymn to the Christ.

Was it a willful, malicious act, as Euodia had insisted all these years? Or was it, as Syntyche maintained, a circumstance brought about by nothing more than a clumsy tongue? Lydia still wasn't sure of the answer.

Eighteen

uodia looked at ease that day for the first time in many weeks, Lydia remembered. Standing in front of the assembly in this same courtyard, all those years ago, holding her son's hand in her right hand and the hand of his intended in her left, she smiled broadly as she announced the impending marriage of Androclus to Flavinia, the daughter of Titus Macrinus. Everyone made a pleased sound at the announcement.

It was a favorable match in every respect. Not content to rest in his villa and spend his military pension, Macrinus had made astute investments in wool trading and mining interests. He exported more finished purple and other costly goods than nearly anyone else in this part of Macedonia. Though he was not a believer in the Christ, his wife and a number of his slaves frequently attended on First Days. If the religious practices of Euodia and her friends disturbed Macrinus's Roman sensibilities, he had never shown it.

And Flavinia was a pretty little thing who seemed perfectly content to be Androclus's wife. Euodia spoke of her in glowing terms—no small recommendation, Lydia thought. Most would have deemed Androclus too young for marriage, but those close to the situation thought that after what had happened a year ago, the sooner he was settled with a wife and the responsibilities of a household, the better. The boy seemed genuinely penitent, but it was best not to take any chances.

Not that it was unknown for pretty slave girls to bear children who strongly resembled the young scion of a house. And Euodia was being more than fair toward the young woman, providing generously for her upkeep and that of her baby. But it was acutely embarrassing to her that her son had been unable to keep his feet on the path of purity. More disturbing was the fact that, by all accounts, the slave girl was deeply smitten. The other slaves had often heard her weeping quietly and whispering his name. For his part, Androclus was almost pathetically eager to take all blame upon himself. Accordingly, it was judged wisest all around to have the girl discreetly moved to Lydia's house during her pregnancy and for as long afterward as needful. Lydia was only too happy to assist. Neria and her other women were very kind to the girl and doted on Lucian, the little boy. Besides, it was good to have a child around the house again, even if the sight of the little fellow playing with pebbles in the courtyard or ambling after one of the cats sometimes dealt Lydia a sharp pang of grief, thinking of Parmenes.

Flavinia's mother had joined the little group at the front as those in the gathering went up to offer their good wishes. Lydia was walking Xerxes to the gate and didn't hear what was said, but Luke told her later that when Syntyche's turn came she had beamed, first at the lovely young bride-to-be, then at a slightly abashed Androclus. She had expressed her happiness for the couple and for Euodia, then she said what a wonderful thing it was that the little baby boy would now be able to grow up in a proper home.

For an instant, Luke said, no one moved or spoke. Syntyche stood there smiling, and the expressions on the faces of Euodia, Flavinia, and her mother slowly melted. Androclus dropped his head and his ears turned almost the color of ripe pomegranates, the physician said.

"What child is she talking about?" the bride's mother wanted to know.

Euodia stared at Syntyche with an expression less of anger than of disbelief.

Flavinia put a hand on Androclus's forearm. "Androclus? What does she mean?"

The young man's mouth moved, but he could form no words. He turned his face from his confused sweetheart to his increasingly alarmed prospective mother-in-law. He swallowed and looked at his mother, then turned and bolted, bouncing off Lydia in his mad rush for the street.

When she regained her balance, Lydia stared after him for a moment, then she turned and saw the shocked, dismayed faces of his mother, his bride-to-be, and the bride's mother. The back of her neck prickled with alarm as she quickly went to them.

"What's the matter?" Syntyche was saying. "Why did Androclus—oh, my," she said, putting a hand over her mouth. She gave Euodia a horrified look. "I thought she knew. I thought it was part of the arrangement."

Euodia, who had been holding her face in her hands, now raised her eyes to Syntyche. "No, she didn't know, you stupid, loose-mouthed jabber bag. Why don't you explain it to her and her mother, now that you've made my son the laughingstock of all Philippi?" Euodia covered her mouth against a sob that got out anyway. She quickly followed her son's path toward the gate.

Within two days, the betrothal was withdrawn. Euodia shut herself up inside her house, and no one entered or left except her servants. Soon, Macrinus's agents came no more to trade with Euodia. And a week afterward, in the dark of the night, Androclus disappeared from Philippi. He left behind a note scribbled on papyrus, saying only that he could not stay and endure the shame he had brought upon himself, his mother, and an innocent slave.

No word of Androclus had ever come back to his mother. Eventually, the grief-stricken Euodia adopted the slave girl as her daughter and raised the little boy as her grandson. Lucian was a fine man, nearly the image of his father, as Lydia remembered him. It wasn't difficult to see why Euodia doted on him.

The homily was ending. Crescens picked up a basket and invited any who cared to make an offering to come forward. Lydia motioned to one of her women, who picked up the purse beside Lydia and carried it to the president of the assembly. Others came, some with loaves of bread, jars of spices, or small cruets of oil, but most with a coin or two. Two of the deacons took the basket from Crescens, for distribution to the poor and ill.

When the collection was finished, Crescens called for Lucian to bring his son forward. The man and boy rose and weaved their way through the seated crowd. Lydia looked at the place where Syntyche was sitting. She was gone.

Crescens turned the youth to face the assembly and placed his hands on the boy's shoulders. "Androclus, son of Lucian and great-grandson of our sister Euodia, will receive baptism today. Any who are able should come to the riverside and welcome our new brother as he is buried with Christ and raised to walk in newness of life. Amen."

Lucian smiled broadly at his son. Euodia's eyes brimmed. A congratulatory murmur rustled through the congregation.

Crescens raised his hands and offered the benediction. He led them in a final, brief hymn of parting, and the congregation rose and began filing toward the gate. The morning sky was paling toward blue, just above the dark line of the walls.

Lydia crooked a finger at Euterpe. "Ask the young men to carry me back to my room. And then you and Clystra come to me. I need to tell you some things about preparing the food for this evening."

Euterpe nodded and padded away. Lydia laid her head back again. She felt a hand brush her arm. She opened her eyes. It was Crescens. He smiled down at her.

"How are you?"

"Dying."

"Yes, I know. But how are you?"

She laughed with a tiny, creaking sound. "Good for you. The rest are mostly more scared of my death than I am."

She put out a hand and he took it. His nails and the creases in his hands were stained with the pigments and grime of his leather trade. She felt the calluses in his palms as he gripped her hand.

"Thank you for not reading the part about Euodia and Syntyche," Lydia said.

"That would have been unkind—especially so today, don't you think?"

Lydia nodded. "I need all my friends to help me be more considerate."

"True enough."

She looked sharply up at him. "Too much honesty is some-times as unbecoming as too little," she said into his grin.

"You'd know."

She laid back her head and waved him away. "Go and pester someone else. Don't you have a baptism to conduct?"

He laughed deep in his chest. "Ah, Mother Lydia. Even on your deathbed, you're better sport than almost anyone I know."

"How nice, that I'm so entertaining. And don't give me that 'Mother' nonsense. You're not that much younger than I am."

He chuckled again. Then, his face straightened as he reached into the pouch at his belt and drew out a small scroll, maybe as long as a man's palm. It was tied with a scrap of linen.

"This came by messenger." He gave her a cautious look. "From Thessalonica."

Lydia stared at him, then at the scroll.

"I sent a letter with the runners. I thought she might answer—me."

"You were always one of her favorites." Lydia turned her face away. "I'm sure she's not coming."

Crescens laid the small packet carefully beside her hand. "I think you ought to read this. Then, if you want to talk about it, we can."

She closed her eyes, imagining all the things the letter might say. She wished Crescens would just read it to her. She didn't want to make this choice; even at such a remove, she dreaded its aftermath. She had so rarely chosen well where Hermeia was concerned.

She turned her head to ask him to read it, but he was gone. The young men, who had been standing at a respectful distance, came now to take her back inside. As they picked up her couch, her fingers spread and took the letter.

They took her into her room and set her carefully in her place, so that she could turn her head one way and see the doorway, and the other way to view the windows in the north wall. One of them asked her if the position suited her and if she needed anything else. She pulled her eyes away from the letter and nodded at the youth, giving him a fleeting smile. The four went out.

Her hand lay limp in her lap, and the letter was cupped in her palm. She unrolled the letter and began reading.

As Lydia was totaling the figures from a day's business, she heard a discreet cough in the doorway. Septimus stood there.

"The master wants to speak with you."

Lydia cocked her head quizzically. "What about?"

The manager huffed an exasperated breath. "That is for you to find out. He didn't tell me."

Lydia's eyes widened. She put down her stylus, trying not to let her smile show. Septimus wouldn't look at her, not even in the oblique, deferential slave way. He was well and truly annoyed.

"All right, then. Please take me to him."

Septimus led her across the main hall toward the small, iron-banded oak door. This was her uncle's private chamber—the quiet apartment opening off the main room where he discussed business with his most important clients. This was where he came to talk about matters he didn't want overheard. Lydia had never been inside.

Menippus stood with his back to the entrance, his hands clasped behind him. At the sound of the door, he turned.

"Lydia. Good." He smiled, then looked past her. "Thank

you, Septimus." The slave bowed himself out the door.

Lydia forced herself to breathe slowly, in and out through her nose. Her uncle was looking at her, studying her, and she willed herself to hold still, not fidget, keep a pleasant, expectant expression on her face, and wait patiently for him to open the talk.

"Would you like some wine?" Menippus walked toward the ebony writing table and picked up a ewer of aquamarine, etched in white. He poured some wine in one of the glazed earthenware cups beside the ewer, then added water from a clay pitcher. He held the ewer toward Lydia, the question still on his face.

"Yes. A little, please."

He poured the wine and watered it, then picked up both cups. He handed one to her as he was taking a sip from the other. He gestured with his cup toward the cushions piled by the low table in a corner of the room. "Let's sit over there."

They settled themselves, and he set his cup carefully on the table between them. "Lydia, your idea for the winter and spring trading was absolutely correct."

She lowered her eyes. "Thank you, Uncle. I'm glad Septimus suggested—"

"I've been watching you, Lydia. And I like what I see. I don't always ask Septimus for permission, you know."

She allowed herself a tiny smile, but she kept her face lowered.

"You were right, you know," he said.

"I try to notice what's going on around me."

"I don't mean about the contracts."

A long space of quiet.

"About what, then?"

"About why you came here, to me. Well." Menippus

slapped his knees and stood, then took several brisk paces toward the center of the room, his hands once more clasped behind his back. "Lydia, I want you to learn the business of this trading house, inside-out and from one end to the other. I want you to know everything: from how we process the madder root to where we ship the finished goods. Nothing is off-limits to you, and you will answer to no one but me." He whirled around to face her, his chin lifted in an appraising look. "How does that sound to you?"

Lydia drew a deep breath. "Uncle, why have you never taken a wife?"

"Why should you ask such a question?"

"Because I need to better understand your intentions for me."

She could feel his stare boring into her, but she sat very still, keeping her eyes on the cup in her lap, waiting.

"I really don't know," he said finally. Lydia glanced up at him. He wasn't looking at her. He was looking at the door, as if maybe he were waiting for something—an answer, an explanation.

"I suppose I never saw the reason, never felt a need. You surmise correctly; I have no heir." He was smiling at her now—a small, sad smile that admitted something, though Lydia couldn't tell what. "And I think you also comprehend that you and I have more in common than blood, little Lydia. Am I right?"

She risked a hesitant smile of her own. "It seems so."

"It is so! Your mind doesn't travel in the usual paths. Or should I say, 'ruts'? You would never be content with the life your father and the rest of them would have forced on you." He looked away. "Distance is the only tonic for that particular malady."

"My husband was a younger son, too."

"Yes. I guessed as much. You loved him very much, didn't you?"

Lydia looked into her cup. "He saw me for who I was. And approved."

"That is very rare. Very rare, indeed," he said in a soft voice. "I'm sorry, Lydia."

She shrugged.

"Now. What do you say to my idea?"

Lydia took a swallow from her cup and set it on the table. She got up and walked the length of the room, her hands tucked beneath her elbows.

"Do you really think you can accomplish this? What if the other buyers won't deal with a woman?"

"They'll have to. We have more product at better prices than anyone else in Philippi—thanks to you. They may balk at first, but their purses will eventually persuade their sensibilties."

"Maybe you have too much confidence in my untried abilities, Uncle."

"Maybe. But I like my chances, anyway."

"I still don't understand why you're doing this."

He stood very still, chewing his lip. "Neither do I, exactly. Maybe it has something to do with my older brother, with righting old wrongs. A wish to change something." Then, he gave her a sly look and a let out a low chuckle. "Or maybe just because it'll be fun to overhear the talk in the forum about that crazy Menippus and the upstart woman who's ruining his trade."

Lydia came home one evening as the women from the adjoining room were taking in a bolt of newly woven wool. They looked to be a mother and daughter. They had spread the fabric on the parapet during the day to let the sun dry and bleach it. As Lydia trudged up the steps, dragging Parmenes and Hermeia behind her, she saw them gathering up their work. Her eyes met those of the daughter, and the girl gave her the flicker of a smile.

Lydia looked at the cloth. Even from the distance of a few paces, she could see the weave was very tight and even.

"Hold a moment," she said, and the two women paused, looking at her. "May I see your cloth?"

The mother hesitated, then gave a quick nod. Lydia sent her children ahead of her into the room. She took the weaving between her fingers and brought it close to her eyes.

"This is good work," she said. "Very good. How much of this can you do in a day?"

While the mother was thinking, her daughter said, "May I go and speak to your little girl?"

"Agatha. Don't be forward," the mother cautioned.

"No, it's all right," Lydia answered. "Her name is Hermeia. She's nine years old. I think she'd like that, very much."

The girl smiled at Lydia and her mother as she went to Lydia's doorway. With a concerned expression, the woman watched her daughter leave.

"I should introduce myself. My name is Lydia. I'm interested in your cloth because I buy and sell dyed goods." She still felt a small, gratifying thrill when she said the words. "I'm always looking for cloth of the highest quality, and yours is some of the best I've seen. I think we'd—I'd like to buy as much of this sort of work as possible. Would you be interested in selling to me?"

The woman plucked nervously at the front of her chiton. "Well, I…Of course, we need to sell as much as we can, but…I ought to talk to—"

"Talit? Who's there? Whom are you speaking to?"

Lydia heard the sound of a stick tapping against brick, and an old, stooped, blind man appeared, feeling his way slowly through the doorway of the room. His beard and the hair straying from beneath his small, round cap were very white.

"Is this the woman from next door?" he asked.

"Yes, Father Seleucus," the woman said. "This is—" She looked at Lydia, putting a hand to her chest. "I'm sorry. Please forgive me. My name is Talit, and this is my husband's father, Seleucus. This is Lydia." She turned toward her father-in-law and put out a hand to guide him toward her. "She says she buys cloth."

"Oh? Well, that's good, then, isn't it? It just so happens we sell cloth." He chuckled softly, ending in a little cough. "Yes, we sell it, don't we?"

"This is some of the finest weaving I've seen," Lydia said. "I was just saying to Talit that I'm always looking for cloth of this quality. How much can you sell to me?"

"Oh, my, well, she doesn't waste any time, does she?" Seleucus rubbed his hand on his robe. "Doesn't waste any time. I—"

"Father."

The voice came from behind Lydia, at the base of the steps. She turned, and two men stood there: one about Talit's age and the other, from his looks, the older brother of the girl Agatha.

"Ah. Clement and Esras. How was the work today, my son?" the old man asked.

The two men came up the stairs with heavy steps. Day laborers, Lydia judged from their dusty, fatigued appearances. A hard way to make any sort of living.

"Could have been worse," the younger one said. "Today we were builders."

"Brick-donkeys, you mean," said Clement with a wry grin at his son.

Lydia moved aside to let them pass. The husband gave her a polite nod. Clement took his wife in a quick embrace, then the same to his father. Esras repeated the greetings. Lydia heard the clink of coins. The old man ran his fingers over the money in his palm.

"Well. Enough to buy another day's bread, anyway."

Lydia did a quick calculation. "I'll pay you three obols and eight per cubit."

A long, thoughtful silence.

"At that price, I should learn weaving," Esras said.

"We've never gotten more than one or two obols before," said Talit quietly.

"How much can you do in a day?" Lydia asked.

"Usually, about two-and-a-half. Three, if Father's joints let him work."

"Wait." Clement was looking back and forth between his family and this woman he didn't know. "How do we know you can afford such rates? What if we agree, and let the rest of the trade go, and you suddenly change your mind? It's taken months to get where we are. Why should we risk it all on your word?"

Lydia held the man's eyes as she reached into the pouch at her belt. She felt the weight and shape of an aureus. For an instant, she let the gold coin glitter on her palm. Then she flicked it toward Clement, and he caught it in his fist. His eyes rounded as he looked in astonishment from the coin to her.

"An aureus?"

"God of Abraham be praised," Seleucus said in a soft voice. "Manna in the wilderness."

"That's enough for nearly a month's worth of cloth," Lydia said. "Call it an advance payment. Will that give you enough time to decide if I can be trusted?"

"Maybe you should come inside," Seleucus said. "Maybe we should talk."

"Why don't we go into my room?" Lydia said. "It's a little bigger." She heard the sound of Agatha's laugh from inside. "And, I think your daughter may not yet be ready to leave."

Nineteen

They were from northern Thrace, Lydia soon learned. Their village was sacked during one of the many skirmishes between the thinly spread Imperial army and the bandits who roamed the rugged mountainsides of their native country. Carrying such meager belongings as remained to them, they followed the river valleys to the Macedonian coast and eventually came to Philippi, the closest city of any size.

There was an unspoken assumption that Hermeia would stay with Agatha and her mother while Lydia was at the trading house. Even though the Jewish girl was nearly four years older than Hermeia, the two became fast friends almost immediately. Hermeia even began begging Talit to teach her to weave.

Parmenes was a bit more of a problem. While he enjoyed Agatha's easy laughter and playfulness, he was easily bored during the time—most of each day—when the girls and Talit had to busy themselves at the looms. Seleucus was as good-natured a grandfather as anyone could imagine, but he could hardly be expected to keep up with a child as active as Parmenes. So, each morning, Lydia would send Hermeia next door, then drag Parmenes, loudly protesting with every step, to the care of her uncle's servants, in the apartment above the trading house.

At sunset on the Day of Aphrodite, the beginning of the day they called "Shabbat," the Jewish family had its sacred gathering. Lydia loved to sit at her doorway and listen to the singing. When Seleucus recited from memory one of their holy stories, he did so in Hebrew. Try as Lydia might, she couldn't get any hint of the actual narrative. But it didn't matter; the sound of the language, the cadence of the words and pauses and murmured responses from the rest of the family—all of it enchanted her, expanded a peaceful space in her spirit. That such music, such language, such people could exist seemed wonderful to Lydia, for reasons she could never have explained.

Lysander wanted an answer quickly; he needed to finish disposing of his property in Philippi and make arrangements for transporting his remaining effects to his new home in Cilicia. He had been a good client of her uncle's through the years, and it was very kind of him to give her first chance at his house on Short Street.

It was spacious—larger than Lydia needed, she had to admit. But its situation was convenient: about halfway between the forum and her uncle's trading house. Actually, it was on the corner of Short Street and the Street of Palms, another fairly busy thoroughfare. And there were three rooms on the side of the house facing the Street of Palms that could be rented. One of them was already occupied by a carpet weaver who paid ten *dēnariī* per month. Lydia even had thoughts of asking Clement and his family to take one of the apartments. With what she was paying them each month for their weaving, they could afford it.

The slave at the well noticed her and bowed. For the last three days, since Lysander had approached her, she had been here almost as much as a member of the household: walking around the courtyard and imagining herself living here; imagining the colonnade as her own place to rest on a sunny afternoon; mentally measuring the rooms and refurnishing them; counting the paces from the well in the atrium to the doorway of the scullery; exulting over Lysander's foresight in building a private latrine that emptied into the city's sewer system. The well was a bit of a worry, actually; she would need to have a good, heavy cover built if Parmenes was going to live here.

The thought of having a real house, all her own, loomed large in her mind. It made her life seem less makeshift. It reassured her this was her place, her city. Lydia wanted this house. It felt right; it suggested things about her that she wanted very much to believe.

There were nearly two hundred Imperial aurei in the bag she kept in her uncle's strongbox in the vault room. From what she could gather by the talk in the forum, she ought to be able to get a well-appointed house for somewhere between one-fifty and two-twenty. The thought of giving over so much of her savings all at once made her a little short of breath. But to have this house all to herself....

"Mistress!"

Lydia turned around. It was Septimus, hurrying toward her from the gate.

"You must come to the trading house, Mistress. The master sent me to find you."

"Can you not manage for even a little while?" Her tone was sharper than she intended.

Septimus stood in front of her with his head bowed. "I humbly beg your forgiveness, Mistress. But you must come. The brother of my master is here to inspect accounts. You are needed."

"The brother...my father! My father is here? In Philippi?"

"Yes, Mistress. And now, will you please come back with me?"

"Yes...of course."

The door to the private chamber was slightly ajar. As she approached, Lydia heard her uncle's voice—then her father's.

"Your trade has increased a great deal," he was saying to Menippus. "I've been grateful for the increased payments. The money has allowed me to make improvements at the plantations."

"I owe it all to that new young trader I told you about," Menippus said.

Lydia reached out a hand, hesitated, then pushed the door open. She stepped inside.

"Ah, here she is now," Menippus said, gesturing toward her.

Her father turned and froze. From somewhere, Lydia forced a smile onto her face.

"Hello, Father. Welcome to Philippi."

"Lydia. So this is where you got off to."

"You never told him?" Menippus said, his eyebrows arching. "I would have said something immediately, but I assumed—"

"Have you found everything to your satisfaction, Father? Has Uncle shown you the pending contracts?"

Her uncle stepped between them. "Threnides, you know I wouldn't have kept such a thing—"

Her father put up a hand. "It's all right, little brother. I see how it is." He measured her with his eyes. "So. You seem to have learned the business quite well."

She folded her hands in front of her, giving him a small bow.

"Menippus was telling me this bright young person he'd discovered had devised new methods, changed the pricing of the contracts, done wonder after wonder. And all the time he was telling me about you." He shook his head. "Still running with the boys."

"Ahead of them, mostly." She kept her face down as she said it, but the lash was in her voice.

"Lydia—"

"No, Menippus. Let her speak her mind. She has been known to become…desperate…when thwarted."

Lydia felt her face warming.

"Well, I suppose I shouldn't care," her father said, moving toward the writing table and the ewer of wine waiting there. "After all, my treasury benefits from her willfulness, it seems." He poured a cup of wine and carefully added water. "I only hope her strange ways don't impair my grandchildren's chances."

"Hermeia and Parmenes are quite well, Father."

"Really? I'm glad to hear it. May I see them?"

"Parmenes is upstairs, in Uncle's apartment." Lydia forced the words through a tightening throat. "Hermeia…Hermeia stays with…some friends of mine."

"And are these friends nearby?"

"Father, I really don't think there's time for this." She willed her fingers to unclench. "And now, will there be anything else?" She looked from her father to Menippus.

Threnides shrugged, then took a long drink from his cup. Menippus spread his hands and shook his head. Lydia turned and walked slowly from the room. When the door closed behind her, she paced quickly across the trading room and out the front gate. She crossed the atrium at a half-trot. As she was going through the front gate, she chanced to remember Parmenes. She grabbed the nearest slave and told him to send her son home with one of the servants. She had some things that had to be attended to, things that had come up rather suddenly. And then she was gone.

Lydia tossed on her bed that night. Her mind was unable to turn loose of her father's words, the line of his mouth, the angle of his head as he appraised her. All this time she had fancied herself free. But now, even Philippi felt constricted, unsafe. The distance, it seemed, was no guarantee. She felt defeated, worn out.

Sometime long before dawn, Lydia got up from her bed. She walked to the doorway of her room and looked out. The city was quiet. The stars sparkled their cheery, false invitation. A sudden, frantic need rose up in her and she couldn't oppose it. Lydia whirled back inside her room, searching urgently with her hands in the darkness around her sleeping place, needing to move quickly but also needing to not wake the children. She found a cord long enough to tie around her waist. She went out-side and down the steps to the street. She twisted her chiton up between her thighs, securing it around her waist with the cord. And then she started running.

When Lydia arrived back at the base of the stairs in the graying dark, she looked up and saw the Jewish girl kneeling at the doorway of her family's apartment. Lydia released the cord holding up her garment and paced for a few moments, her hands in the small of her back, catching her breath. When she could speak in a somewhat even voice, she quietly asked the girl why she was awake so early.

"Aren't you afraid?" Agatha asked.

"Afraid of what?"

"Afraid to be out in the streets, in the dark. By yourself."

Lydia took some breaths and let them go out as slowly as she could. She looked up at the girl's huddled form.

"I was more afraid of what would happen if I didn't go."

Lydia could see Agatha's face, a grayish blur against the darker color of the blanket wrapped around her shoulders. She sat very still for a long time. Then she got up and went back inside.

The next morning, when Lydia mounted the steps to her room, Agatha was there, lying across the doorway. She stirred when Lydia came in.

"Oh. You're back."

"Why are you here, Agatha?"

"Someone needed to stay with the children."

Clement was not at all opposed to the idea of moving into the apartment in front of Lydia's new house. It was bigger than their quarters on the roof, and not much more expensive. It hadn't taken long for him to realize the truth of his son's assessment; they could make more money by helping with the woolworking than they could ever hope to scrape together as day laborers. The five of them were now supplying the trading house with nearly five bolts of good quality cloth per month. And Lydia didn't mind at all that Hermeia, whether she realized it or not, was absorbing Talit's secrets for turning out a fine, straight weave.

Lydia was pleased to find that Lysander also had a female slave he would sell along with the house. Her name was Neria, and she looked to be about Lydia's age, or slightly older, though with Nubians it was always more difficult for Lydia to tell. She had a sister who was a slave in another household nearby, and she had begged her former master to let her stay in Philippi with the house. Lydia pretended, for the sake of the final haggling, to be put off by the unexpected expense of a slave, but it was good to have someone on hand who knew the layout of the house. It was also helpful to have someone to watch Parmenes during the day. Her standing with her uncle's household servants was much improved by the change.

The Nubian woman seemed oddly attached to her. Lydia supposed it was because of her gratitude at not being separated from her sister. Neria would find a way to make almost every household task take her near Lydia. Lydia might be filling a jar from the well, and she would turn to find Neria squatted by the colonnade outside the scullery door, quietly cleaning a bowl from the previous meal. Or, she might be tending the brazier nearest the children's sleeping place in the corner of her room, and she would hear Neria's soft footsteps through the doorway, perhaps carrying in an armload of faggots to see the fire through the night.

Neria rarely spoke, and when she did it was in a soft voice, with eyes averted. But Lydia often heard her laughing with the children in the mornings, before she left for the trading house. Her service seemed so agreeable, Lydia sometimes wondered if it was mere coincidence that had placed the black woman in her household.

The Jewish family's day of Shabbat was becoming for Lydia a longed-for respite in the scurry of each week. She had long since dispensed with lurking near the doorway; now she sat in the room with the family as they sang and prayed to their formless, nameless god. They even allowed her to accompany them when they went to the place on the riverbank where they sometimes worshipped.

Lydia was amazed to discover that some of their sacred writings had been rendered in Greek. On the night after she first heard Esras read from one of the handful of precious scrolls the family owned—the words of a prophet they called Amos—she could no more sleep than she could fly. The thundering pronouncements of doom for the nations that had oppressed the Jewish people rang in her ears like a hammer on an anvil. And this jealous, angry god would not spare even his own favored people, the prophet asserted. Amos rained down curses on them for violating the laws of hospitality and decency that their god had given them generations before, in a time, to hear Seleucus tell it, when giants still walked on the land and rivers and mountains still lay unnamed.

The sheer ancientness of the Jewish legends captured Lydia's mind. By their reckoning, the Jews' earliest forefathers arose thousands of years before anything dreamed by Homer. Why, by the time Homer happened along, the old blind Jew told her, there were kings in Israel who held under tribute all the lands from the Mediterranean Sea to the distant frontiers east of the Tigris and Euphrates rivers: kings whose palaces gleamed with gold and shone with ivory, whose gardens echoed with the call of exotic animals and birds.

And yet, he sadly went on, all this splendor and strength amounted to nothing, once the kings and people of Israel began ignoring the commands of their god. Within a few generations, they were reduced to slavery in a foreign land, just as their ancestors had been, ages before. Everything threatened by Amos and the other prophets had been carried out against the nation, he said, because the people would not heed, nor turn from the wickedness of their ways.

Though breathtaking in its scope and gripping in its

poignancy, the lore of the Jews was still very strange to Lydia. How could a single god so captivate and define a people? Even Athens, the city of Athena, was crowded with altars and temples for all the gods of the Greeks, and many of the gods of Asia Minor and the Parthians, as well. Yet this Jewish god, who had no proper image or cult that Lydia had ever seen, had such a grip on the people that they interpreted even the dissolution of their nation as a just punishment rather than a failure or weakness of their deity. She began to realize that the Jews understood their history less as a series of tales about the deeds of heroes and kings than as a tally of the ways they pleased or displeased their god.

"Why do you have no temple or holy place in which to worship?" she asked Seleucus one evening.

"Ah, but we do. The Temple of Herod in Jerusalem is one of the most amazing structures in the world—I've heard even Romans say so. I've never seen it, of course. I had hoped one day to go there, to be in Jerusalem at the great Feast of the Passover. But I'm too old and blind, now. I'll never make it."

"Only one temple? For all the Jews, everywhere in the world?"

"Yes. Only one. But you should have seen our little synagogue in Carpaeum—that was our village, in Thrace. It wasn't at all grand, no precious stones or gold, nothing of that sort. But it was clean. And one of the men in our minyan had some skill as a painter of pictures, and the walls—ah! It was a fine place to be on Shabbat, I tell you." He leaned back against the wall, remembering. His smile slowly faded. "It's gone now, of course. Burned to the ground, like the rest of the village."

"But, still, Father Seleucus, I don't understand how you can worship your god without a temple, and altars, and sacrifices."

He closed his eyes. For a moment, Lydia thought he had fallen asleep.

"'But will God really dwell on earth?'" he said finally, in a low, musing voice. "'The heavens, even the highest heaven, cannot contain you. How much less this temple I have built! Yet give attention to your servant's prayer and his plea for mercy, O LORD my God. Hear the cry and the prayer that your servant is praying in your presence this day. May your eyes be open toward this temple night and day, this place of which you said, "My Name shall be there," so that you will hear the prayer your servant prays toward this place.'"

He opened his eyes. His blind, unguided orbs tumbled this way and that. "Part of the prayer of Solomon, the greatest king of our people, when he built the Temple. The first one." He sighed. "It's gone now, too. For a long time."

Lydia hugged her knees to her chest. She looked into the fire, slowly dying in the brazier.

"I don't understand a god who is so careless about his temples," she said, more to herself than to Seleucus.

"Ah, but do you still not comprehend, little Lydia, after all you've heard?" said the old man in a breathy voice that sounded like a plea. "The temple doesn't contain him. He contains it."

Lydia felt a warm place, deep in the middle of her chest. The old man's words sounded almost like something Menander might have said.

Her footfalls pattered back at her from the walls on either side as she ran down the alley between the north side of the forum and the rear walls of the large houses that fronted on the Via Egnatia. The early winter air was chill, but at least there was no wind. The stars gave all the light Lydia needed to negotiate the route that had become so familiar.

She came out of the alley into New Street, starting the final leg of her course. This was a wide, straight thoroughfare, built by Imperial labor crews during the early days of the colony. Though it was one of the older thoroughfares in Philippi, it was the newest when it was built, and for some reason the name had stuck all these years. Houses of some of the oldest Roman settler families lined the street on both sides; many of the residents were regular patrons of the trading house. Ornate archways, some surmounted with Latin inscriptions and family mottos, adorned the gates of the houses and villas. She needed to learn to read Latin. Surely Menippus knew someone who would be willing to tutor her. Maybe one of their customers owned a skilled pedagogue or *grammaticus* he would be willing to lend or hire out.

Lydia heard a sound behind her. She felt a little thrill of fear along her spine. She had never encountered anyone or anything during this time between night and dawn. Should she turn and look, or was it best to keep going? Her house was not far.

The opening of an alley appeared, between the walls of two villas. On an impulse, Lydia ducked into the narrow space. She thought she remembered that this alley connected New Street with Short Street, not far from her gate. She increased her pace.

She heard the sound behind her, at the mouth of the alley. By now there was no mistaking the sound of pursuing feet. Lydia's throat went dry; her breath sawed in and out of her with a quick, whimpering sound.

The end of the alley rushed toward her, and to Lydia's horror the dim starlight revealed a blank wall, twice her height, barring the way. Her head spun around. Her pursuer was maybe a stone's throw away, coming steadily at a run. Lydia sprinted toward the wall. With a cry, she hurled herself upward, grasping desperately for a finger- or toehold. Her chin smashed into the stone of the wall and she fell in a heap. She sprang to her feet, her back to the wall, watching the figure break stride, slowing to a walk, coming toward her with a deliberate, knowing pace. Lydia gathered herself for a scream.

"Don't be afraid," the figure said.

A woman's voice. The figure reached toward her, and the sleeve of her cloak fell away. The skin of her arm was a deeper dark in the blackness of the predawn.

Twenty

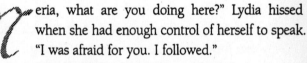

eria, what are you doing here?" Lydia hissed
when she had enough control of herself to speak.
"I was afraid for you. I followed."

"You nearly frightened me to death."

Neria bowed her head. "I should have been more careful.
I'm sorry, Mistress."

"How long have you been running behind me?"

"Since the second night."

"The second night I had the house?"

Neria nodded, her face still lowered.

"You've been following me all this time, and I just now
heard you?"

"I should have been more careful," the Nubian mumbled.

"How fast could you run if you weren't trying to be quiet?"

Neria shrugged.

Lydia felt a laugh bubbling up inside her. The last traces of
her fright and anger dissolved in amusement at this surprising,
loyal, apparently quite sturdy slave woman. Neria peered at her
curiously, then worriedly, as she kept laughing. Lydia wanted to

explain, to reassure her, but she couldn't stop laughing. She finally managed to rein herself in and gave Neria a sidelong, appraising look. "Well, let's find out, what do you say?"

The black woman tilted her face in confusion.

"Shall we have a race to the front gate? I presume you know the way."

Neria looked at her for a long time before the smile started. And when it did, it was big and broad. She nodded.

"Go!" Lydia said, and they sprinted the length of the alley. They turned the corner and whirled away down New Street in a flashing of legs and outflung arms.

Hermeia, faithful wife of Livius of Thessalonica, to Crescens, my dear friend whom I love as a father: Greetings.

Your couriers reached me on the third after the twentieth of last month. I have read your words about my mother, and I have considered very carefully within myself as to what I should do. I am at war with myself, dear friend, and I confess to you that even as I begin to write this letter I do not know what answer I will give.

You judge truly, of course, that as a dutiful child, I should attend my mother's sickbed. But you cannot understand, beloved Crescens, how the thought of her afflicts me....

Lydia let the parchment fall through her fingers. She turned her face to one side and stared out the window into the morning as it broadened into day. An affliction. She was an affliction to her daughter. Why should she bother to read any more?

She looked at the parchment in her lap. With the backs of her fingers, she slowly stroked the letter. She smoothed it out flat in her lap and stroked the firm, curved characters made by her daughter, tracing with a fingertip the graceful track of Hermeia's writing. Hermeia had developed a fine hand. She must write many letters. Was that how she spent her days?

Maybe she was a gracious, respected lady who entertained the wives of her husband's friends. Maybe her house was calm and well ordered; maybe she moved serenely among well-tended gardens, where ivy climbed the colonnades and the smell of mint and thyme soothed the senses. Maybe she had a servant who was skilled with the *kithara* or the pipes, one who sang to Hermeia as she drowsed in the shade during the heat of the afternoon. Maybe her daughters brought their children to her; maybe she showed the boys how to rob the nectar from honeysuckles. Maybe she taught the girls to plait garlands from the blossoms of clover.

How many great-grandchildren did Lydia have by this time? Had Hermeia ever mentioned her to them? Probably not. Why should she?

A spasm tore at her abdomen. Lydia's eyes squeezed shut as she clenched her jaw against the pain. Always busy, always moving. Moving where? Had she ever stopped long enough to ask herself?

Paul had known. He had seen, hadn't he? The morning she came back to find him already awake and pacing in the atrium, she stopped, her hand on the gate latch, and watched him as he stalked the length of the courtyard. He wheeled and came back the other way. He nearly bumped into her before he saw her. He pulled up short, looking at her in surprise. Hastily, she undid the belt that held her skirts out of the way for running.

"Where have you been?"

"I—I run in the early mornings." She was oddly embarrassed to admit it to him. Why?

"It's still dark."

"Yes. That's the best time, I think." A pause, as he kept watching her. "I don't go alone. Several other women join me, usually."

"To run?"

She nodded.

"Are you training for a race?"

"No, not really."

"What, then?"

She coiled the belt in her hands and slowly smoothed the front of her chiton. "I don't know, really. Only…because I must."

He was looking at her in that unblinking, disturbing way he had. She squared her shoulders and returned his stare.

"Why are you pacing my courtyard at such an hour?" she asked.

His eyes widened a little, then softened around the edges. A tiny, guilty smile sidled onto his face. "Because I must."

She turned her head slightly and gave him a sidelong look. "And what are you training for?"

"A race, of sorts. I suppose."

She heard the sudden longing in his voice, and it saddened and lifted her, all at once. Neither of them moved or spoke. The moment stretched between them, absorbed in the knowing and the not knowing.

"Shall we take some refreshment, then?" she asked, finally. "There are fresh pears and apricots in the larder, and some good cheese."

He gave a quick nod and a tiny bow, and she went into the kitchen. Lydia put some fruit and cheese in a bowl while Paul drew a pail of water up from the well. He filled two cups, and they went back into the atrium. They set the food and water in the center of one of the stone benches and seated themselves on either side. Lydia selected a pear of just the right greenish yellow shade, and Paul scooped a palmful of soft, white cheese. They ate and watched the slow brightening of dawn.

"So...which kind of running do you do?" he asked.

"What do you mean? How many different kinds are there?"

"Two, that I can think of. Running to and running from."

Lydia studied the pear. "Can a person do both, do you think?"

"I suppose so."

A long quiet passed.

"You teach that the Christ came to bring us to God," she said in a low, thinking voice. "That by believing in him we can be saved. How long before the saving comes? When does it start, and how can we know?"

He picked up an apricot and popped it whole into his mouth, chewed a moment, then cupped his palm to his lips and spat out the pit.

"It has already begun in you, Lydia. It began the moment you believed, and it will continue in you as long as you hold to your faith and live as a child of the light."

"Why then does the darkness still seem so real?"

"Ah. So it *is* running from."

"Sometimes." She got up from the bench and paced toward the kitchen, then back. "Mostly, maybe. Don't you ever run from anything?"

"Yes, I suppose I do, sometimes. But I try not to. I try to leave behind what's past, and move forward toward the destination God has given me."

"And how far away is that?"

"Of that, I'm not sure. But I think I must keep going anyway."

She walked back over to the bench and sat down. "Maybe

that's all any of us can do—keep pushing forward. But don't you sometimes wish you knew how much farther you had to go? How much effort to spend and how much to save? Don't you wish you knew exactly where the finish line was?"

He chuckled and nodded. "I confess it, yes. But the Christ gives me enough strength for each day. So far, at least, that's been enough."

He met her in the atrium nearly every morning after that. Sometimes they barely said a word to each other, sitting on the stone bench and taking an early breakfast, sharing the solitude of their private thoughts. Other times he spoke to her of the Christ. He talked about sin and righteousness, law and grace. Lydia had never known grace as anything other than a word people used when meeting in the street or the forum. But when Paul talked of grace, he spoke of the plans God had laid since the beginnings of time, plans to restore humanity to its place by his side. His words sounded like the talk of philosophers, but he spoke with such certainty: not as if he were spinning webs of suppositions, but as if he was trying to get his hands around something he had glimpsed, something he needed more than anything to put into words.

Lydia thought sometimes he was talking more to himself than to her. But it didn't matter; his talk gave her mind a peaceful place to stroll, a place where all the past hurts and mistakes didn't lie in wait for her at every turn. And that itself would have been enough to earn him her gratitude.

Then there was the morning when she let herself back in at the gate and saw him sitting on the ground in the middle of the atrium, his back to her.

She smiled. "Not all of the benches are taken, just yet. Why don't you use one of them?"

He didn't answer.

"Paul?"

No response—no movement.

"Are you well?" She went over to him and knelt in front of him. His face was slack, his eyes staring. His mouth hung open in a rigid position, as if frozen in the midst of a grimace. He was drooling like a helpless child.

"Paul! What's the matter? Paul!"

She shook him, but he made no response; no recognition flickered behind his eyes. Lydia dashed into the main hall, to the corner where Luke slept.

"Luke! Come quickly! Something's wrong with Paul."

The physician stirred sleepily and sat up, rubbing his face. "Paul? Oh…yes. Never mind, I know what to do."

Paul had these episodes every once in a great while, Luke later told her. They had started as the result of some great vision or dream, many years ago. They came without warning: in the middle of a busy street, as he lay asleep in his bed, when he was speaking or writing a letter. They vexed him deeply, and he forbade his companions to mention them. Even the physician was not permitted to speak of the seizures. All that could be done was to make Paul comfortable until the fit passed, which it usually did in less time than it takes a small lamp to burn all its oil, he told her. And then, they must all pretend as if nothing had happened.

We all have our afflictions, don't we, Paul? Lydia thought as she looked at Hermeia's letter. And none of us admit them too readily. She took up the parchment.

As long as I can remember, dear Crescens, I have been confused by my mother. I am an old woman myself now, with grand-children of my own, and still my heart is led strangely by thoughts of her. I suppose I love her, and yet the love is mingled with all the painful memories that lead, by one path or another, back to her.

I think you will remember the family of Jews who lived in one of the apartments in the front of our house. Maybe they're still there. These were the people I stayed with each day while Mother went to work in the trading house. She thought I liked being there because of Agatha, the daughter who was a few years older than I. She thought I spent all those days carding wool and weaving because of the friend-ship between us. But I now know that was wrong. I loved Agatha, it is true. But the real reason I stayed with them was to watch and listen to how a mother and daughter behave toward one another: the things they talk about, the ways they teach each other what it means to become a woman, what it meant to have been a girl. I never learned that from my mother, Crescens. From my very earliest memory, she was too busy escaping her own hurts to recog-nize my need for her. And I was too young to understand how to tell her, or how to separate her woundedness from some undiscovered flaw of my own. My brother's death, too, became one more reason for silence between us, a silence that taught me to doubt my own worth. It was a terrible burden for a young girl to bear, especially when she didn't own the words, even the thoughts, to explain it to herself, much less anyone else.

Lydia closed her eyes. The memory came, sliding into its accustomed place in her mind with the familiarity of an old adversary.

Neria started the unpleasantness innocently enough by saying something to her sister, who served a household nearby. The matron of that house, Euodia by name, was indignant that any self-respecting woman would run through the streets like a common harlot. "Of course," she would explain, "I wouldn't put anything past this Thyatiran. I hear she goes to her trading house every day to buy and sell, just like the men."

Euodia widely advertised her indignation, but it had a result she would never have suspected. Before long, Lydia and Neria were being greeted by one or two cautious figures waiting in the shadows near her gate in the darkness just before dawn. Then, one or two more. Would she let them run with her? they wanted to know. They didn't want anyone to find out, but.... Before long, Lydia found herself at the head of a pack of ten or twelve female runners. When she stopped to consider it, she was astounded. She had never imagined her regimen as anything other than her own way of staking a claim to at least the beginning of each day.

Then she began to notice the change in the manner of some of her customers. Men she had been conducting business with suddenly became ill at ease in her presence. They fretted and shied like cats caught in a downpour. They wouldn't answer her questions; they treated her every request for explanation like an accusation. She finally put it all together the day a customer abruptly turned and stalked out of the trading house, flinging over his shoulder that he had no more time to waste on a woman who wasn't content with shaving away an honest merchant's profits, but also talked his wife into parading herself through the streets every morning at an hour when decent women were in bed with their husbands.

If her trade hadn't been so well established, it might have ruined her. She wanted to talk to Menippus about it, but his health was poor lately, and she was afraid this might make him worse. She had certainly never intended to be a point of contention between the men of Philippi and their wives. And yet, the thought of abandoning her morning exercises made her angry. Why should some petulant husband force her to choose between her livelihood and her self-nourishment? She kept coming to work each day as if nothing were amiss and kept running every morning as if her life depended on it.

In the end, she was never certain whether her good pricing brought them back, or whether it was that year's disastrous madder crop, combined with the stockpiles of dried root in her storage vaults. It might even have had something to do with a pointed comment she made one morning to some of her running companions. However it was, the traders began returning with guarded, sometimes sheepish, expressions and asking whether they might still have the terms they had been used to before. That was as close as any of them ever came to talking about the disagreement.

Lydia heard from her servants, later, that there was some persistent muttering in the forum about "that pack of bacchantes," but in the trading house the men of Philippi approached her with courtesy at least, if not their former amiability. And the women kept coming in the mornings.

Surviving the ire of the men of Philippi refreshed her, made her feel invincible. She decided to accelerate the course she had lately begun, of steering the house's trade almost entirely toward finished purple goods. The others could keep selling the dye and the woven stock to each other, if they wanted. It was too complicated, maintaining two kinds of pricing for two different types of customers. Besides, the real profits were in the long bolts of richly hued wools and linens so coveted by the wealthy families of Philippi and the other cities of Macedonia. Let the *bouleutēs* and decurions pass their ordinances and carve their names above the doorways of the temples and public buildings; their wives would never let them hear the end of it if they didn't get their finery. And they would be willing to pay for the quality they thought they deserved. Lydia knew that more certainly now than ever before.

Menippus had retired more and more from the daily operation of the business. Still, Lydia thought she ought to consult with him on her decision, if only to ask his blessing.

She went up the stairs to his apartment. He rarely came down to the working areas anymore. The private chamber off the trading room was still kept for his use, but she couldn't remember the last time she'd seen her uncle in there. A serving woman answered her knock. The woman had a worried look on her face.

"Please tell my uncle I'm here to see him."

She scurried away and returned only moments later. Lydia watched her coming, alternately looking back over her shoulder and shaking her head.

"The physician says no one is permitted to see the master."

"Physician? If my uncle is so ill, why wasn't I told?"

The slave woman stood still, her face down.

"Take me to him, at once!"

"Mistress, I just—"

"You let me worry about the physician. I will see my uncle immediately."

The woman gave her the smallest possible bow and led the way to Menippus's chamber. Long before she got there, Lydia smelled the strong, acrid odor of burning asafetida. When she came to the doorway of her uncle's room, she saw him stretched on a couch and another person huddled beside him. The asafetida was smoking in a large clay bowl beside the couch. Her uncle's face was a sickly, yellow color. Lydia covered her mouth with her hand as she quickly knelt beside him.

Menippus slowly turned his face toward her. "Ah, Lydia. You've outrun everyone else in Philippi, and now you've come to challenge your poor, old uncle."

She forced a smile. "Uncle! I hoped you hadn't heard about all that silliness. I didn't want to bother you. I heard you were—ill."

"True enough," he said with a weak smile.

"I instructed that woman to allow no one in here." The physician glared across the couch at her, then at the slave, who wilted in the doorway.

"I ordered her to bring me to my uncle."

"Peace, Phiteles. This is my brother's daughter. I'm glad she's here."

The physician busied himself with the smoking bowl, grumbling under his breath.

"Why didn't you send for me sooner?" Lydia asked, taking Menippus's cold hand in both of hers. "I've been busy, but you know I would have come immediately—"

"Of course, of course," he said. "I had hoped to spare you this a little while yet, but…."

"Spare me what?"

"Your leaving Thyatira when you did was no mere chance. Ever since you came to Philippi, I have known that some god or fate brought you to me, so that when my time came—"

"What are you talking about, Uncle?"

"Lydia, I'm dying. I've known it since just before your arrival. Phiteles here has done everything in his power to slow the progress of the disease, but he is only human, after all."

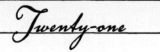

ydia stared at the man on the other side of the couch, then at her uncle. "Dying? But—"

"And you have proved out just as I would have wished," Menippus went on. "No, better. I can die, knowing my house and people are in competent hands."

"Uncle—"

"And, there is this. It pleases me—ah!" A sudden pain caught him and he sank back on his couch. His eyes clenched shut and his breath became a shallow, quick panting.

"Is there nothing you can do?" Lydia asked the physician. "He's in pain!"

Phiteles put a hand on her uncle's forehead. With the other, he tightly gripped Menippus's free hand. Lydia noticed that his fingers were long and slender, almost feminine. He gently stroked her uncle's forehead and face.

"He has taken scarcely anything but poppy resin for the last week," Phiteles explained. "There is little other comfort I can give him." His eyes never left the face of his patient. Lydia instantly forgave the physician's brusque manner.

As the spasm eased, Menippus leaned closer to her. "It pleases me that my brother will have to reckon with you."

Lydia had her uncle's favorite cup buried with him. She had his body dressed in a robe of purple linen, trimmed in gold. She paid for mourners and musicians to follow the casket through the streets and down the middle of the forum, then up to the interment site on the slope of Mount Orbelos. She amended his will to provide a yearly stipend for food and drink to be taken to the grave.

On the day after the funeral, Lydia went into the trading house. She stopped the first servant she saw and told him to call Septimus to her. "I'll be in the private chamber," she said. She paused long enough to see the slave's eyes widen in surprise. Then she turned and walked away.

When Septimus came in, she was seated behind the ebony writing table. She saw the way his eyes flickered toward her, then away. His head was lowered in the customary, deferential way, but she saw his jaw clench and unclench.

"Septimus, you have served my uncle well for many years," she said. "I want you to have the apartment to use as your own residence, for as long as you need it."

The old slave's face jerked up in a startled look. "My master's—you're giving it to me?"

She nodded, smiling. "If that would please you."

He stared at her. It was the longest time he had ever looked directly at her. Lydia waited, enjoying his perplexity.

"Mistress, I—I don't know what to say. This is...most unexpected."

"Why don't you just say 'thank you'?"

Instead, he dropped to his knees on the other side of the table. "I am your humble servant, Mistress."

"Please rise, Septimus. Now, then. I want to know how much dye we have on hand, ready for use, and how much root we have that can be processed within the next few days. I also need to know how much undyed cloth we have in inventory, and how long it will take our dyers to process it into finished purple goods."

Septimus nodded.

"I intend to sell only finished goods. From now on, we won't be furnishing other dyers with raw cloth, dye, madder root, or anything else."

"That may upset some of your uncle's—some of your colleagues. They've grown accustomed—"

"Never mind that. They'll adjust, or not, as may be. We have a more reliable supply of product than any house in Philippi—maybe in all northern Macedonia. I think we can take better advantage of that strength than we have."

Septimus bowed and turned to leave.

"Oh, and Septimus. If anyone comes to buy raw cloth or root—send him in here to me. And have one of the servants bring me a fresh amphora of wine, a pitcher of water, and several cups—the bronze ones with the silver rims, not the clay. I may have several interviews today."

The old slave bowed again, but not before she saw his smile.

That night, she dreamed of Felix. The old slave stood in the doorway of her house in Thyatira, and three ravens perched on the wall above his head. He was looking at her and speaking, but Lydia couldn't understand the words. She realized he was speaking in Hebrew. She tried to tell him to talk plain Greek, but her own voice was muffled and unclear to her, as if the air around her head were filled with drifts of wool. Felix stood in a puddle of purple dye, holding an empty bowl. He raised it to his face and Lydia could hear the beginnings of one of the Hebrew songs, but the words and the sound were distorted by the bowl. Why wouldn't he put down the bowl and speak plainly to her?

She felt herself growing more angry and disturbed, but her feet wouldn't move her toward him. Then the ravens began calling to each other in squawks that sounded like brittle laughter. They flew up from their perch and shattered in midair into a thousand tiny shards of black that turned to purple as they fell about her like drops of rain. Her hands, her arms, and her face were spattered with purple. She looked up, and Felix was gone.

Lydia woke with a keen pang of loss in her chest. She was thinking of Menander, and for the first time in many months, his memory brought her to tears. She got up and dressed herself for running. She glanced out her window at the stars. It was probably too early yet for the other women to be gathered, but she didn't care. Today, she needed the cleansing of solitary exertion.

A man approached her as she was leaving her house to go to work. Was she the woman who owned the house, the one with the three rooms on the front? Was she willing to rent the remaining room? He was a leatherworker and his name was Crescens, he said. He had a good trade, he assured her. The carpet weaver in the middle apartment told him the room was servants' quarters, but said the woman who owned the house might let it, just the same.

"Marcus talks a lot," Lydia said, shaking her head. "What else did he tell you?"

Crescens smiled and ducked his face. More than he wanted to know, certainly. He would be able to pay on time each month, and his family would be no trouble at all, he went on. The place they were staying, on one of the narrow, crooked streets of the old Thasian mining settlement east of the forum, was small and crowded. His wife was most eager to move to more comfortable surroundings. And on a better street, he could make even more money, most likely. Would she please consider letting him move into one of her rooms?

She had been letting Neria and some of her other serving women sleep in the untenanted room, but the rental income would be welcome. The slave women could always sleep in a corner of the dining hall or the kitchen.

"The rate is eight dēnariī per month. Are you still interested?"

"Well...yes, I—Are you sure? Eight?"

"What did Marcus say?"

He looked crestfallen. "Ten."

"I charge Marcus more for putting up with his constant jabber."

Crescens laughed out loud. Lydia liked the sound; his voice had a ring to it, a clear resonance. He had a broad, round face and a wide, deep chest. His arms hung like a tradesman's: long, wiry, with muscles bunched tight in his forearms, angled at the elbows, even when he was standing erect. His hands and knuckles wore the nicks and scars of someone who spent his days cutting thick hides and sewing with rawhide string and sharp awls.

"Now, Crescens, you don't do tanning, do you?"

"Oh, no. All my goods are cured before I bring them into my shop. No smelly brine vats, nothing like that."

"Good. Eight, then?"

He smiled. "Done. Eight. Ten if I talk too much to suit you."

It was Lydia's turn to laugh.

"When can we move in?"

"As soon as you like. I'll have my servants clear out all their things."

Crescens quickly proved a welcome addition to her little community. He was always sitting in his doorway by the time the sun was up, fashioning a strap for a pair of sandals or putting the final touches on a set of the hobnail boots favored by the soldiers at the garrison. He displayed his finished products on a wooden rack just outside the doorway, and there was hardly a time during the day when at least one prospective purchaser wasn't eyeing Crescens' wares. The leatherworker greeted Hermeia each morning when she made her way around the corner from the gate of the house to the entry of Clement's apartment, where she spent her days working the looms with Agatha and her mother. Like everyone else, Lydia's daughter soon came to enjoy the easy smile and deep-throated, musical laughter of the busy artisan.

Seleucus took ill on the same day the first grayish blue bank of winter clouds moved in over the northwestern flanks of Mount Orbelos. For days on end, the old Jew lay under stacks of blankets on his pallet near the brazier and coughed with a wet, wheezing sound. Agatha and Talit brought him broths of onion and garlic and held his head while he sipped. Each day, Lydia hurried home from the trading house and sat beside him, talking gaily of things about the Jewish religion she wanted him to explain as soon as he was better. As she talked, she did her best to keep the dread out of her voice.

On the night he died, Lydia and the rest of the family were sitting by his pallet. It was days since he'd had the strength to speak, longer since he'd been able to swallow even the weak broths they made for him. The fire in the brazier crumbled toward embers. In the dull glow, Lydia could see the shadows in their faces as they huddled around him, listening to the halting, raspy sound of his shallow breathing.

Hermeia sat beside her, unable to take her eyes off the sunken, pale face of the old man. At each pause in Seleucus's weak breathing, her hand would tighten on Lydia's arm. The breaths became fainter and fainter, slower and slower. At last, sometime in the watches just past the middle of the night, Seleucus made a sound like a sigh, or the final, deep breath a child takes when dropping off to sleep. Then he breathed no more.

"The LORD gives, and the LORD takes away. Blessed be the name of the LORD." It was Clement's voice, low and toneless in the near dark. He leaned forward and brushed the backs of his fingers on his father's cheek. Agatha began sobbing quietly into her mother's chest. When Hermeia saw her friend's grief, she started to cry, also.

"He never got to Jerusalem," said Esras.

"I wish we could at least send his bones," said Agatha, wiping her eyes with the back of her hand.

"Send his bones? How is that done?" Lydia asked.

"Sometimes, we dig up the bones of the dead, after…after a time," Clement explained. "We put them in caskets and rebury them. I've known families who sent the bones of their dead to Jerusalem for burial. But it's a long way, and it costs too much."

"I'll pay for it," Lydia said.

"Oh, I could never ask you to—"

"You aren't asking. I'm offering."

Clement looked at Talit, then at her. "Lydia, you've done so much already. Our family owes you—"

"You owe me nothing. Clement, I humbly ask you to let me perform this service for Father Seleucus."

He didn't answer, but Lydia saw the look on Agatha's face, and for now, that was enough.

She didn't go running that morning. She sent word to the trading house that Septimus should tend her customers. Lydia stayed with the Jewish family to watch and help as she could while they prepared Seleucus's body for burial. First, they lit two lamps and placed one at Seleucus's head and one at his feet. They carefully washed the corpse and anointed it with oil. Then, Clement and Esras wrapped the body in strips of clean linen, starting with the feet. They wrapped each limb separately, then bound his head. Lydia felt a catch in her throat when, just before wrapping the linen over his father's face, Clement bent and kissed his forehead.

Lydia sent runners to a spice seller she knew and had them bring back bales of dried aloe, cakes of myrrh, bundles of dried mint. Talit and Agatha spread the sweet-smelling mixture over the body before wrapping it in a final layer of linen, binding together the limbs and completely enfolding the figure from head to toe.

Often while they labored over the body, one or another of the family members would intone a slow, rhythmic chorus in the Hebrew tongue. Clement sometimes recited some words in Hebrew, to which the others would make the one-word answer, "Amen." They told Lydia the word's rough meaning was, "Let it be so."

Amen. The word rolled around in Lydia's mind as she

watched them give the last, tender service to their beloved one; as she followed them on the slow walk out of town and up the hillside to the burial place; as she watched Esras and Clement dig a hole in the flinty, gray slope, in an unclaimed space among the markers of the other dead. Let it be so. Even death could be borne with composure and faith. The departure, the permanent absence of the wise and patient Seleucus—a loving father, a kind and generous grandfather—could be, after all, woven into the fabric of life. Let it be so. Though it wound them, though it drag them through an empty place inhabited only by dull, grinding hurt, let it be so. Their God waited for them, they supposed, somewhere on the other side of the hurt, or maybe in its midst. They were willing to make even this dreary trek, if somehow it brought them to a holy place. Let it be so. Amen. Who were these people? Who was their God? What had taught them such hope in the face of the end of all hope?

When the hole was deep and wide enough, Clement and his son passed ropes beneath the bound corpse. Lying on the ground beside the freshly dug grave, Seleucus's linen-wrapped figure looked like a huge cocoon, waiting for springtime. The two men grunted as they moved the body closer to the edge of the grave. They straddled the hole they had dug and let the body down into the ground. When it was settled at the bottom, each member of the family picked up a handful of soil and dropped it into the grave. It made a hollow, muffled pattering as it hit the corpse.

Clement turned to Lydia. "Do you want to help us give him back to the dust?"

"I thought—the family…."

Clement gave her a tired smile. "I think he thought of you that way."

Lydia walked slowly to the pile of dirt and rocks. She took up a handful and stood over the grave. She unclenched her fist and let the dirt and small chips of rock drain away through her fingers. She looked down into the grave. The small scatterings of dirt made a sharp contrast against the clean, white linen wrapping, even in the shadow of the deep hole.

Clement closed his eyes and raised his arms toward the overcast sky. "Blessed is the LORD, the king of the universe."

"Amen," his family answered.

"Blessed and praised be the great name of the LORD throughout the world which he has created according to his will. May he establish his kingdom in our lifetime."

"May his holy name be forever blessed."

"Blessed, praised, glorified, and exalted be the name of the Holy One, far beyond all the blessings and hymns and praises that are ever spoken in the world."

"Amen."

"May there be peace from heaven and life for all Israel."

"Amen."

"May the Holy One, blessed be he, create peace for us and for all Israel."

"Amen."

Clement bowed his head and lowered his arms. "May the Holy One, blessed be he, preserve the soul of our father Seleucus, son of Yehudah, and raise him up again in the day of Messiah."

This was delivered in a near whisper, and there was no response from the others. For several moments, the only sound was the wind brushing past the grave markers on its way toward the town walls.

Clement raised his face and turned toward them. "It's getting colder. Talit, you, Agatha, and Lydia should go back. Esras and I can finish here."

Talit and Agatha began picking their way down the slope toward the town. Lydia started with them, then stopped and turned around. Clement and Esras were shoveling earth into the grave. In the sky just over the shoulder of Mount Orbelos, a dark bird wheeled back and forth across the face of the breeze.

"When they've covered him well with a blanket of earth, they'll start carrying stones to put on top of him," came Talit's voice at her elbow.

"Stones?"

"To discourage the animals. Even with a good, deep grave, sometimes...."

They stood and watched the men work for a moment longer, then went down the slope.

Lydia was surprised and confused by the depth of her sadness. After all, Seleucus was well over seventy years of age; death at such a time was surely not entirely unexpected. But however she tried to explain it to herself, still she felt the old man's dying as a personal disaster, a ripping away. Or maybe her despair over the old Jew's passing was joined in some way to the loss of Menippus. Maybe loss was revisited at each sundering; maybe it brought another hungry guest each time it came calling.

In the mornings that winter, Lydia woke early and wrapped her legs and arms in wool to stave off the deepening chill. Once outside, she ran ferociously, as if she were trying to punish the streets, or her body, or both. The other women couldn't hope to keep up with her. Even the fleet and hard-bodied Neria could barely manage the angry pace set by her mistress.

Lydia threw herself at her business. She arrived early and stayed late. She constantly roved the trading house. She paced around the rendering vats, stalked the counting room, the warehouses. She inspected the contracts, the counting-room records, the dye storage urns. She questioned her servants about everything they did. She ordered the cedar planking in the wool closets ripped out and replaced and made the workmen start the job over three times, until the corners lined up to her satisfaction. She had Septimus report to her several times each day. She insisted on dealing personally with each customer, and on the days when there were too few callers, she herself would go to the forum and make inquiries: "Don't you need purple? We've just acquired some very fine Thracian wool; wouldn't you like to come see for yourself?" "I have a special price right now on some bolts of linen that I've had too long. Your wife prefers linen for her formal attire, as I recall. Can I persuade you to come and look?"

At home, she tired easily and frequently lost her patience with her children and the servants. Hermeia simply took to avoiding her whenever possible, but Parmenes was a different story. The more irritable and fatigued Lydia felt, the more insistent he was that she watch him turn handsprings in the atrium, or find him something to eat, or notice how high he could jump, or hear the halting, tangled narrative of his latest exploit with his schoolmates. Lydia found herself idly wondering if the boy's grammaticus couldn't be paid a little extra to keep him in the evenings, then immediately despised herself for having the thought.

A certain buyer had begun frequenting the trading house more and more. His name was Stephanos, and even in her hurried, bothered state Lydia noticed how he studied her without seeming to.

Stephanos was from Galatia, and he had the straw-colored

hair and fair skin to prove it. He had entered the army at a young enough age that upon his retirement to Philippi, he was still under forty. Evidently, military service had been good to him; he owned a great deal of land around Philippi. Lydia frequently saw him in the forum, standing near the bema and talking with the city elders. He had no wife.

Stephanos was good-looking, in a rustic, unassuming sort of way. He had a wide, honest face and pale, blue eyes that always seemed opened a bit wider than strictly necessary. He smiled a lot. He was tall, as those with Gaulish blood often were. Lydia's dealings with him had always been pleasant.

He usually bought smaller quantities of purple, just enough to hem his togas and robes with the narrow equite band. But today, as he came through the door just before closing time, he seemed to have something special in mind. He waved at Lydia and walked directly up to her.

"Lydia, I need to make a purchase today."

"Of course, Stephanos. Why else would you have come?"

"No. I mean a real purchase. A large one."

"Oh?"

"Can we go inside?" He waved toward the private chamber.

"Well...yes, Stephanos. Of course."

She signaled a slave for wine, water, and cups, and led the way to the heavy-hinged oak door.

She seated herself behind the small table and motioned toward a three-legged stool nearby. She saw Stephanos's eyes flicker toward the table and cushions in the corner and his very slight grimace of disappointment.

"Lydia, I want to buy three bolts of your best dyed linen," he said when he had pulled the stool to the table and seated himself.

The slave brought in a tray with two long-necked pitchers and two carved rosewood cups. He set the vessels on the ebony table and padded silently out, carrying the tray.

Her eyebrows arched. "Three? This must be an unusual occasion, indeed. May I ask what it is?"

He leaned forward on his elbows. His blue eyes opened even wider, if that were possible.

"I'm getting married."

"Well, congratulations. And who, if you don't mind my asking, is the fortunate woman?"

He showed nearly all his teeth in a huge, boyish grin. "You."

Twenty-two

The laugh bubbled over without warning, surprising Lydia before she could do anything to stop it. "Me? Marry you? Oh, Stephanos, forgive me, but I'm afraid you've taken me rather aback."

The corners of his smile wilted. "Well, maybe I could have prefaced it a little more carefully, but it would have still come down to the same thing. Consider, Lydia. I have some wealth. The mines on my property are still producing a decent quantity of silver. I have some of the best barley and millet fields in the country, but they could just as easily be growing madder. I have slaves enough so that you might never have to do more again than lift your hand to have whatever you wanted. It could be a very advantageous alliance."

He leaned closer. Lydia pulled her arms into her lap. "I have been watching you for a long time, Lydia, almost since the day you came to stay with your uncle. You have great strength and determination. I like that. And—" She saw the color rising up his neck, into his cheeks, above his beard. "—and you are very pleasing to look at."

His eyes dropped then. He seemed to be searching for more words and not finding them. Or maybe the shocked, closed expression on her face had daunted him at last.

"Stephanos, I...I don't know—"

Quickly he put up a hand. "Then don't answer. Give some thought to what I've said. Combining our houses could be a good thing, Lydia. I have high regard for you. I would be a good husband...and a doting father to your little boy."

Lydia stood. "Well, Stephanos, I—I thank you. I presume you'll want to delay the final decision about the cloth until...until you know more?"

He looked up at her for a moment, then got up slowly. "Yes. I'll wait."

He leaned toward her slightly, but something in her attitude warned him away. He gave her an embarrassed half-smile and walked out.

She watched Stephanos leave, then found Septimus and told him to close down the trading house for the night. Walking home, she couldn't decide if astonishment or anger had the upper hand in her. Imagine! To stride in and propose marriage, just like that! But...was there something about her manner or circumstances that had encouraged Stephanos, without her realizing it? She tried to recall every interchange she had ever had with him. Had she encouraged him, without meaning to?

She was still puzzling over this when she reached her gate. She swung it open and crossed the entry portico. She came into the atrium and heard Parmenes shouting at her from behind the colonnade enclosing the small courtyard in front of the dining hall.

"Mother, watch me! I can jump all the way over the well!"

Her head jerked up and the command to stop was in her

throat, but he was already dashing across the courtyard. Just as he leaped, his foot slipped. His head struck the side of the well with a sickening thud, and he toppled in.

Lydia screamed and raced toward the well. Neria was already there in front of her, shouting down the well. "Parmenes, grab the rope! The rope—hold on to it!"

There was no answer.

Neria rose up and wheeled around, her eyes big. "Doris! There is a heavy rope in the corner of the storeroom. Bring it here!"

The kitchen girl flew around the corner and came back moments later, carrying a thick cord of plaited flax. Lydia looked wildly around the courtyard. Hermeia stood nearby, her face white and slack as she stared at the well.

"Go and get Crescens, Clement, Esras—whoever you can find! We need help!" Hermeia spun and dashed for the gate.

They tied the cord around Neria, just beneath her arms. Lydia and three of the other women held it as the Nubian clambered over the low stone wall circling the well. They braced their feet against the wall and paid out the rope as evenly as they could. Lydia heard a sound coming from her throat that was half a pant, half a whimper. She clenched her teeth and forced her eyes to stay on the rope running through her hands.

She felt arms reaching between her and the rope, shoulders moving in front of her. "Let us take this," said Clement. "You talk to her and guide us."

Lydia leaned over the well, her eyes straining, following the light as far as it reached down into the hole. Even in the driest summers, there was always water in the bottom of this well. She had always thought that a good thing. Why, oh, why hadn't she ever had that cover built?

"Do you have him?" she called, hearing her voice slapping around the stones of the shaft. "Neria?"

"More. Let me down more," came the reply from the well.

The men paid out more rope. Lydia heard splashing sounds.

"Is he all right?" asked Hermeia in a quavery voice. "He was doing that earlier, when he came home from his classes. I told him to stop, but—"

"Quiet!" Lydia hissed. She turned her face back toward the shaft. "Do you have him? Do you?"

"Pull! Pull us up!" Neria shouted.

"Pull them up!" Lydia said. "Hurry! Get them up here!"

The men strained and pulled. Lydia watched the rope rising from the darkness. She pounded her fists bloody on the stone wall.

"Oh, please hurry. Can't you go any faster?"

The men grunted and the rope crawled out of the well. Lydia saw Neria's shadowy form rise slowly into view. She was holding him. Lydia could see the white of his face against Neria's arms. As the rope crawled higher, she could see Neria holding his head against her chest, talking to him in a low voice.

When they reached the top, Lydia took Parmenes from Neria's arms while the others helped her climb out of the well. Lydia laid her son on the ground beside the well. His head lolled at a strange angle, as if he were trying to scratch his ear with his shoulder. Water spilled loosely from his slack mouth. There was a huge, oozing gash on his forehead. His chest wasn't moving.

"Parmenes! Parmenes, can you hear me?" She fell to her knees and straddled him, taking his face in her hands. "Parmenes!" She shook him, and his body was slack. "Parmenes!" she screamed. She felt hands on her shoulders, pulling her away. "No! No, let me have my son! Parmenes! Don't take me away from him! My baby! Parmenes!"

Lydia of Thyatira placed this tablet in memory of her esteemed son, Parmenes, son of Menander, who died at the age of seven years and six months, departing this life on the seventh after the twentieth of Dystros, two days before the Calends of March by the Roman reckoning.

It was odd what one noticed. As Lydia looked at the memorial stone she had commissioned, all she could think was that if the day was called "two before the Calends of March," wouldn't everyone realize it was the Roman reckoning, without being told? But she lacked the will to call the stonecutter's attention to the redundancy. The words looked so solid and official, carved with right-angled ruts into the milky white marble slab.

The stonecutter was asking her where she wanted the tablet mounted. He was a stubby, battered-looking man with a few strands of straggling, yellowish white hair. Where, indeed? One of the temples would probably permit the marker, especially if it carried with it the promise of a payment to the god's treasury. Or she might place the tablet on one of the columns surrounding the forum. Her reputation might even entitle her to have it placed on a plinth near the bema.

She thought about Seleucus's grave, on the hillside above the town. Just a simple, hand-lettered wooden plaque driven into the ground near the place he was buried. Enough to enable the family to find the site, but not much more. Maybe the Jewish God had a better memory than the others.

The man had said something else; Lydia didn't hear what. The sound of his voice registered only faintly, barely enough to cause her to look at him. A question waited on his grizzled face.

"Oh. It doesn't matter. Somewhere in the forum, I suppose." She waved vaguely in that direction. "And enter a copy in the city archives." She took some coins from her purse and gave them to the stonecutter before leaving.

When she arrived back home, Talit and Agatha were sitting on a stone bench in the atrium, beneath the colonnade of the well yard. Hermeia sat between them, and the two Jewish women had their arms around Lydia's daughter. At the sound of the gate's closing, Talit looked up and saw Lydia. She got up and came toward her.

"Is it done?"

Lydia nodded. "The forum, I think."

"You don't know? What did you tell him?"

Lydia shrugged and went toward her room. Talit walked beside her.

"A man was here, while you were gone. He said his name was Stephanos."

"What did he want?"

"Nothing. He left that." She pointed to the place beside the kitchen doorway, where two of Lydia's women squatted with knives, cutting steaks and strips of meat from the hanging carcass of a yearling pig. "He said it was for the funeral meal. He said he was very sorry to hear about Parmenes."

"Oh." Lydia stood a moment and looked at her servants, at their hands smeared with gore. The hanging carcass dripped blood onto the paving stones of her courtyard; the servants stepped in it, tracking it around the area where they worked. Someone would have to have them clean away all that blood. She turned away and went on toward her room. She wanted to go inside, lie down on her couch, and know nothing for as long as possible.

"Lydia." Talit's hand was on her shoulder, turning her. Why wouldn't Talit let her go lie down? Consciousness was such a burden. Didn't the Jewish woman understand?

"What is it?" she asked.

"Lydia, letting your life ebb away won't bring him back. You know that. You have a daughter. You have a fine trade, a good house."

She looked at Talit. She let her eyes rove the courtyard, the columns, the frescoes on the walls. No. It weighed nothing, made no difference. None of it.

"I'm going to lie down."

She went into her room and fell onto her couch. She didn't bother to remove her shoes.

She woke up in the dark, but she didn't have the strength to go running. She doubted she even had the strength to roll over. She knew if she turned her head to one side, she would see the stars through her window. She didn't want to see the stars. There were too many reminders there, too many false promises. There was no escape; she knew that now.

"If you are who they say you are, why didn't you do something?" she said into the darkness. "Maybe you can't; maybe you aren't who they say. And if you can, but won't, then I despise you."

The words felt stark and strong in her ears. It felt good to say them, and it felt horrible.

"Wasn't Menander enough? Wasn't it enough to take him from me before he even had the chance to see his son? And then, my uncle, the only other person who believed in me. And Seleucus? Would it have been too hard to let him stay a little longer? After all, it was he who told me the most about you. But now, my little boy. You have taken my son, or let him be taken.

Why? Which of your purposes is served by slowly robbing me of everyone I hold dear?"

She felt the deep, wracking sobs surfacing and flung her arms across her face. She gave herself to the sadness, submerged herself in it. A single question pounded from her, again and again: Why? Why, why, why....

After a time, she slept. And then, she was walking beneath the plane tree, in the green and shady space beneath—but wasn't it still winter?

"Why won't you answer me?" she was saying.

"How do you know I won't?" said the hide-clothed stranger.

"But when I ask, you say nothing in reply."

"There are answers that come in words, but there are also those that come in the spaces between, those that come down to you along the pathways of days, and months, and years. Answers that find their place in you, though you can't know them until you're ready. There are answers that come only in silence."

"How will I know?"

"You will."

"How?"

"You will."

"How can I endure?"

"You can."

"How?"

"You can. You will."

When she woke again, it was broad daylight. She was still in her clothes from the day before, but her sandals were gone and the dust wiped from her feet. She sat up and saw Neria, sitting on the floor near the doorway, leaning against the wall. Her eyes were closed, her head bent to one side.

Lydia swung her feet down to the floor and stood. Neria's eyes fluttered and opened. The two women looked at each other. There was a word in Lydia's mind, a word she couldn't yet permit herself to say aloud. Maybe one day, she would be able.

Amen.

It was another grief that finally brought her back—at least, part way. She would never have expected such, but that was exactly how it happened.

Neria brought her sister to Lydia, sobbing inconsolably. The two women clung to each other as Neria told Lydia that her sister's master had died, and his wife was going to sell her entire household, even her house. Neria's sister—Anetis was her name—was afraid she would be sold to someone in another town and she would never again see Neria, the only relative left to her.

"Why is she selling everything?" Lydia wanted to know.

"The master had large debts," Anetis said, wiping her eyes. "Now that he is dead, all his creditors are demanding their money. And there isn't any money to pay them."

"I don't see what can be done, then. I certainly don't need any more servants."

But the agony in Neria's face as she looked first at Lydia, then at her weeping sister, proved more potent than Lydia's lethargy. She got herself dressed. She walked to her gate and opened it, part of her a little surprised that she had made it this far. She went to the house on New Street where Anetis's mistress lived. Just as she reached out her hand to knock at the gate, Lydia remembered that this was the woman who had such noisy disapproval for her morning exercises. Yes—Euodia, wasn't it? She knocked anyway.

A eunuch with a face as devastated as Anetis's answered the summons. Lydia told him she had come to see his mistress. He replied that the mistress wasn't seeing anyone, then reached across her to close the gate.

Her back arching with indignation, Lydia brushed aside the eunuch's arm and firmly stepped across the threshold. The eunuch repeated his message. She told him to announce her, anyway, and to do it at once. He stared at her a moment, then rolled his eyes and padded away across the courtyard.

Before long, the eunuch stepped out of a doorway in the center of the walkway, opposite the gate. He gestured to Lydia. She strode across the courtyard and into the room where his mistress waited. She didn't look at the eunuch.

Euodia was seated by a brazier on which a low flame burned in sporadic flickers. She had a dark woolen blanket wrapped around her. She looked up.

"Well. The running woman. Here to gloat, I assume."

Twenty-three

The first thing Lydia noticed about Euodia was her eyes and the dark circles under them. She was a handsome woman, one who was probably accustomed to attracting notice; even in her devastation, she held herself with the bearing of one who assumes others are watching her. But she wore a discarded expression—hollowed out from the inside.

"I ought to have that Nubian girl whipped," Euodia was saying. "No doubt, she blabbered to that sister of hers. I'm sure her sister tells you everything."

"They don't want to be parted. I can understand that."

"Yes. Well. Sometimes, partings can't be avoided."

"I know." Lydia saw the change on Euodia's face. "May I sit down?"

Euodia shrugged and inclined her head toward another chair, not far from the brazier. Lydia pulled the chair closer to the fire and tugged her cloak around her shoulders. She sat quietly, her eyes on Euodia, waiting.

"Aren't you going to say anything?" Euodia asked. She wouldn't look at Lydia.

"I don't know what you want to hear."

"How should I know? How should I know anything?"

A while later, Lydia said, "How bad is it?"

Euodia looked at her then. "You presume quite a lot."

"I know more than I want to know about how much grief can weigh. I'm here to listen, if you want to talk."

Another long silence.

"The first notice I had was when one of Tyrimachus's business partners showed up here, the day after the burial, with one of the magistrates," Euodia said at last. "He showed me a letter in my husband's handwriting, with his name affixed, acknowledging the loan of five hundred dēnariī." She gave a harsh laugh. "The due date was the same as the day he died. That was just the first, of course. Within three days, I saw debts of nearly four Imperial talents.

"Apparently, Tyrimachus had been gambling for years. I never knew. I suppose he was able to juggle the debts and keep it mostly hidden. We were married for thirteen years. I bore him a son and two daughters. We may not have always been the happiest of partners, but our household was respectable. Or so I thought." Her lips were trembling. She covered her mouth with her hand.

"How old is your son?" Lydia asked after a few moments had passed.

"Androclus is seven—our oldest. And he so admired his father."

"My son is—was seven. But he never knew his father."

A space of quiet.

"It…must have been terrible, to lose him that way—so young," Euodia said, finally.

"The girls?"

"Eugenia is five, and Cassandra is three." She gave Lydia a guilty glance that slid away to the side. "Your coming here—it was very kind, especially under the circumstances."

"I came here to offer to buy the Nubian from you."

"Ah. Well, just name your price. I'm not in much of a position to bargain."

Lydia gave Euodia a careful, appraising look. "How many servants do you have that really know how to handle a loom?"

"Loom? What are you talking about?"

"How many do you have that are skilled weavers? Tight, even work, and fast—able to turn out, say, two or three cubits a day? How many looms do you own?"

"Are you trying to buy out everything I have?"

"No." Lydia smiled at her. "I'm looking for a partner."

Even after all these many years, good Crescens, the confusion of that silence besets me, sorrows me.

I know you are a follower of the one they call Christ. I know some people here who believe in him, also. I have heard them say this Christ can call into being that which is not, that he can reach into a human soul. They even say he can unmake death. I don't know. I've never seen death let slip any of his holds. I've never had much belief in anything beyond the touch of a hand, the comfort of a bed at night, the safety of a strong, locked door. I think she taught me that, Crescens. I think I learned my doubt from her.

Maybe this Christ has changed my mother. Maybe she really is different than the woman I remember. If I could believe that, even for your sake, then I might be able to come. I will think about what you've said. But you must understand how hard it is for me. You must make allowance for the years, the unanswered questions, the caresses that never came. If it comes to it, you must forgive me. Maybe this Christ of yours and my mother's can help her forgive me, too. I wish I knew more about forgiving and being forgiven.

Farewell.

Lydia let the parchment tumble from her hand onto the floor beside her couch. How could she blame Hermeia for not coming? Everything her daughter said was true. And had she really changed? Was she any different now, as she rocked impatiently on the edge of death's precipice, than when she was young and determined and heedful only of going forward, forward, always forward?

She tilted her head back and closed her eyes and tried to think of what she would say to Hermeia, if she did come. Maybe she'd keep to something safe. Maybe she'd ask about the journey from Thessalonica, about the weather and the condition of the road. Maybe she'd talk about her servants, and the difficulty of finding anyone who really knew how to bake bread, or how to wait on a person without being in the way.

One of the girls came in. It was that Euterpe, with the voice that grated on Lydia's ears like a chalkstone on slate. Did Mother Lydia need anything? Was she thirsty? Hungry? Cold?

Yes. All of these.

"A few sticks for the brazier might be nice."

Euterpe nodded and bowed her way back out the door.

The day Hermeia left Philippi was much like today, Lydia remembered: spring was well underway; the air was still cool at night and in the early mornings, but the sun was growing stronger each day.

It was good for them to be going, Lydia decided. Hermeia's husband had opportunities in the large seaport city. And besides, with Hermeia gone from her household, Lydia wouldn't be so constantly reminded of how little they really had to say to each other.

They had stopped at her house before taking to the highway. It was early; Lydia had not yet gone to her place of business. Neria answered the knock at the gate, and there stood Hermeia. Livius stood in the road a little way behind her, fidgeting and studying the sky, eager to be away.

"I wish you well, daughter," Lydia said. "Mind your household. Your husband is a fine man. May you have every happiness."

Lydia wished she knew something better to say, some magic trick of speech to shatter the invisible wall dividing them, undo the harm that had somehow crept unnoticed between them. How was it she had managed to lose her living child, as well as her dead one?

Hermeia didn't answer for a long time, didn't even look at Lydia. She just stood there, her hands folded demurely in front of her, her eyes on the ground near Lydia's feet. Finally, she looked up, met her mother's eyes. "Thank you."

Hermeia turned and went to her husband, and they started down the street. Lydia watched them go until they were nearly to the corner. Sudden words sprouted in her mind.

"Hermeia! Thessalonica isn't so far, is it?"

Hermeia stopped and turned around. Lydia saw her cup a hand to her mouth. "Yes. Too far to run."

There was a fluttering and rapid beating at the lattices of her window. Lydia turned her head. A small, bluish blur fell through the bars and onto the floor, just as a large shadow swept across the opening—a swallow, probably dodging a hawk's talons. The little bird quickly righted itself and sat on the floor, blinking and twitching its head this way and that. It flicked its wings nervously a few times, then sprang up, flying around the room and beating at the ceiling. Lydia could hear its small, peeping cries of alarm.

The bird kept swooping near the window and striking against the bars of the lattice, hovering and chattering there before making another long loop across the room, then back.

Why won't it light on the sill and go through the lattice to the outside? she wondered. The openings between the bars are certainly big enough for such a small bird to negotiate.

The bird settled on the wall near the doorway, clinging precariously to a crack or seam between the courses of brick. It appeared to be looking over its shoulder at the windows in the opposite wall, but it clung to its perpendicular perch, too exhausted or confused to try again for freedom.

Lydia heard footsteps scuffing toward the opening. Euterpe came in, carrying a few sticks for the brazier, and the startled bird launched itself again around the room, twittering in fright.

"Oh!"

Euterpe flung her hands in front of her face, scattering the sticks on the floor. She started spinning this way and that, waving her arms in the air as she tried to follow the bird's frenetic flight and shoo it toward the doorway. Finally, the swallow dove through the opening into the courtyard and arrowed away into the morning.

"Well done, Euterpe. You freed the prisoner."

"Pardon, Mother Lydia?" The flustered servant panted, one hand on her chest, as she bent over to regather the flung sticks.

"Never mind. Just leave those sticks beside the brazier; I'm warm enough, right now. But bring me a cup of water, please."

Looking a little annoyed, the girl piled the sticks near the brazier and went out.

Lydia thought about what she would see if she were able to peer out the windows, high in the north wall of her room. For years a large elm had stood opposite her window, just across Short Street. In the mornings the starlings and sparrows that roosted there would wake, calling sleepily and hesitantly to each other at first, and as dawn brightened, more and more insistently. Often, after her run, Lydia would sit in her room and, as she used the strigil or bound her hair, listen to the waking-up of the elm tree. In the late evenings, too—especially in the summer—the birds would come back to the elm and argue noisily over who should sleep where that night. Some years, when the rains were plentiful and the nights grew cold at just the right time, the leaves would turn a brilliant, golden yellow, all at once. Looking at the tree on such autumn afternoons was like beholding a canopy of mellowed sunlight.

But a few years ago, someone had purchased the land across from her to build a house, and the elm tree was not part of his plans. Lydia was sorry the day the workmen came with axes and saws to take down the elm. Too late, she wished she had bought the small parcel where the elm sat, so she could keep on judging her days by the rhythm of the tree. It would be a comfort, right now, to hear the wind rustling through the rough-edged leaves and see the faint green shadow of the new leaves falling through the lattice.

She heard Euterpe's feet slapping across the courtyard. Why didn't Euodia teach these poor girls to pick up their feet when they walked? She brought Lydia a cup of water and bent to help her drink.

"Thank you, dear. Just set the rest on my table."

The pain drew a thin, screaming line across her belly, then drove up under her breastbone. Euterpe heard her tiny grunt and saw the clenched jaw, the squinted eyes.

"Mother Lydia, what's wrong?"

Lydia held up a hand and the servant grabbed it in both of hers. Lydia squeezed Euterpe's hands and tried to make her breath go slowly, in and out through her nose. But the pain wouldn't let go. It twisted in her like a snake with a spiked tail, it twined tighter and tighter until Lydia thought she would lose consciousness from the agony. It had never been this bad before.

"Clystra! Bring the opium powder!" Euterpe shouted.

Lydia shook her head. "No," she gasped. "None of that."

She opened her mouth and panted like a dog. The edges of her vision sprouted black spots that quickly spread and threw a dark curtain across her sight. And then, the pain started to withdraw, as slowly as the tide receding. Lydia felt the muscles in her jaws and face releasing, smoothing.

"Why don't you want the opium?" Euterpe asked. "If it hurts so much—"

"No. I want to know the pain."

Euterpe gave her an uncomprehending look.

"We must test ourselves against it, don't you know?"

"I don't understand, Mother Lydia."

Nothing worthwhile comes without pain, Lydia thought. Without it, we don't know how far we've come. We don't know where we are or what we might be able to do. The pain tells us; it measures us. Haven't you heard the story of the Christ refusing wine when he was on the cross? He knew. He knows.

How could she say all this to a simple girl who only knew about eating as soon as she was hungry, resting when she was a little tired, and taking opium when she hurt? Instead, Lydia closed her eyes.

"Never mind, child. You may leave me, now."

Euterpe went out, with many worried glances over her shoulder.

Lydia lay back, still breathing hard, and thought about the knowing that comes only through pain. Paul understood. He was another who was tutored by lack, by mishap, by discomfort, and even distress. Maybe it was the common language between the two of them. Maybe it accounted for the awareness they shared, the discernment that came from a place beyond knowledge. They had learned from the same teacher. Maybe that was it.

When he came through Philippi for the very last time, she remembered, he seemed constantly ringed about by watchful eyes: Trophimus, Tychicus, Sopater, and the rest of them who had accompanied Paul through Asia Minor. They had maybe learned caution from the threats of angry synagogue presidents and the shouting of the mob in the amphitheater at Ephesus; they guarded him like a treasure. Even young Timothy had acquired a wary sheen, a vigilance that aged him more quickly than the seven or so years that had passed since he first came to Philippi with Paul.

Nearly everyone in the little band of believers wanted to help with Paul's collection effort. Even Xerxes somewhere found a copper or two, bless him. They all gathered to Paul in the courtyard of Lydia's house, before dawn on that First Day. After they had sung a few choruses and listened to Paul wind through a long prayer that sounded more like a homily, one of Lydia's women brought out a large basket and set it at Paul's feet. He had a word for each of them as they came forward to place their offerings in the basket. When Syntyche stepped up to him, he talked earnestly to her for several moments. She gave him a flustered, open-mouthed look and moved away. When at last Euodia approached, Lydia was only close enough to hear the tone of his voice—not the words. It sounded as if he asked her but a single question. She answered with a terse shake of the head and refused to look at him any more.

"May this help those in Judea who need it most," Lydia said to Paul when her turn came. She put the pouch of gold in his hands and turned to go, but his hands covered hers and held her there.

"Thank you, Lydia. It's good of you to share the burden of those who labor for the Lord." The smile he gave her reminded her more of a farewell than a greeting.

"We owe a great debt to Jerusalem," she answered, doing her best to keep her eyes level with his, instead of looking at their intertwined hands. "It's only fair."

"I don't mean only those in Jerusalem. I've never stopped being glad of your hospitality that very first Sabbath. It was a kindness then, and in the years since, it has only seemed better to me."

It was hushed in the courtyard; there was just a little low talk here and there. Lydia could hear the sound of feet shuffling quietly, a woman softly clearing her throat, someone sniffing. A few houses over, a cock had started to notice the sunrise. The scent of wood smoke came from the kitchen.

What did Paul mean? Lydia was conscious of those waiting to see him, even more of those who had made their offerings and still stood about, watching this unexpected tableau unfolding between them. But she knew he was not long for Philippi. He wanted to get on to Corinth and Athens, and who knew whether he would come back this way before going to Jerusalem with his collection? There were things she wanted to say to him. Now? Here?

"It was an offer freely made," she said, slowly pulling her hands from his.

He released her, and his eyes flickered shut for an instant. The thin lips curved gently upward, and his gaze met hers again.

"Yes. And that makes it the more precious."

He didn't stay at her house when he came back. Paul sent most of his traveling companions ahead to take a ship to Troas with the money, while he stayed in Philippi for the seder. They held the feast at Euodia's, where Luke had been staying, and all during that time, Paul kept mostly to himself, unless he was closeted with the physician. Some worried talk leaked out from among them: of the anger of the synagogues in Asia Minor and the necessity of staying away from Ephesus and the interior, of the need to get to Jerusalem before the Jews of Asia Minor poisoned the well. As soon as the week was over, they left for the seaport at Neapolis. His course was set, Lydia realized. There was no use in thinking otherwise.

A few of them walked with the travelers as far as the pōmērium on the morning of their leaving, watched them continue along the Via Egnatia, waved now and then at their receding figures until the contour of the falling land and the curves in the road took them out of sight. There was no chance to speak to him as she wished. And, watching him leave, she realized she wasn't completely sure of what she would have said, even if the chance had come.

About that time, copies of his letters began circulating among the believers. Now and then, someone would come to the First Day gathering or to the following agapē and announce a new writing. They would hear the reading, and Lydia or Euodia or someone else would pay a scribe to make a good copy or two before the messenger went on his way. Lydia smiled, thinking about the first time they had heard the reading of Paul's letter written to the Corinthian believers. A thorn, he called it. He had learned to glory in it, he said, since it displayed the power of God, couched in the weakness of his own body. To delight in weakness for Christ's sake: to find the grace in a hardship. Yes.

How was it they first heard of his trouble in Jerusalem? Oh, yes—Seleucus, the son of Agatha, returning from the Feast of Weeks. Lydia smiled. She remembered the joy on the faces of Talit, his grandmother, and Agatha, his mother, as the young man set out on the pilgrimage. Lydia wondered if his great-grandfather somehow knew of his namesake's journey to the sacred city. She hoped so.

Seleucus told them what he knew of the uproar in the temple, of Paul's arrest. Listening to his account, it seemed to Lydia she was hearing something she already knew. And then, not long after, Paul's letter to them arrived in the hands of Epaphroditus. They had first listened to it here, gathered together in Lydia's house. Epaphroditus had read the letter, she remembered. She also recalled the silence that followed the reading. A long silence—a thinking silence.

Lydia had thought often about that silence. Maybe they stopped listening when the letter revealed them to themselves or everyone else. The Jews from Asia left quickly after the gathering, she remembered. They went out, not looking at anyone else. Crescens and the other non-Jewish men stood together, watching them go.

When Euodia and Syntyche heard their names read aloud,

heard their private bitterness announced and its quick resolution enjoined, how could they have heard anything else the letter said? Seated on opposite sides of the atrium from each other, jaws clenched and cheeks reddening, it had seemed to Lydia each could look anywhere except at the other.

And when Lydia heard the secret way he called her out, remembering and naming her, her quiet joy muffled her hearing to all else that came after. Only days later did anyone—Clement, wasn't it?—approach her and quietly ask why, she supposed, did Paul fail to greet her or mention her in his writing? Her kind friend and tenant only wondered, only wanted to honor her feelings. She smiled at him, Lydia remembered. She gave him some noncommittal answer or other. Revealing to him what Paul had intended as a private message between them would spoil the intimacy he had intended. She would not share that with anyone, she decided.

When the reading ended, Lydia remembered, they all sat very quietly for some time, trying to understand all that Paul had said, trying to return from the scattered places their individual reactions had sent them. Lydia wondered how much they would remember from this single hearing. How much difference would this letter make? How could anyone keep it all in a useful place? But this was Paul's last gift to them, she knew. It was all he could offer, and he meant it for their strengthening.

Lydia thought about Euterpe and Clystra. Week after week, they sat with the others in Lydia's courtyard, or Euodia's, and listened to someone read from the letters, or even from Moses, the prophets, the songs of David. The words struck their ears, and maybe some of them went in, for a time, at least. How much would they remember? How would unlearned, illiterate slaves receive and keep the words that were meant to bring life? And how much hearing was enough? Lydia thought about Neria and her sister, in their new home in Ephesus for these several months, now. She wondered if they gathered with the Christ-believers there. Had all that hearing changed them any? Were the words implanted in them, or had they assumed whatever life was easiest, once they left Lydia's household? That any human being could be changed by words seemed a ludicrous notion to Lydia sometimes, until she remembered how Paul's words had changed and quickened her, that day beside the river.

Epaphroditus told them what he learned from Paul: of his trial before the procurator Felix, of his appeal to Nero, of his tumultuous voyage to Rome and the adventures he and his companions faced on the way. Years later, they would receive word of his execution during the emperor's vindictive abuse of the believers, following the great fire. But none of it came as a surprise to Lydia.

She heard sandaled feet coming through the doorway. She opened her eyes. It was Euodia. And she had been crying.

PART THREE

The Reward

ydia had no idea how long Pericles had been waiting at the doorway of the private chamber before she noticed him. She waved him forward impatiently. This new manager was too quiet. Septimus would have contrived some noise or motion to attract her attention, but Pericles moved about the trading house like a shadow. She would have to say something to him about it; he made the other workers nervous.

"A patron waits outside, Mistress."

"Who?"

"Stephanos, son of Antiochus, I believe."

Lydia let out an exasperated breath. "I don't want to see him. Tell him to leave."

The manager gave her a confused, uncomfortable look.

"Oh, well, all right, then…Euodia, you go talk to him."

"Me?"

"Yes. Maybe he wants to buy some purple. Go sell it to him."

"But, Lydia, I don't know what to—"

"You know more than you think you do. You've been watching me for nearly two months, now. Go sell him some purple."

Pericles made a hesitant motion with one hand.

"What now, Pericles?" Lydia said.

"Master Stephanos asked to see you, Mistress."

Lydia put a hand to her forehead and drew several slow breaths. "All right. Tell him I'll be with him in a moment."

Pericles bowed himself out the door.

"What will I say to him, Euodia?"

"How should I know? You're the experienced trader, not me." She smiled sweetly as she said it.

Lydia gave her a look of pure malice, then wheeled about and went into the main room. Stephanos stood in the center of the floor. For all his stature, he looked like a lost boy. She walked up to him, giving him the best smile she could manage.

"Grace to you, Stephanos. How may we assist you today?"

"Can we go in there?" he asked, tilting his head toward the private room.

"I'm sorry, no. My partner is in there—studying some figures."

He crossed his arms in front of him and studied the tops of his sandals. "Lydia, you have never answered me."

"Please forgive me, Stephanos. Things have been so busy lately: teaching my partner the business, helping her settle her affairs—you knew the widow of Tyrimachus had come into business with me, didn't you?"

He was still looking down. "You won't marry me, will you?"

"Stephanos, I…I can't. I'm honored by your proposal but— no. I can't marry you."

He stood for several moments without moving. Then he lifted his head. His eyes moved over her face, and he pulled a smile from somewhere. He nodded, once, and turned toward the door.

Within the month he was married to the young daughter of another wealthy citizen. Euodia sold him a huge order of purple linen for the occasion.

That summer in Macedonia was one of the driest in anyone's memory. Though the usual amount of dried root arrived from the plantations near Thyatira, the local madder crop was a disaster. Lydia's storage bins were being depleted by constant demand. As stores elsewhere evaporated, she and Euodia began to see clients from farther and farther afield. Even the legate of Macedonia sent his factor from Thessalonica to purchase from them.

Lydia and Euodia were in the counting room totaling up the month's receipts when the letter arrived.

"...forty, forty-five, fifty," Euodia counted, making marks on a tally board. She leaned back and rubbed her eyes. "I need to stop for a while, Lydia. I'm getting cross-eyed."

Lydia smiled, stacking the gold aurei carefully in a small casket of aromatic cedar. "Does counting your money tire you so easily?"

She handed the casket to a slave, who carried it to the vault, carved into the rock of the hillside at the back of the house.

Euodia stood, reaching behind her back and interlocking her fingertips. She stretched her arms behind her, then took a deep breath, rubbing the back of her neck and slowly turning her head from side to side.

"Being prosperous is hard work, Lydia. I never knew."

One of the boys came in, carrying a small message pouch.

"What is it, Chrestus?" Lydia asked, motioning him forward.

The slave handed her the pouch. It was a letter, bound by a strip of black linen.

From Philip, son of Threnides of Thyatira, to Lydia, his sister, of Philippi: Greetings. May this message find you and your children well and prosperous.

Know that our father died three days after the first of Hyperberetaios, being seventy-seven years of age, beloved of Apollo and his sister, respected by his household, esteemed by all good men, a patron of the city, and an elder of the boule.

In consideration of your good efforts, sister, I have decided to continue our father's custom of sending to you such quantities of the produce of our plantations as you judge fit. I will expect, of course, to continue receiving from you the agreed-upon share of the profits from the house our uncle established in Philippi with our father's sponsorship.

Mother sends her greeting to you, as do your sisters.

May the gods smile upon you.

I will expect, then, to receive your courier at the usual time.

Farewell.

"What's the matter?" Euodia wanted to know.

Lydia looked at her strangely for a moment, then righted herself. "What? Oh, this? Nothing, really." She crumpled the letter in her hand and tucked it into her belt. "Why don't we finish counting this before it gets any later? I'll take a turn counting and you can put it away, if you want."

She took the tally board from Euodia and sat down in front of the pile of coins. Euodia gave her a doubtful look, then seated herself slowly on the other side of the table.

As Lydia walked home that evening, each step felt odd, out of place. When she noticed, it reminded her of the sensation of coming down stairs in the dark and reaching the bottom step a stride too early. The ground wasn't quite where she thought it should be; she fancied sometimes she ought to slow down, touch the ground lightly with her toe before putting her full weight on it.

She went through the gate to her house. Hermeia was just coming out of the latrine, and her face turned aside from her mother's. The girl went into the atrium as quickly as she could. For an instant, Lydia considered asking her daughter a question, making a request, complimenting her dress. But she didn't have the strength to withstand the likely disappointment, so she just watched as Hermeia paced across the courtyard and past the colonnade, toward the well and the entrance to the main hall, just beyond.

Neria came out to her and led her to a bench beside the well. She had poured water in a basin of baked clay and a fresh linen cloth was folded on the bench. The Nubian woman motioned toward one of the younger girls, a mousy, silent child with thin, lank hair and teeth that protruded slightly. She kneeled in front of Lydia and removed her sandals, then eased her mistress's feet into the cool water of the basin. Lydia stared straight ahead, feeling the small hands run over her arches, along her soles, flutter briefly between her toes. The girl had an annoying habit of sucking at her teeth, and usually Lydia rebuked her, but this evening it seemed too much trouble.

She wondered why, in all the long years of escape from her father, she had never stopped to think about what she would feel upon receiving today's news. For all of her resentment toward him, the knowledge of his death had created an empty place. Or, maybe it announced to her a void that was already there, and waiting.

The slave girl slid her feet out of the basin onto one end of the soft linen towel. With the other end, she dried Lydia's feet, all the while sucking noisily at her large teeth. She brought out a clean pair of shoes, slippers of kid leather as pliable as Lydia's own skin.

Lydia stood and walked toward the door of the dining hall. She could smell the aroma of roast meat and onions, of boiled barley and freshly baked bread. She motioned to Neria's sister, who was placing on the table a lamp she had just lit.

"Bring my food to my room. I won't be eating in here tonight."

Later, picking at her food, Lydia found herself imagining her father's funeral. She pictured the forum at Thyatira, crowded with paid mourners. She could hear the skirling of the aulos racketing back and forth between the facades of the temples and the monuments to heroes and public benefactors. Was her father inhumed, or had he instructed cremation? She imagined her father's corpse, rendered into smoke and ash by the flames of the pyre, pluming into the skies above Thyatira to be gathered up by the clouds and rained back upon his native city, to run down the streets and into the cracks between the paving stones; to soak into the earth and become food and drink for the grasses.

Which part of him had Mother ordered cut off for burial? A hand, maybe. The right hand, which distributed the largesse of his coffers to the priests and civic leaders, the hand that commissioned public buildings and waved to the adoring, forgetful crowds at the feasts of dedication. That was the part of him they all saw. That was the part of Threnides of Thyatira they'd want to remember. His memorial marker would be grand. Year after year, her father's memory would be saluted by the officers of the Guild of Fullers and Dyers as they gathered at his monument for the refrigerium.

She thought of Seleucus, dying on his pallet beside the brazier of his son's house, mourned by his grandchildren. She thought of the honest tears of the Jewish family, the quiet singing as they prepared the body, the simple prayers to the one they never named. She thought of Esras, working beside his father as they layered the stones atop the body, to keep it safe from marauding scavengers. The simple, homely wooden marker driven into the rocky soil of the hillside. In a few years, the winds and rain would weather away the rude, hand-carved lettering that announced the grave's tenant.

Amen.

Lydia wondered if, when her time came, anyone would say the amen. Would she say it? Would she rather be remembered as her father would be remembered—or as Seleucus? She thought of Hermeia's face, distant as the stars and as isolated. The divide between them was great, and growing. Lydia feared she already lacked the strength to bridge it. Would someone bring Hermeia a letter one day, a dispatch bound in a black band? Would she trace back the course of her days and wonder, as Lydia now wondered, how she could have spent so much time occupied with evasion, only to realize she had finally managed to evade herself?

Amen.

Tomorrow was the Jews' Sabbath. Lydia would be with them in their house. Or maybe they would go to the place beside the river. And the next day, Euodia would ask why Lydia hadn't come to the trading house the day before. Lydia would remind her, as she always did, that she kept the Jewish holy day with her friends. Euodia would ask, as she always did, why Lydia always wanted to attend the strange, unadorned worship of Clement and his family. Usually, Lydia would engage in a fruitless attempt to explain the Jews' strict codes of behavior, or their haunting, captivating songs, or even the ancient wisdom of their suffering. But tomorrow, when Euodia asked, Lydia knew what her answer would be.

Amen.

"What's wrong?"

Euodia shook her head, swiping at her eyes with the back of a hand.

"Can I have one of the girls bring you something?" Lydia asked.

Euodia didn't answer. She sank onto the footstool at the end of the couch, her face angled toward the floor. She didn't move for a long time. Lydia waited. Euodia straightened and pulled in a long breath, then let it go back out through her teeth. She stood and walked toward the window. She lingered beneath it for a moment and looked up at the sky, then paced slowly back toward Lydia's couch.

"I should never have gone to Androclus's baptism," Euodia said, idly fingering the back of the chair beside Lydia's resting place.

"But you're his great-grandmother. What a foolish thing to say."

"Yes, of course it is. Still…"

"What happened, dear? What upset you?"

Euodia came around to the front of the chair and sat heavily. "I don't know. Nothing, really. But somehow, standing there at the edge of the river, hearing Crescens saying those words over him as they stood in the water—it took me back to that day."

"Ah."

"What did we really know then, Lydia? Just some things Paul said, some teaching from the Prophets and the Law that he saw reflected in the Christ. And it was enough—we all knew it was. But why did we know that?"

"Because it was true, I suppose. Surely you aren't doubting—"

"Oh, no. Not doubting. But wondering things. Wondering why it still seems so easy to drift from the way. Wondering why, if Christ is completing me, I'm still broken and flawed. Wondering why I can see some things so clearly and be blind to others, even after all this time."

"Do you think you're different from anyone else?"

"I suppose not. But I know my failures more intimately than I know anyone else's."

"Thank God for that. Your own are enough. Adding mine would swamp your vessel."

Euodia smiled at her, nodding her head. Lydia was glad to see the smile. Then the pincers clamped her abdomen. She hissed. Euodia came quickly to her, kneeling beside her bed and gripping Lydia's hands.

"You're hurting."

Lydia nodded, grimacing. The spots were back, and darker this time, spreading faster.

"Do you want the opium?"

Lydia gritted her teeth and shook her head. A bright wedge of pain started at the back of her skull and slowly expanded, squeezing out everything else. Lydia felt a low humming in her chest and realized she was moaning.

"Oh, Lydia! Is there anything I can do?"

"Sing."

"What?"

"Sing. A song."

"Well, I…I'll try. But I can't think of anything."

"The plough," Lydia panted.

"The what?"

"The plough, the plough. Do I have to do everything for you?"

"As the work of the farmer is his plough," Euodia began in a quavery voice,

> And the work of the navigator is the steering of the ship,
> So is my work to sing the praises of the Lord;
> It is my work, my daily task to offer him praise
> Because his love has given sustenance to my heart….

"One…of my…favorites."

"Lydia, I cannot permit you to hold the agapē this evening."

"Not…evening…yet."

"You must let me send for my physician."

"What will you do…if I refuse?"

A long silence. "Honor your wish."

"That…was the right answer, dear." Her breath was coming easier now. She opened her eyes. "So…thinking of that first day, when Paul and the others came—that made you cry?"

Euodia looked at her carefully, then slowly released her hand. She moved back to the footstool. She sat, hugging herself and rocking slightly.

"That was where it started. Thinking of that time reminded me of other times."

Euodia stood again. She walked toward the doorway, cupping her elbows in her hands.

Lydia watched her, watched the shape of her shoulders, the

angle of her head. "Euodia. Listen to me. I would give up every-thing I ever owned to be able to get up from this bed and go to my daughter. Even if she rejected me, I would own the peace of having tried. Will you wait until waiting is all you can do? Or will you go while you still have the choice?"

Euodia turned then, all the way back toward Lydia. She let her hands fall to her sides. She stared at her, and Lydia couldn't read what was behind her friend's face. Then Euodia turned and left.

Twenty-five

*A*fter Euodia left, Lydia thought for a long time about what she had said, and left unsaid. She thought about the mystery of believing. She wondered, with Euodia, how it was that a person could know and even believe, and yet lack so much. If Christ was the linchpin of everything that was made, as Paul wrote, if he made his dwelling in those who believed in him, why was he content to whisper so quietly amidst the shouting disorder of a human life? She had lived her years looking for this answer, and was now nearly at the end, and still she wondered. How could that be?

She wondered what Seleucus had known, deep inside the quiet of his dying mind, as he lay on his pallet, slowly smothering from his final illness. Was he as uncertain of final meaning as she? What regrets were hidden beneath that kindly, fading brow? Lydia found it hard to imagine the old, blind Jew having any regrets, any ghosts whispering to him as he passed from this life. But, maybe. Maybe regrets, things left undone and unsaid, disagreements left unmended, were common to everyone who had journeyed as far through life as Seleucus and, now, Lydia had. Maybe God had the answers. Maybe he saved them, waiting until the souls of humans were in the place apart before he parceled them out. She would soon know.

Clystra came in, wanting to know how much food they should prepare for the agapē. There were twenty loaves ready in the larder; did Mother Lydia think they would need more? Maybe twelve *sēxtarii* of beans remained in the kitchen urns, and maybe half that many of chickpeas. Would that be enough? And should they send to the market for more meat?

"Go buy a kid or a lamb," Lydia told her. "But make sure it comes from one of the secular vendors; there'll be some here tonight who won't eat meat from the temple stalls. And see if we have any dried apricots or pears left. Some fruit would be nice."

The girl bowed and started out, wiping her hands on the front of her chiton. "And make sure we have plenty of wine," Lydia called after her.

Clystra was probably none too happy. Poor thing. When Euodia sent the two over, they hadn't realized they'd be cooking and cleaning for a crowd, along with nursing a dying old woman.

Lydia shivered. The day was rolling from morning into afternoon. She knew by now the sun had driven all the chill from the air, and still she was cold. But earlier she had been warm enough. She supposed her body had given up on cooling and heating itself. After all, why go to the trouble to decorate a temple that was about to be torn down?

She thought about those who would gather here later for the meal. She hoped Epaphroditus was right about Theon feeling better by tonight. She wanted to see him. She wanted very much to see everyone.

On that first Sabbath, after they had returned to her house and changed from their wet clothes, they had gathered in the courtyard to hear Paul talk more about the Christ, the one the Jews called Messiah. Before long, Clement and his family came in, too. Lydia remembered feeling a twinge of jealousy; this man and his words belonged to her. She had invited him in, not the others. Her heart was hungry for hope, and she wasn't ready to share whatever he might be offering. But when she saw the rapt expression on Talit's face, on the faces of Agatha and her young husband, she felt foolish and ashamed.

Through the years, Clement had spoken now and again to her of the one the Jews were looking for, the deliverer they sometimes called the Son of Man, or the Anointed One. When he came, Clement explained, all would be set right. The poor would be fed, the blind would see, and the lame would walk. Some even thought the dead would come back to life. He would reign as God's sovereign on earth, and war would be no more.

Lydia had never heard such talk, and it thrilled and repelled her, at once. She remembered the earnest prayer of Clement at his father's graveside, his evocation of the day of Messiah. She remembered the hope hanging on the words, the longing that made her know how deeply he missed his father's presence. And if she could see her son again, and her husband.... For such uses, something like a resurrection seemed a good thing.

But there were other considerations, Lydia realized as she counted up her dead. There were those she didn't want to revisit. What about them? And how could a shade, once departed, be forced back into the flesh it had escaped? Nothing she had ever heard prepared her for such a notion. But then, everything else she knew about the God of the Jews was outside the boundaries of what her previous experience had prepared her for.

And then, she heard Paul announce with such authority that the day of Messiah had come—not in the way Clement had explained it, maybe, but come, nonetheless—and that death had, indeed, been reversed. Only once, true, but that one instance, Paul said, was but the precursor, the announcement of a general reversal still to come, a reversal that would transform the heavens and the earth. All the ancient stories and prophecies, Paul said, all the long, dry years of teaching and correction and anger and loss and blessing were gathered together in this Jesus. To know him and to believe in him was to own every promise God had ever made to his people.

Lydia needed that hope. She wanted desperately to own those promises, to be connected with the God who loved so long, so arduously, so extravagantly, and so shamelessly. He was coming soon, Paul said, perhaps before the sun rose again. Lydia wanted to greet him as one of his own when he came. If Paul had said she had to mutilate herself, like a Greek man who converted to the Jewish faith, she would have done it. If he had commanded her to be immersed in hot oil, instead of merely water, she would have built the fire herself. Of course she would take the washing in his name, as would her whole household.

So many years ago. And Lydia did not, for an instant, regret the purity of her conviction that day. True, it had come too late to teach her a better way of being with her daughter; Hermeia had walled herself off in Thessalonica with her husband three or four years before Paul's coming. Time and the daily wear and tear of living had chipped her belief, scored its once shiny surface. But her faith was still there. Old, worn, and battered, like a pot used too many times, for too many years, for too many different tasks. But still holding together inside her. Her body was wasting away, but Lydia husbanded her belief, saved it for the very end. It was all she had. Maybe it would be enough. She would soon know.

The last day of the Thesmophoria festival brought with it a brilliant autumn sky so blue it made Lydia's eyes ache. The day was one of those few warm days that return after the heat of summer has ended and just before winter hangs its long, dull drape over the land.

Euodia hadn't gone up to the campsite with the other women this year. They could sing about Demeter and Persephone without her, she said. There was too much to be done around the trading house for her to spend three days sleeping on the mountainside, listening to the ritual cursing, and smelling the odor of decaying pork.

Lydia suspected there was more to Euodia's absence from the festival than commercial necessity. She had been asking more and more questions lately about the Jewish beliefs; Lydia thought she was attracted, despite the sidelong remarks she made sometimes, to the austerity and straightforwardness of the ancient traditions of Clement and his family. Maybe one day soon, she would ask Clement if Euodia could attend one of the Sabbath gatherings.

They sat in the atrium of the trading house, soaking in the afternoon sun. There wouldn't be many more such fine days before winter, and it seemed a shame to waste it sitting inside. There weren't many customers today, anyway; most of the men were home grumbling about their wives' and daughters' three-day absence from their homes. The light in the courtyard seemed to drape itself all about; it had a presence, a kind of sad sweetness. On such an afternoon, Lydia felt herself opening to everything. She felt as if she could take the entire world in her arms.

They could hear the echoes of singing from the amphitheater, around the shoulder of Mount Orbelos. The sound of the women's voices caromed off the buildings of the forum and rang along the streets of Philippi. This hymn was the final, exuberant remembrance of the reunion of Demeter and Persephone, and at its conclusion, this year's priestesses would sow the ceremonial seeds, mixed with the decayed pork and serpent-shaped cakes the women had carried to the grottos on the mountainside, signifying the beginning of the autumn planting time. Then they would go back to their homes and their impatient, scowling husbands.

"My sister is a priestess this year, did I tell you?" Euodia said.

"No. Have I ever met her?"

"I don't think so. She doesn't leave the house too much; her husband is rather traditional."

"Really? Why did he ever allow her to be a priestess?"

"Maybe he decided it was a good omen for him."

"I wonder if he felt the same when she told him she had to stay out of his bed for three days before the festival."

Euodia laughed. "Omens only count for so much, don't they?"

"Especially where a man's desires are concerned."

They chuckled a moment more, then a quiet came. The hymn in the amphitheater was reaching its conclusion.

"Ah, but don't you sometimes miss it, Lydia?" Euodia asked.

"Miss what?"

"Being held by a man. Wrapping yourself around him.

Thinking, even just for a little while, that you can enfold him, keep him. That he can keep you."

A tender agony welled up in her. Yes, she missed it. She missed the smell of Menander, the gentle brush of his downy beard on her neck, the sweet weight of his head on her shoulder as he fell asleep.

"It's been a long time, Euodia. But, yes, I do. Sometimes."

Their hands found each other.

The street gate creaked open, and a woman came in. Her hair strayed out in several directions from what had been, probably a day or two ago, a complex and very modish hairstyle. Her chiton, himation, and cloak were dirt-stained, and the palms of her hands were caked with grime. There was a smudge of dirt across the bridge of her nose. The thong of one of her sandals trailed on the ground behind her.

"Oh, Euodia! There you are! I thought I was following your directions to this place, but somehow I kept winding up in the forum. Still, I've found you now, haven't I? Is there any water I can use to clean my hands? Planting the seeds with all that filth on them is a nasty business, and there just isn't any place to wash between the amphitheater and here."

"Hello, Syntyche," Euodia said. "There are pitchers and a basin in the back, through here."

She got up and walked toward the door of the main room. The priestess followed, then stopped short when she came abreast of the place Lydia sat.

"Oh! Who are you?"

"Syntyche, this is Lydia," Euodia said. "Surely you remember. How many times have I told you about her?"

"Oh, of course! Lydia. Yes, Euodia has told me so much, and—"

At the catch in Syntyche's voice, Lydia looked up. Tears were quickly gathering in the corners of Syntyche's eyes.

"How can I ever thank you for being of such help to my sister?" Syntyche said. "You saved her. That's all there is to say."

"Your sister is a very capable—"

"And after her husband shamed her so."

"Syntyche. This way." Euodia stood in the open doorway, motioning her sister inside.

"Well, excuse me. I have to go."

Syntyche flounced toward the place Euodia waited. She went inside, and Euodia followed her, closing the door behind them. Lydia saw the irritated way Euodia raised her eyes to the sky when her sister had passed. She smiled and shook her head. Poor Euodia. To have such a sister.

The courier brought the package to Lydia in her private chamber, and she knew immediately what it was. A wide grin spread across her face, and her fingers flew at the bindings. She slipped down the leather cover and slid out the vellum scroll. Her discreet inquiries had paid off. She could hardly wait till the next Sabbath, to see Clement's face when she presented it to him.

So often she had heard him quote snatches from one of their ancient wise men—one he called "Isaiah." Sometimes he would get part way through the citation, and his voice would falter. He would make a few false starts, and then fall silent, shaking his head.

"I can't remember any more," he would say. "When I was a boy, the rabbi would drill us over and over. 'Put these words in your minds,' he would say. 'You'll want them, one day.' But now I've lost too much."

Esras might put a hand on his father's shoulder. "If only we'd had more time, Father. We could have looked more carefully at the synagogue."

Talit or Agatha might begin a song, and the Sabbath time would move on. But sometimes, Lydia could see the brooding that wouldn't quite leave Clement's face, the faraway look. Isaiah. Always it was the words of Isaiah that surfaced that longing in him.

She ran her fingers over the creamy, supple vellum. Well, after the next Sabbath, he wouldn't have to search his memory anymore. She resisted the urge to unroll the parchment, to look on the neat, clipped rows of Hebrew writing. No. Let Clement's eyes be the first to see these beloved lines.

The day came, and Lydia could hardly sit still. Euodia was with her that day, and she had her friend slip the parchment behind her, between her chiton and her outer robe. They sang one or two of the songs of the ancient king called David, and Clement offered a prayer of blessing and thanks. Then he motioned for Esras to fetch one of their few scrolls for the reading.

"Wait, Esras," Lydia said, "I brought something I want you to read."

She reached behind Euodia, who was already grinning from ear to ear, and extracted the scroll in its leather case. She handed it to the young man, who opened the binding and slid out the scroll. His eyes widened when he began unrolling it. Without a word, he handed it to his father.

"There's a synagogue in Thessalonica," Lydia blurted. "They have a scribe there."

"The scroll of Isaiah," Clement said. "I never thought—"

"Read something." Lydia's voice felt constricted and tears itched in her eyes. "Please."

Clement searched along the columns with a finger. He found the place he wanted. With a quavering smile at Lydia, he began reading.

This is what the LORD says:
"Maintain justice and do what is right,
for my salvation is close at hand
and my righteousness will soon be revealed.
Blessed is the man who does this, the man who holds it fast,
who keeps the Sabbath without desecrating it,
and keeps his hand from doing any evil."
Let no foreigner who has joined himself to the LORD say,
"The LORD will surely exclude me from his people."
And let not any eunuch complain, "I am only a dry tree."
For this is what the LORD says:
"To the eunuchs who keep my Sabbaths, who choose what
pleases me
and hold fast to my covenant—
to them I will give within my temple and its walls a memo-
rial and a name
better than sons and daughters;
I will give them an everlasting name that will not be cut off.
And foreigners who bind themselves to the LORD —

He looked up at Lydia, and his eyes were brimming.

—foreigners who bind themselves to the LORD to serve him,
to love the name of the LORD and to worship him,

all who keep the Sabbath without desecrating it
and who hold fast to my covenant—
these I will bring to my holy mountain and give them joy
in my house of prayer.
Their burnt offerings and sacrifices will be accepted on my
    altar;
for my house will be called a house of prayer for all nations."
The Sovereign LORD *declares—*
he who gathers the exiles of Israel:
"I will gather still others to them besides those already gathered."

By the time he finished, all of them were weeping softly—even Euodia.

These were prosperous days for purple merchants. Claudius Caesar had just annexed Lycia and, closer to home, there was talk from the north that Thrace might soon come into the empire. The Via Egnatia bustled with more traffic than ever. New colonies were being founded; new equites were being created; new villas were being built; new wardrobes were being assembled. Lydia and Euodia had never been busier.

Euodia came into the private chamber with a troubled look on her face. Lydia set aside the document she had been studying. Old Septimus, having grown rapidly feebler in these last months, had died a few days before, and Lydia was reviewing the terms of his will before registering it in the city records. The old *oikonomikos* had accumulated a good deal of money through the years of his service to Lydia and her uncle, and he had many nephews and cousins he wished to remember with his estate. Sorting it all out was no small task. But Euodia clearly had something on her mind. Septimus's will could wait.

They made themselves comfortable on the cushions beside

the low table. A pitcher of wine sat nearby, but Euodia declined Lydia's offer.

"Our trade is very healthy these days," she began, and stopped, looking worriedly at Lydia. "The new commerce in the east and the increased traffic to the north has given us quite a number of new customers."

"Yes. And so far, you've said nothing to explain the creases between your eyebrows."

"Some of the people I've been working with—they've never seen you at all. They don't even know you."

"True enough. And you've done very well with them, I might add."

"Thank you." Euodia squirmed a moment, resettling herself. She pulled in a deep breath and looked directly at Lydia. "I think it's time for me to go out on my own."

"Ah."

Lydia stretched her hand to the wine pitcher and poured a few swallows in a cup of hammered silver. She peered around; there was no water vessel. She gave Euodia a guilty look.

"This is good Thracian wine. You won't tell on me, will you?"

Euodia smiled and made a dismissing wave. Lydia drank, then set down the cup and looked carefully at her friend.

"So…you think you're ready?"

Euodia nodded decisively.

"I do too."

"Really?"

"You sound surprised. Are you really so sure?"

"Yes, I am, but…I never thought you'd—"

"Agree?"

She laughed then, a relieved sound. "I've been working up

to this for months, dreading it, but knowing I had to ask. And you said 'Yes,' just like that."

Lydia shrugged.

"Is there another cup?" Euodia asked. "Pour me some of that wine."

"Do you have a place in mind?" Lydia asked.

"I can work from my house for now. It's big enough, and there's an extra room I can use for storage."

"You're welcome to use some of my warehouse space, as long as you need it." She gave Euodia a sidelong smile. "You've changed quite a bit from the hesitant, nervous newcomer who was afraid to wrangle with men over the price for her goods."

"You've been so kind to me, Lydia. And we didn't start on the best of terms."

"So, you think your house will give you enough room?"

"For a while. And it'll be better for Syntyche. I can stay close to her, this way."

"What's wrong with her?"

"Hadn't I told you? Her husband divorced her."

"Why?"

"You saw her, Lydia. Surely you can guess."

"Poor thing."

"Yes. All her life, that's been the case."

"What will she do?"

"Well, of course Patroclus had to return the dowry, and that was no small sum. With or without me, she isn't likely to starve."

"The two of you are so different."

"You can't imagine."

Euodia began moving her things out of the trading house the next day.

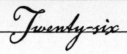

ow this is the law for the Nazirite when the period of his separation is over. He is to be brought to the entrance to the Tent of Meeting. There he is to present his offerings to the LORD: a year-old male lamb without defect for a burnt offering, a year-old ewe lamb without defect for a sin offering, a ram without defect for a fellowship offering, together with their grain offerings and drink offerings...."

Lydia shifted on the rock where she sat. Neria, ever watchful, offered her a rolled-up cloak to soften the seat. Lydia waved it away. In her mind, she was seeing the weird figure of an ancient Hebrew, wild haired and crazy from solitude, drunk from communion with the Holy. What inner compulsion would drive one who was already swarthy with the desert sun, whose feet were already calloused and hard from wandering among the rocks and dust of the wild places, to go alone into the barrenness, away from his people? What would God say to such a one, to mark him and pull him apart, even more apart than a homeless people already were? She thought about the maker of the oath coming down from the purity and desolation of some waste place, down into the camp of the people of God, back to his father's tent. She imagined him walking into the pens, among the sheep, to select the victims for the completion of his vow. Would the animals shy and mill away from him, pressing into each other to escape the dreadful notice of his wild, God-crazed eyes? Would God guide his vision among the shuffling, bleating crowd, enable him to find the three, the ones whose blood would be perfect, spilling from a body without blemish?

"If a man or woman wants to make a special vow," Clement had read at the beginning. What would a woman Nazirite look like? Off by herself in the midst of a stark and wild land, her hair long and rank from her covenant, what would she think about? Would she be afraid? What would be her covering, her protection from the uncaring elements and the mishaps of chance?

She thought about the lambs and the ram, led to the door of the holy tent by the returning pilgrim. Would they sense the knife, burning silently in the hand of the robed priest? Would the shadow of the Tent of Meeting fall on them, darken them before the snatching, the hard hand gripping the jaw, the stretching back of the neck, the swift, freezing burn of the blade across their throats? She imagined the hot, metallic smell of the blood, gushing crimson across the flawless hide of the chosen sacrifices.

"Then at the entrance to the Tent of Meeting, the Nazirite must shave off the hair that he dedicated. He is to take the hair and put it in the fire that is under the sacrifice of the fellowship offering…."

Yes. This had a familiar shape. This would complete the marking, wouldn't it? Even though the vow was now satisfied, all who saw the naked head would know. The Nazirite would be plainly signed out for them. But what could they really know of the mind, the heart of the shaved, completed one? How could they know about the power of strangeness and purpose?

Lydia thought of Menander's confused, saddened face, contemplating her hair on the family altar. She recalled the hesitancy in her father's voice, the day he came to fetch her from the oracle. How much greater the awe of an oracle from the true God. Who could withstand it? Who was strong enough?

Clement stood, signaling that they should all rise for the final blessing.

> "The Lord bless you, and keep you;
> the Lord make his face to shine upon you;
> and be gracious unto you;
> the Lord turn his face toward you,
> and give you peace."

"Amen," Lydia said, along with Euodia, Syntyche, and the rest of Clement's family. Clement put the scroll back in its sheath as the rest of them gathered their things for the walk from the bank of the Krenides back to the house on Short Street.

There was quite a little group of them, these days. Besides Clement, Talit, and their two children, there was Lydia and most of her household, Euodia, Syntyche, and their handful of male and female servants.

Hermeia was absent again. More and more lately, she had been staying away from Agatha and the rest of them, and it saddened Lydia to admit it was her presence that encouraged her daughter to find other things to do on Sabbath days. She was harder and harder to approach, and Lydia didn't know what to do about it. This morning, she worked up her nerve enough to look in on Hermeia where she sat in the colonnade by the well, studiously working at her loom.

"That's good work, dear."

No answer.

"Are you coming to Sabbath?"

A shake of the head, busy fingers tucking the shuttle in and out of the warp.

"You seem in a hurry, Hermeia. Is this piece of cloth so urgent?"

The fingers paused, then resumed. "I'm working on my dowry."

"Well, when the time comes, I'm sure I can help you gather plenty of things that will serve. Surely you don't have to occupy every—"

"You're too busy to trouble yourself."

"Oh, well. I didn't know you had such immediate prospects."

Lydia bit her lip, knowing immediately the words had come out sharper than she intended. The fingers stopped. Hermeia looked up at her, and her face made Lydia dread whatever she was about to say.

"Neria found this loom for me. Maybe she'll help me find a husband."

As Lydia walked away, Hermeia's next words reached her, pitched just loud enough to register:

"Unless, of course, you sell her, too."

Hermeia was already gone in her mind, Lydia knew. It was only a matter of time before some eligible man noticed her.

"What was that blessing you read, at the end?" she asked Clement as they walked, to force her mind onto another path.

"Those were the words with which God commanded Aaron and his sons to bless the people of Israel. He gave it at the same time he numbered our people and gave us the laws for the service in the holy tabernacle."

"What a strange thing—that God should have been worshipped in a tent."

"It was a time of wandering," he answered. "The Tabernacle was God's mercy, made visible among us."

The path toward the town gates wound along the river's edge for maybe forty paces, then twisted between the shaggy trunks of three large elms before it angled up the slope toward the main road. As they rustled through the drifts of fallen leaves beneath the elms, Lydia had a fleeting memory of a little girl in a plane tree beside another river, near another town, in another life. Such a strange journey that little girl had taken. Such strange voices had sometimes called to her, moved her this way or that along the winding course of her pilgrimage. How long before she came at last to the land of promise?

She felt a hand on her shoulder. Talit had moved in beside her.

"Your face is troubled, Lydia."

They took a few paces. "Hermeia," Lydia said, finally.

"Yes. I've gotten concerned for Agatha, lately."

"Agatha? She's a wonderful girl—young woman, I mean."

"Young woman. Nearly eighteen. I don't know what we'll do to find her a husband. Send to Thessalonica, maybe. But we don't know many people there."

"I know many good families. I could—what am I saying? You want her to marry a Jewish man."

"That has always been our wish. Some girls do otherwise, but...."

"What about Esras?"

Talit shrugged. "The same problem. He's not getting any

younger, either. But he's a man, so it's not as bad."

"Why is that, do you suppose, Talit?"

"What?"

"A man who waits until he's twenty, or even thirty, is considered no more than prudent. This is even truer among my people than yours. But a woman who passes her twentieth birthday without a husband is thought a strumpet, or barren, or otherwise unfit. Why?"

"I've never thought of it, Lydia. Maybe because childbearing is a hard thing, best started when the woman is young and strong."

"Is anyone ever strong enough for children?"

Talit gave her a sad smile.

"What about you, Talit? Did you ever dream of anything other than being a wife and mother?"

"Clement is a good—"

"Yes, I know. It's easy to see that. But deep down inside you, in your most secret place, did you ever wonder what it would be like to…to travel, maybe? To see places no one else from your village had ever seen? To go somewhere just for the sheer joy of going. Jerusalem, or Alexandria, or even Rome?"

"We came here. That's enough traveling." Talit stopped walking, and put a hand on Lydia's arm. "Let me ask you something, Lydia. Who sang to your babies?"

Lydia stared at her. Talit measured Lydia with her eyes. After a while, she turned and trudged on up the slope to the main road.

With Euodia gone, it became even easier for Lydia to find things that needed doing at her place of business. The servants who lived there grew accustomed to seeing the lamplight leaking from beneath the door of her private chamber, sometimes until the far watches of the night. She took to making long lists of tasks and leaving them for Pericles to find in the morning. Sometimes, when she could think of nothing else to give her mind to, she woke one of the slaves and had him accompany her back to her house. Sometimes she walked back by herself. Sometimes she slept in her chamber.

She prided herself for maintaining a calm countenance when the father of Livius came to strike the bargain for Hermeia. Her one moment of enjoyment came after Prosculus had laid out his pedigree, his son's qualifications, and his prospects. She listened carefully, nodding at all the right places, then told him the value of the dowry she proposed. Prosculus's cheeks reddened above his beard and he swallowed at least twice. The amount was sufficiently above his expectations to have the exact effect she had hoped for. It would also guarantee that Livius would think long and hard before putting Hermeia away. Lydia enjoyed Prosculus's moment of discomfort. She might be only a woman, and her daughter might despise her, but none of them could accuse her of parsimony. And she owed Hermeia that much, at least.

How soon might the marriage be concluded? he wanted to know. The sooner the better, she told him; how about the first day of the new month? And would the, ah, dowry be available for delivery so soon? he asked, with a discreet little cough. Lydia wanted to laugh at him. Yes, she assured him, all would be in order. She had Pericles draw up the agreement. Two citizens were there on business, and they signed their names as witnesses.

On the day of the wedding, she didn't bother trying to give

Hermeia any final words of maternal wisdom. In a way, it was just. She remembered her own wedding day, and the acrimony between her, her mother, and her sisters. Hermeia's distance was, in a strange way, the closing of a bitter circle.

The day Esras left for Thessalonica was overcast and cool. A thin, hunting wind furled around the sides of Mount Orbelos and caught at the edges of their cloaks as they stood just outside the city gate.

Talit's face glistened with tear-shine as she stood, clutching her wrap across her shoulders. They had hoped a good Jewish family might find its way to Philippi, and when Clement met the two brothers in the forum, making inquiries about places they might house themselves and their wives and children, it seemed their prayers were answered. But the brothers had sons, not daughters. While Agatha seemed to bloom, acquiring a new attentiveness to her unfolding prospects, Esras began turning elsewhere in his thoughts. By the time Agatha's betrothal was announced, they all knew he had made up his mind to go. He would wait until after his sister's wedding, he told them.

There were synagogues in the seaport, a large Jewish community there. A fine, industrious man like Esras would have no lack of marital prospects. Maybe he would even bring his new wife back to Philippi. They could still hope.

The quarter-bolt of purple wool was rolled up and stuffed in the bottom of the large satchel slung across Esras's shoulder. Along with the money Euodia had pressed into his hands, the cloth would probably bring enough to make a good start. Lydia had given him letters to some merchants she knew.

Agatha's husband embraced Esras and kissed him. Then Agatha went to her brother, holding him close and long. He held her away from him.

"Sister. Why the weeping? Busy yourself with your husband, and don't worry about me."

He winked at Autolychus, who promptly blushed to the roots of his hair. Autolychus was the oldest son of the older of the two brothers. He was painfully shy, and Agatha, from all appearances, adored him.

Clement was next. He and Esras gripped each other's wrists, then wrapped their arms around each other.

"The Most High guard your steps, my son," Clement said.

"His peace be on your house, Father."

"I wish I could sit with you in one of the synagogues of Thessalonica. It would be good to hear the Torah read by a real rabbi. Listen to the words, Esras. Keep them always in your mind, and hold them in your heart like treasure."

"When I hear the Torah in Thessalonica, I will think of you. And the rabbi's voice will not seem as good to me as when I listened to your reading, beside the river."

Clement's eyes were bright with emotion. Again he took his son in his arms. Their hands thumped on each other's backs. Their eyes were tightly closed. Clement released Esras and held out a hand to his wife. Talit's lips quivered as she came to her son.

"Mother," he said.

He held her for a long time, his face buried in her shoulder. He released her, and she stepped back, her hand in front of her mouth. Clement put a hand on his wife's shoulder, and she leaned into him.

Esras looked at them all for a moment, then turned to hurry after the group of merchants and tradesmen, already disappearing around a bend in the Via Egnatia. They heard the quick slapping of his sandals against the paving stones, gradually fading into the gray light of the day.

Lydia watched him go, thinking of Hermeia. Would Esras ever chance to see her? Would she walk past his stall in the forum at Thessalonica, and stop, and look, and recognize him? Lydia tried to think of what her daughter might say to Esras, what the two of them might find to talk about. She wanted to think Hermeia might ask after her health, at least. She might ask Esras, as he worked his loom or showed his cloth to her, how her mother spent her days, whether she seemed well, if she still knew her way toward a smile. Lydia wanted to run after Esras, to beg him to allow her to travel with him. She wanted to walk through the crowded streets of the city and look into the faces of its people, to maybe find her daughter. She wanted to try one more time to outrun her mistakes and Hermeia's hurt and arrive at a place where mother and daughter could rest in each other, recover some of what they had lost, without meaning to.

But, no. Thessalonica was a big place. And too far to run.

The pains were coming closer together now—never really left her, in fact. It was a curious thing, Lydia thought; it reminded her of giving birth. Pain was her messenger; it pointed the way toward her culmination. And she waited for it, unable to do anything else. She could feel through her doorway the warmth of the sun on the flagstones of the courtyard. She could hear Clystra and Euterpe clattering at each other in the kitchen, across from her room. But her vision was almost gone, and there was no sensation in her legs or her hands. She decided not to tell anyone; it would serve no purpose. Her soul was pulling down into the center of her, maybe, abandoning the perimeter and hiding as deep as it could. Not that it would matter. God's summons would find her anyway.

She wanted to hold out until the agapē. She wanted, one more time, to hear the sounds of voices filling her main hall and courtyard, to know her friends and fellow believers were gathered in her house, sharing food and the sanctuary of each other. Maybe God would grant her this grace. Lydia hoped so.

She wished Neria were here. Neria had an uncanny knack for anticipating her needs and wishes. She would often bring Lydia a cup of wine or a piece of bread, just as she was raising a hand to send one of the other servants for it. Why shouldn't Neria, after all those years, have been able to judge her? Lydia hoped she and her sister were doing well in Ephesus. She remembered the day she granted them their freedom.

It wasn't too long after the day she realized she wouldn't be able to go back to her business; that this was probably her last illness and the stuff in her warehouse might as well go to someone who could use it. She remembered the look on Pericles' face when she instructed him to sell it, all of it, and keep two parts of every ten of the proceeds for himself, distribute four parts among the other servants, and bring her the rest. Then she handed him the script that freed him and the rest of them.

She remembered how strange and lost he looked, standing in the center of the floor of her room, here at the house. She could count on her fingers the number of times he had been to her home. At the trading house or in the forum, talking with the other managers, he was relaxed and confident. Here, he was ill at ease. He took the document she gave him, read it quickly, and bowed, once. Then he left.

Euodia bought most of the goods. Lydia thought she remembered hearing that Pericles went back to Cenchrea, near Corinth, where he was born.

When Neria came to her, she was lying on this exact couch.

It was underneath the window; she was still well enough in those days to enjoy watching the sparrows that sometimes perched on the ledge. Neria came in, her face a taut, unreadable mask.

"Here, Neria," she said, holding out a folded piece of parchment.

Neria's eyes never left Lydia's face as she took the paper. She unfolded it and glanced at it. She shook her head.

"What is this?"

"It says you're free, Neria. You and your sister."

"What?"

"You can go anywhere you like. You're free. Both of you."

"You're sending us away?"

"No, Neria, listen to me. I'm old and sick. I don't have much longer. You've been faithful for so many years. You shouldn't spend any more of your life as a slave in this house."

"You're freeing us? We're not slaves anymore?"

"Yes, dear. Don't you have a brother in Ephesus? You could go to him. You could all be together again."

"Go...to Ephesus?"

"Of course. Why not?"

She covered her mouth with her hands and fell to her knees. She wailed aloud and held her face in her hands. Her sister, apparently standing just outside, rushed in to her. She wrapped her arms around Neria, speaking frantically to her in the tongue of their homeland. The two dark women batted rapid words back and forth, and in a moment, the sister turned wondering eyes on Lydia. She began crying, staggering over to the old woman and laying her head in her lap.

She gave them a generous parting allowance: enough to take them to Ephesus and have almost a year's living expenses, as well. Over the next few months, she freed her other slaves, too. She wouldn't be needing them. Euodia's girls could take care of such few requirements as she had in her remaining days.

Now those requirements were trimmed down to nothing. Lydia wondered what time of day it was. She hoped it was nearing sunset, when the believers would start gathering for the agapē. There wasn't much time left. The pain had acquired a cold, dark center, and it was spreading.

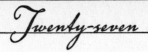

o harm, no harm. Where is friend Lydia? Xerxes wants to talk to her, no harm."

Good. If Xerxes was here, the others would be arriving soon. He had probably brought three or four others with him, poor ones for whom the agapē was the principal source of nourishment each week. Lydia hoped someone remembered to tell the girls to save aside some of the food to send to Tryphinus's family. It was too bad he had gotten hurt, just after the new baby came. And they shouldn't forget about poor Daphne. Her sons had looked dreadfully tired the last time Lydia saw them here. How much longer could the dear old thing hold on? Then Lydia realized Daphne would surely outlive her. She would have laughed at herself, had she the strength.

"Friend Lydia, it's old Xerxes, no harm."

She heard him coming across the floor, sliding one foot cautiously in front of him, then the other.

"Hello, Xerxes. I'm so glad you're here." She tried to raise a hand in greeting, but she couldn't. "I'd love to hear a story."

She felt him standing over her, heard the slight wheeze in

his breathing. His hand lightly touched her shoulder.

"Lydia is leaving." The words were quiet, more to himself than to her, maybe.

"Yes, Xerxes. I am. Soon I'll be with God."

"God is good. He will be good to Lydia."

"Yes. He will."

There was a long silence. She felt a slight puff of air in front of her face, something waving, maybe.

"What are you doing, Xerxes?"

"Friend Lydia's eyes don't work?"

She hesitated. She really didn't want to alarm everyone, and she especially didn't want them all crowding around her. And how could he tell, anyway? He was more than half blind, himself.

"Not very well, they don't," she answered, finally.

"That is good."

"It is?"

"Yes. Lydia has to see with inside eyes, like Xerxes. Now she has to learn to listen. Then she can be found."

More people were coming through the gate. Lydia could hear them talking to each other. She could hear the scrape of the extra tables being dragged across the flagstones into place in the colonnade by the well. She heard the upturned, questioning voices of Euodia's other women, asking Euterpe and Clystra where this should go, or that.

It was funny: when she bought this house, it seemed so spacious. In those days, she couldn't imagine needing more room. And in the time after Hermeia left, when she was left here with just Neria and the other servants, the house had echoed with silence and wounding memories. But now there wasn't enough elbowroom for everyone in the church to eat in her main hall.

When Crescens said the benediction before the meal, he would have to stand in the doorway to be heard by everyone.

She thought about this community, about the many years of its life: about the friends they had buried, the births they had celebrated. Those who had left Philippi and gone to other places. Those who had stayed in Philippi, but left the community. She remembered the times when the magistrates here watched them with suspicious eyes, when they had had to wait for the cover of full dark before making their way through the back streets and alleys to the house where the agapē was being held. And the easier times, when they had been able to greet each other with the kiss of meeting, even in the broad light of day in the middle of the forum. She remembered the time the fever came through, when nearly every house in Philippi, from the wealthiest to the humblest, had at least one who was stricken. That was when Agatha and Autolychus had lost their youngest daughter. Lydia remembered the tablet she had placed in the child's memory. She remembered when Talit died. Much of Clement had gone with her.

She remembered the bad drought in northern Macedonia and the food shortage that followed, when she and Euodia and some of the others gathered money and took it to the magistrates. They put it in their hands and told them it was the way of their belief to share with everyone in need, no matter what god he worshipped. They told them to use it to have grain brought in from Alexandria, to distribute to the many in Philippi who were having more and more difficulty finding enough to eat. She remembered the surprise on their faces, mixed with gratitude. Not long after, a slave of one of the officials received the washing in the name of the Christ. The magistrate never came to one of their gatherings, but Lydia always wondered if the slave found a chance to say something to his master.

And always there were new ones coming among them, ones who heard about the Christ and yearned for the chance to hope again. Slaves, tradesmen, artisans, merchants, widows, divorced women, even a few soldiers and officials. She thought of Stratius and his fine family, and smiled inside. All of them—all came to the table from many, many places and somehow, there was always just room enough. They seated themselves side-by-side, ready to fill themselves with good food and the peace of the holy time that was always too brief. Their memories and thoughts and faces and voices, their griefs and their joys—all of it pooled in her mind, blended like wine and water in a cup, the clear with the dark.

Xerxes stirred beside her. She heard the sound of his breathing come down, hovering beside her ear. She wished she could turn her face toward him, but now the muscles of her neck had ceased obeying her mind's bidding. She thought about this beautiful, pitiful man, smiling and weeping his erratic way through life, telling stories and making faces—speaking truth in surprising and hidden ways.

"Don't you want to be found, Xerxes?"

"Xerxes will be found. When it is time."

"Is my time almost here?"

"Yes, friend Lydia. Soon, you won't be lost anymore."

The young men thought she was asleep when they came in to bring her to the meal. They started to tiptoe out, but Xerxes convinced them to move her. Lydia felt herself rise and hover, then move toward the doorway. Xerxes walked beside her, his hand covering hers. She tried to squeeze his fingers, and thought once, maybe she did, but she couldn't be sure.

The air of the courtyard opened out above her. She floated

down a corridor of familiar voices, but as she came by they quieted. She wished they'd keep talking, that she could just be among them without attracting such notice. She felt like someone on display, laid out on a bier, in a funeral procession. There would be plenty of time for that later, she thought, annoyed. Oh, well.

"She's gone down so much, just since this morning," she heard some woman say. It sounded like Crescens' wife. "Poor thing," someone agreed.

They turned her through the archway of the colonnade and went into the main hall. They carried her the length of the room, to the long wall opposite the entrance. They were going to put her at the head table. Just put me in the corner, she thought, out of the way. I only want to be here; I don't want to be the centerpiece. But they set her down at the front, anyway. Androclus would be at this table, she thought, in honor of his baptism this morning. His mother and father and Euodia, his great-grandmother, would be here, too.

She could hear the clumping of bowls and platters being placed on the tables. She could smell the roast meat, the still-warm bread, the steaming beans and lentils. From the sound of the shuffling feet and the low voices, she guessed they were gathering in, near their tables, that Crescens or one of the other elders was about to initiate the feast with a prayer of blessing.

"Welcome to this house, brothers and sisters," Crescens said, his voice coming clear and strong from the entrance to the hall. Lydia did so much like to hear Crescens' voice. "Let us join our hearts together in this feast of love."

Lydia imagined them, standing in here and out in the courtyard, turning their eyes toward the president of the assembly. The mothers were pulling the young children close, quieting them. The shuffling feet were stilled, the voices hushed as Crescens began praying.

"O Lord God, blessed father of our Savior, Jesus Christ, may your name be praised for ever and ever. You have fed us from your bounty since the beginning of our days, and you have provided for every living thing. Gladden our hearts in your presence and give us what we need, so that we may be strong and able to do good to all men in the name of Jesus Christ our Lord, through whom honor and blessing are due you until the end of all days. Amen."

"Amen," chorused the assembly, and they seated themselves around the low tables and began to eat.

"Where is Grandmother Euodia?" asked a voice to Lydia's right. It was Androclus.

"Hush, son. I don't know," said Lucian. "She'll be here, I'm sure. Now be quiet and don't disturb Mother Lydia."

Let the boy talk, she thought. He ought to know why his great-grandmother isn't here, tonight of all nights.

Lydia heard Crescens coming to the place just to her left, settling himself. There was a pause in his movements, and she heard him say, "Why is she here? Shouldn't she be in her room, where it's quiet?"

"No harm," came Xerxes' voice, next to her. "Friend Lydia needs to be here, with her family. It is best. No harm." She felt his hand on her arm again.

It must have persuaded Crescens. After a moment, she heard him ask, "Where is your grandmother?"

Lydia heard no answer from Lucian.

Gradually, the enjoyment of the food and the wine enlivened the gathering, even those seated near Lydia. The talk was still quiet, but the tone was engaged and interesting: the sound of friends catching up on events, reminding one another who they were. Some of the younger men moved from table to table, refilling bowls and offering more wine or water. Later, they would take food to those who hadn't been able to be here. Lydia wished the pain in her wouldn't yell so loudly. She wanted to hear the voices of her friends. She wanted to place them, see them in her mind.

She felt someone's breath on her ear. "I'm glad to see you, Lydia. I'm sorry I wasn't here for the service this morning, but I'm feeling better this evening."

It was Theon. She wished she could tell him not to shout. There wasn't anything wrong with her hearing, even if her eyes were closed and she wasn't moving. He patted her hand and moved back toward his table. Nice of him to drop by.

She was sitting up, looking out at them. For some reason, they had left an aisle down the center of the main hall. Reclining around their tables, they looked at her, smiling. They were watching her, waiting for her to do something. What?

She let her eyes move down the aisle in the hall and through the doorway. Framed in the doorway was the arch of the colonnade and the opening to the entry yard. Her front gate was open—who had forgotten to shut it?—and a wide, shining street led straight away from her door. Where were the houses across the street? Where, come to think of it, was the street? Only this broad thoroughfare, going away from her gate as if her house were its source, rising up a gradual slope for maybe twenty paces, then ascending sharply.

Xerxes held out a hand to her, winking at her and making a face. His eyes were clear, she noticed, dark and twinkling with mischief. She put her hand in his, and all of them watched as she stood up from her couch. She realized she was wearing a silly smile as she started walking, down the aisle and through the doorway to the hall. She was quickening her pace as she passed the archway. By the time she reached the front gate, she was trotting. She heard them behind her, pouring through the front gate to watch, cheering as she started up the gentle slope. "Io! Io!" they shouted.

She kept waiting for the burning in her calves, ready for the familiar discomfort, ready to lean into it and work through it. But as the slope grew steeper, the way became easier. Soon she was running at full tilt, straight up the shining slope. The higher she went, the faster she could go. She was laughing as she ran, laughing as she tried to keep up with her flying feet.

"Brothers and sisters," Crescens was saying, "let us together raise a cup of blessing."

The talk rapidly stilled and Lydia heard the sound of cups clicking against dishes, then an expectant silence.

"Blessed be the Lord God, father of our Savior, Jesus Christ. May his name gladden our hearts always, and may he richly bless Lydia, his servant, in whose house we gather tonight. Amen."

"Amen," answered the church. A quiet followed, then the sound of cups being placed on the tables.

"Let the brothers bring the bread for the blessing."

She heard the sound of feet moving among the tables, of baskets being gathered. The men came and stood in the opening of the triclinium.

"O Lord our God, we give thanks—"

His voice stopped. In the instant before the low murmuring started, Androclus said, "There's Grandmother Euodia. And Aunt Syntyche is with her! But who's that other woman with them?"

Faster and faster she went, running up the glowing way. Light was all around, and at first she thought it was the light that seemed to rise up from the surface on which she ran, but she gradually became aware that there was another, greater light. It lay ahead of her, at the summit she was running toward. Though she seemed to herself to be running as fast as even the swiftest birds could fly, the summit was approaching only slowly. But that didn't matter. The longer it took, the longer she could savor this exhilarating sense of going faster, and faster, and faster still. She laughed again, and the light was inside her mouth, inside all of her. It tasted like joy. And the light at the summit was a greater joy, she suddenly knew. She laughed even louder, and longer. And still she was increasing her speed.

Lydia heard the three women's footsteps in the silent hall. They came toward her.

"The little girl has come back," Xerxes breathed. "No harm."

"Lydia, there's someone here who wants to speak to you," Euodia said.

"She was standing outside the gate when we got here," Syntyche added. "I hope she can hear," she said in a doubtful voice.

"Mother. It's Hermeia. I'm here. Can you hear me?"

Hermeia. You came, after all. How could I ever have imagined the sound of your voice would be so much like mine? When you left, you still had the mellow, pure tones of a young woman. But now—

"I almost didn't come in, Mother, even after the long journey. But, Euodia—"

"She was looking at the gate, and I knew immediately who she was," Euodia said. "I knew. And Syntyche knew what needed to happen."

Lydia heard Euodia make the small sound that was half a laugh, half a sob.

Are you pleased, Paul? I did as you asked. Your loyal yoke-fellow has at last helped them follow your urging. And my daughter, my Hermeia....If only I could tell her how much I've longed for this day, knowing it would never happen. If only I could touch her face, one last time.

Lydia could hear the quiet sobs, coming from many places in the hall. She could feel the pounding of her own heart. The constant pain had even receded slightly, enough to allow her to feel the tears pooling beneath her closed eyelids, seeping from beneath, sliding down her cheeks.

"Look!" Syntyche said. "She weeps!"

"Oh, Mother. You can hear, then, can't you?"

Hermeia was on her knees, beside her. Lydia felt dry, wrinkled hands touching her face. Her daughter's hands—aged. Her daughter's face, near hers, kissing her.

Lydia felt a strange surging in her right arm, a tingling as the motionless limb somehow woke itself from slumber. With agonizing slowness, her right hand began to move, sliding from her chest, across Hermeia's back, to the place just below her right shoulder. Then she was able to pat her daughter: once, twice. And to whisper the words, so soft they were barely more than a shaped breath: "Hermeia. Forgive."

Lydia heard Crescens then, his voice raspy with emotion. Once more, he began the blessing of the bread. And this time, he was not interrupted.

Faster and faster she went, in the light and toward the light. And then, someone was running beside her. It was Paul. His head was thrown back, and he was laughing. She realized it was the first time she had ever seen him laugh out loud.

"Paul! What is that light ahead?"

"Haven't you guessed, dear yokefellow?"

"Joy?"

"Yes, it is joy! The end and beginning of all joy!"

They ran together, up, and up, and up. Laughing and shouting, they ran toward the joy.

The Daughters of Faith Series

ISBN 1-57673-477-3

DAUGHTER OF JERUSALEM

THOM LEMMONS

Go back to the time of Jesus and be on the scene as Mary Magdalene—one who was lost, then found—reaches in compassion toward other wandering sheep of the house of Israel. Through Mary's eyes, one will experience the birth of the infant church and the excitement of the early days following Pentecost.